MINNESOTA

WISCONSIN

MICHIGAN

IOWA

NEW HAMPSHIRE
VERMONT

MAINE

NEW
YORK

MASSACHUSETTS

RHODE ISLAND
CONNECTICUT

PENNSYLVANIA

NEW JERSEY

DELAWARE
MARYLAND

ILLINOIS

INDIANA

OHIO

WEST
VIRGINIA

VIRGINIA

MISSOURI

KENTUCKY

NORTH
CAROLINA

ARKANSAS

TENNESSEE

SOUTH
CAROLINA

MISSISSIPPI

ALABAMA

GEORGIA

LOUISIANA

FLORIDA

LAKES

RIVERS

NAVIGABLE WATERWAYS

OFFSHORE AREAS

THE WONDERFUL WORLD OF HOUSEBOATING

by DUANE NEWCOMB

Maps by Theodore R. Miller

PRENTICE-HALL, Inc., Englewood Cliffs, N.J.

I wish to give special thanks to the many individuals, companies, and agencies that helped in the preparation of this book. Photographs used in the interior were supplied by the following: Aluminum Cruisers, Inc., Louisville, Ky., Beyer Manufacturing Co., Fresno, Calif., Boatel Company, Inc., Mora, Minn., Chris-Craft Corporation, Pompano Beach, Fla., Culver Boat Co., Center Hill, Fla., Cutter (Division of Cargile, Inc.), Nashville, Tenn., Dometic Sales Corp., Drifter (House Boating Corporation of America), Gallatin, Tenn., ERA Dynamics Corporation, Cedar Grove, N.J., Fischer-Pierce Co., Inc., Rockland, Mass., Heath Co., Benton Harbor, Mich., Holiday Mansion (Division of Mohawk, Inc.), Salina, Kans., Kayot, Inc. Marine Division, Mankato, Minn., Kenner Boat Co., Knoxville, Ark., Kings Craft Corp., Florence, Ala., Land N' Sea Craft, Inc., San Jose, Calif., Lazy Days Manufacturing Co., Inc., Buford, Ga., Magic Chef, City of Industry, Ga., Marine Products Operations, Chrysler Corporation, Detroit, Mich., Marine Travelift, Inc., Mercruiser Division, Kiekhaefer Mercury, Fond Du Lac, Wis., Monogram Industries, Inc., Nauta-Line, Inc., Hendersonville, Tenn., Northernaire Floating Lodges, International Falls, Minn., Perkins Engines, Inc., Farmington, Mich., Princess Mfg. Corp., Alhambra, Calif., Ray Jefferson, Philadelphia, Pa., River Queen Boat Works, Douglas, Mich., Rubbermaid Marine and Recreational Products Division, Wooster, Ohio, SeaCamper (Farenwald Enterprises of Florida), Green Cove Springs, Fla., Sea Rover Marine, Inc., St. Petersburg, Fla., Ship-A-Shore Corp., Mishawaka, Ind., Trail or Float, Vancouver, Wash., Thompson and Associates, Tulsa, Okla., Uniflite, Inc., Bellingham, Wash., Watercraft, Inc., Gallatin, Tenn.

Sincere thanks also, for photographs and invaluable assistance, to the U.S. Coast Guard (particularly the Governor's Island, N.Y., Headquarters), the U.S. Department of the Interior, Bureau of Reclamation and National Park Service, the U.S. Army Corps of Engineers (particularly Nashville, Mobile, and Omaha districts), the Tennessee Valley Authority, American National Red Cross, Arkansas Publicity and Parks Commission, Florida Development Commission, Florida News Bureau, Florida Department of Commerce, Maine Department of Economic Development, Ohio Division of Parks and Recreation, and Washington State Department of Commerce and Economic Development. Also Richard DeShazer.

The cooperation of *Family Houseboating* magazine and Rent-A-Cruise of America is gratefully noted, as well as the cheerful and speedy assistance of many concerns not specifically listed here.

The Wonderful World of Houseboating, by Duane Newcomb
Copyright © 1974 by Duane Newcomb
Copyright © 1974 by Prentice-Hall, Inc., for all maps

Printed in the United States of America

Prentice-Hall International, Inc., London
Prentice-Hall of Australia, Pty. Ltd., North Sydney
Prentice-Hall of Canada, Ltd., Toronto
Prentice-Hall of India Private Ltd., New Delhi
Prentice-Hall of Japan, Inc., Tokyo

Library of Congress Cataloging in Publication Data
Newcomb, Duane G
The wonderful world of houseboating.
Includes bibliographical references.
1. House-boats. I. Title.
GV836.N48   797.1'2   73-14733
ISBN 0-13-962472-4

10   9   8   7   6   5   4   3   2   1

CONTENTS

LIST OF MAPS

Maps planned and executed by Theodore R. Miller

CHAPTER ONE

The Joys of Houseboating

Most of us can remember when family houseboating as we know it today was virtually unheard of. People went water-skiing in droves or out for an afternoon's cruise or sail, but who would have thought of taking the entire family on a lazy two-week water vacation?

Today, however, the world of houseboating has dramatically changed. A drive along any waterside community shows that water-skiing, Sunday afternoon cruising and sailing are as popular as ever, if not more so. But now literally hundreds of thousands of families also go houseboating each year, enjoying a leisurely week or two of water exploration many proclaim to be the most exhilarating adventure they've ever had. And chances are good that the following year many of them will come back for more, joining the thousands of new houseboating families.

Probably the chief reason for this tremendous upsurge in houseboat vacationing is that each year more and more families are discovering that life on the water provides a refreshing change for each and every member of the family—with the houseboat offering an almost ideal base of operations.

What are some of the factors that contribute to the houseboat's ever-increasing popularity?

First and foremost, houseboating offers a tremendous opportunity for browsing afloat. America's extensive network of waterways is studded with varied and picturesque sights. Along one short stretch of California's delta country, for instance, a houseboater might encounter a seagoing freighter, pass by row upon row of unusual waterside dwellings, come upon an old sternwheeler sitting out in the middle of an asparagus field and glide through dramatic backwater country abounding with wildlife. Other areas of the country offer the additional diversity of glimpses of semiswampland, the opportunity to observe locks in action, water exploration of back-country lakes and fascinating views of industrial water traffic.

Houseboat explorers can also tie up and investigate remote islands, examine caves, tour old towns and visit nearby museums.

Houseboating as a family activity has literally exploded onto the vacation scene.

1

Many houseboaters like this combination of land and sea exploration. They therefore keep a car available at their houseboat base to use for visits to nearby attractions. Those taking longer cruises stop off at major towns along the way and rent a car on the spot to investigate the local points of interest.

For example, houseboaters cruising the Mississippi often dock at Clinton, Iowa, and go ashore to visit the Buffalo Bill and Lone Star museums, General Grant's home, Effigy Mounds National Monument and other attractions. Or on Lake Ouachita, Arkansas, they can tour such scenic spots as Hot Springs National Park, the Ouachita National Forest and Crystal Mountain. Other areas offer similar opportunities for exploring the nearby countryside.

Another favorite pastime for which the houseboat is ideally suited is fishing, for America's houseboating waters are also some of the country's best fishing waters. Family houseboaters across the nation, including children, have caught huge striped bass in California, 36-inch rainbow trout in Idaho's lake country, sauger in Kentucky Lake, pike, channel catfish, bluegill, perch, paddlefish and many other varieties of marine life in other areas. Marinas along the route gladly provide information on the best bait for local waters, thus increasing chances of a good catch.

In addition to these activities, the top deck of a houseboat makes an excellent observation platform from which to observe the abundant birdlife on and alongside the water. Alert birdwatchers will be rewarded with glimpses of species of a variety of sizes and colors, especially during the twilight hours of dawn and dusk.

There is a variety of other wildlife along the banks as well. Freshwater areas shelter amphibians, snails and snakes, while the saltwater shores harbor a host of sea plants, seashells, sea crabs and other crustaceans.

Houseboaters have also discovered that many houseboating areas, especially in the Southwest, are in rockhound country. This provides the entire family with the opportunity to collect unusual rocks and minerals for later identification. These are not only fun to gather but make attractive display mementos back home.

Houseboating families can even try their hand at that historical American pastime, gold panning. In some sections of the country you are likely to come up with "color" (gold flakes) in almost every panful.

Another plus for the houseboat is the "new," almost unbelievable look the heavens take on from the deck (there are fewer lights to cut star visibility, and most bodies of water offer a clear unobstructed view in all directions). It's a real thrill to pick out a planet, identify one of the brighter stars or locate the constellations.

A houseboat also makes a good base for swimming, for underwater exploration with a mask and snorkle and for skin diving. It is even possible to water-ski behind some of the most powerful houseboats, but the gas consumption necessary to bring that much weight up to skiing speed makes for an extremely expensive ride.

Finally, houseboating offers the entire family a much needed change of pace, providing each family member with his own special

A vacation for every taste: Cocktails for two at the end of a day afloat.

2

All aboard for a day of family fun in the sun.

Houseboat get-togethers like these are part of the fun. Sometimes three or four houseboats join up for a big picnic on shore.

reason for enjoying life on board. The lady of the house will find herself surrounded with all the familiar conveniences: a complete kitchen (galley) with hot and cold running water, a stove, an oven and a refrigerator. There is plenty of working and storage space on the boat, plus a shower. She can thus enjoy life on the water with all of home's comforts but few of its problems.

Children will find their days jam-packed with such activities as fishing, swimming, exploring and helping with the boat. All this plus a snug bed at night and a built-in playground on deck.

For the skipper there is the fun and freedom of adventure behind the wheel of his own boat. There are no alarm clocks here, nor the pressure of being somewhere at a given time.

One last practical point. A family houseboating vacation is extremely easy to plan. Just answer one of the ads in magazines such as *Sunset, Family Houseboating, Motor Boating, Rudder, Boating,* etc., select the area and the houseboat that look the most appealing and make a reservation. From then on it is simply a matter of arriving at the dock on the given day.

Why a Houseboat?

Although long-time cruiser owners deny it fiercely, there isn't a boat type better suited for a real water vacation than a houseboat. The facts speak for themselves.

A conventional cruiser is a compromise between performance and good looks. Its V-type hull handles well under all sorts of water conditions and provides good speed, but for real vacation living a cruiser lacks space. Because of its hull design, the cruiser's galley will be small, its bunks crammed into tight corners and its living space (unless you are lucky enough to be aboard a really deluxe model) decidedly cramped.

Take a 35-foot cabin cruiser, for example. Only a portion of its overall space is livable, and a party of eight would feel crowded. The cabin accommodations of one popular 35-footer, for instance, consist of a single 9 by 12 foot cabin plus two forward V-shaped berths. A 4 by 4 foot galley, two convertible lounges, a drop-leaf table and a head (toilet) are compressed into this space.

In contrast, a popular 34-foot houseboat offers its occupants over 50 feet of usable space. It boasts a long 9 by 21½ foot cabin plus a lower stateroom that sleeps two. The living area is divided into a 7 by 9 foot forward cabin, a large galley, a head, storage areas and a 7 by 8 foot aft (rear) cabin. There are convertible lounges in both the forward and aft cabins, plus a dinette area that converts into a bed sleeping two. Passengers can relax in the forward cabin, utilizing both the forward and aft lounges; they can sit or lounge on the forward deck; they can stretch out on the sundeck above. Ten to twelve people can really spread out and enjoy themselves in this amount of space.

A houseboat of this type offers other advantages as well. Its galley provides at least twice the working space of a similarly sized cruiser, over twice the counter space and two to three times as much storage area. Most 34-foot models feature double sinks (as compared to the cruiser's single variety), plus larger ovens and refrigerators. Houseboats this size are generally equipped with a shower and a spacious vanity area.

Besides offering its passengers comfort and roominess, the houseboat, with its emphasis on drapes, carpets and other "homey" touches, provides an atmosphere of coziness not generally found on the more Spartan cruiser.

America's network of waterways is studded with a variety of sights. Boldt Castle at Alexandria Bay in the fascinating Thousand Islands area.

Another definite plus for the houseboat is its initial cost—roughly half that of a cruiser of the same size. One popular 30-foot houseboat, for instance, retails at $10,000; a cruiser of similar size and quality is $20,000.

There is also the safety factor to consider. The houseboat's shallow draft makes it less susceptible to damage by underwater objects than a cruiser of comparable size. Also, the guard rail that runs all the way around most houseboats offers greater protection against falling overboard than what is available on most cruisers.

A further matter that should not be overlooked is the question of accessibility. Houseboat rentals, because of their popularity, are available at several hundred diverse locations. Cruiser rentals are neither as plentiful nor as widely scattered. In addition, agencies renting houseboats cater to family skippers, many of whom have never been on the water before; most cruiser rentals are limited to experienced helmsmen.

Operating costs are about the same for either type of boat. Maintenance and care of houseboats and cruisers constructed from similar materials are also comparable.

Evolution of the Houseboat

It has taken a long time for the houseboat to come into its own. The first houseboats in the United States probably date back to the "shanty boats"—shacks on logs or rafts—that appeared on our inland rivers during the late 1700s and early 1800s. These primitive dwellings were followed by more sophisticated crafts with a deckhouse or cabin designed to carry both freight and passengers. In turn, they led to the creation of the legendary "sin" or pleasure boats peopled by mustachioed gamblers and their ladies.

It was not until the early 1930s that water enthusiasts first began constructing what amounted to conventional homes on pontoons.

A picturesque Florida byway. The miles of interconnecting waterways make this state a top houseboating area.

Some of these initial efforts boasted awnings, porches and even gardens. A few could be floated from place to place, but most were permanently moored at one location. But even the most ambitious of these waterborne dwellings was a far cry from the houseboat as we know it today.

Several backyard builders began putting a more modernized house cabin on pontoons in the late 1930s. During the next decade houseboat engineering took a stride forward with the appearance along the Kentucky, Ohio and Tennessee rivers of steel houseboats designed by builder/designer Bob Darling. Roland T. Peterson of Gary, Ind., built *River Queen*, the nation's first assembly-line produced steel hull houseboat, in 1954.

This innovation was followed in 1959 by the development of the rental concept, conceived by George Ladd of Stockton, Calif. Ladd designed and built his own rental fleet of standardized houseboats, which were primarily "houses" or houseboat cabins built on round pontoons. They could travel up to eight miles an hour and were restricted to quiet waters.

An additional breakthrough occurred in 1960, when Jack McKee, a boat dealer in Gallatin, Tennessee, started tinkering with a fiberglass-hulled houseboat that performed well and could even plane (come up out of the water to ride on a portion of the hull) and pull water-skiers when powered by a 50-horsepower Mercury outboard. Various manufacturers went on to experiment with a variety of new hull designs; diverse hull materials including fiberglass, steel, aluminum and Ferro-cement; and multilevel craft and stern drive propulsion, powered with a variety of power packages.

The new emphasis on speed has narrowed the performance gap between houseboats and cruisers amazingly in recent years. Some cruiser-hull houseboats, for example, can now attain speeds over 30 mph and some have handled 10- to 12-foot waves and 40-knot wind gusts. Modern houseboat designers have developed craft that are highly resistant to the tendency to roll or broach (veer suddenly into the wind) in rough water.

Another major factor in the evolution of the houseboat as we know it today has been the desire to entice the women of the family aboard by providing in effect comfortable vacation cottages on the water. Taking a tip from the travel trailer manufacturers, houseboat manufacturers began equipping their crafts with LP (liquefied petroleum) gas ranges with ovens, LP or electric refrigerators, hot water tanks, pressurized water systems and a 12/110 electrical system. Some of the larger houseboats even sport gasoline-powered generators to handle lighting and the operation of electric ovens and refrigerators.

And the influence of the trailer boom has not stopped here. The latest and most ingenious developments in the houseboat field include sleekly modern amphibious trailerables that are equally at home in a trailer camp and afloat. For a detailed discussion of these popular newcomers to the boating scene see Chapter 6.

Today's comfortable, self-contained units stressing livability and all-round performance can easily accommodate a family for two weeks while providing a boat versatile enough to satisfy even a veteran sailor. The average 14-inch draft of most modern houseboats makes it possible to leave the channel and cruise close to shore and into shallow, winding

Locking through at Guntersville Dam, one of the popular TVA houseboating reservoirs.

Industrial water traffic along the Gulf Intracoastal Waterway.

backwaters that a conventional craft would not dare tackle. Many models can be grounded bow first on a sandy beach if the family decides to step ashore to picnic, swim, explore or spend the night.

In an attempt to provide a boat for every kind of water, houseboat design today is developing in two main directions. One type of craft is evolving toward the cruiser, stressing high speed and rough-weather performance . . . the other is geared towards the pleasures of still water.

Rough-water houseboats have water-tightness, safety glass and electrical and mechanical systems that meet cruiser standards. They can be operated safely in coastal waters in calm weather, and in rough water with an experienced skipper. They are now used in coastal waters from Seattle to Maine. One recently made the 1900-mile run in open water from San Diego to Acapulco, encountering 35-foot waves and 40-to 50-knot winds. Another set a speed record for boats over 50 feet, in the Miami to Nassau Power Boat Race.

Protected-water houseboats, on the other hand, are built with an eye to pleasure cruising on inland lakes, rivers and protected bays. They feature large expanses of glass, a flat or semiflat bottom and a low freeboard (the distance between the deck and the waterline).

Full-Time Living Aboard

More and more people are living full-time aboard houseboats. Two factors have contributed to this. First, as we have seen, houseboats have begun to add all the comforts of home, such as 10 cu. ft. refrigerators, ovens with rotisseries, freezers, and more. In addition, there is more storage than ever before. Living areas, such as the galley (kitchen), lounges, staterooms ,and other sleeping facilities are completely separate and don't interfere with each other. This makes a houseboat extremely comfortable for extended living. *Family Houseboating* magazine regularly carries articles about couples who live aboard full-time, giving complete details on how they do it.

Exclusive houseboating communities designed for full-time houseboat living are beginning to spring up across the country. These closely resemble modern mobile home-park developments, some with clubhouses and other common recreational facilities. All provide electricity, water and sewage hookups. Many houseboaters living aboard simply utilize conventional marinas at a nominal monthly charge.

Growing numbers of retirees also boat northern waters in the summer, headquartering at a marina of their choice; then pull anchor in the fall and migrate to warmer southern waters. Currently, many retirees with their houseboat completely paid for find they can live comfortably on a houseboat for as little as $300 a month. These costs vary depending on the type of marina you select, the amount of cruising you do and your general lifestyle (see Chapter 6 for a general discussion of houseboat expenses).

Pontoons or cruisers? A boat for every vacation need. Pontoon boats make excellent beach explorers. They can be pulled up almost anywhere.

Cruiser hulls offer speed and maneuverability, plus plenty of loafing space.

Renting a Houseboat

Until quite recently, houseboat rentals were only available in the most popular and sheltered recreational areas such as Florida's waterways and the California Sacramento-San Joaquin Delta. Today the scene has changed dramatically. With more and more families discovering the tremendous fun of houseboat adventuring, houseboat marinas have sprung up throughout the nation, including the coastal areas. Now there is hardly a state or a good-size body of water anywhere in the United States (and much of Canada) that doesn't offer some type of rental unit.

It is possible, for example, to rent houseboats to explore New York's Barge Canal System, Long Island Sound, the Ohio River, the entire Mississippi River system, the coast of Southern California, the 1000-mile Sacramento Delta, the Florida Keys and the Bahamas.

The nature of the waters you plan to explore will influence the type of boat you require. Whereas rentals in the past were almost exclusively limited to slow-moving, pontoon-type craft, today's selections range from such leisurely models—for the family that wants a relaxing ride—to the streamlined houseboat cruiser that can travel over 30 mph.

Today's houseboat emphasizes livability.

Vacationing Aboard

The special peacefulness and lack of pressure of a houseboat vacation has been enthusiastically described by Erle Stanley Gardner in his *Drifting Down the Delta* (William Morrow Co., 1969).

"One can sleep in the morning as late as he desires. He can press a button and turn on the coffee percolator. He can dress or not as he pleases. If he chooses to lie around in pajamas after having his coffee, he can stretch out on one of the beds, prop pillows behind his head, and look out over the sunkissed waters, watching the fish arching up to slap the water with their tails before again descending into the depths. Or he can step out on deck, draw up a chair, and be fishing in a matter of seconds. . . .

Under such circumstances as this, the blood pressure in human beings tends to drop to normal limits. . . . And the nice thing is that one doesn't need to go to some distant point in order to achieve this privacy and luxury. Everything is built in. There is no necessity for breathless pursuit of any object. The only thing that is necessary is to get aboard and cast off the lines, start the motors, and move slowly along the surface of the river."

This general atmosphere of tranquility is spiced with the fun of taking part in "water life." The dealings and details involved in water travel include pulling into the dock for fuel, dropping anchor for the night, getting splashed by the waves from a freighter, chatting with other houseboaters, locking through a series of locks and watching a drawbridge raise up just for you.

Many types of sleeping arrangements are available in today's houseboats. This guest stateroom offers peace and privacy.

Houseboat galleys combine good storage space with the latest time-saving kitchen aids.

A feeling of space and grace are two major concerns in modern houseboat design. Note the cleverly designed dining table.

Different people have different vacation needs. The houseboat can cater to a variety of these at one time.

Here's how one novice skipper describes his family's experiences: "When we eased the throttle into reverse and backed away from the dock at Lake Shasta [California], we had an awful lot of doubts. After all, none of us had ever handled a boat before.

"The kids directed us out, then I turned the helm to the right. At first nothing happened. Then the boat began to respond. The dock gradually disappeared from sight and we were on our way down lake.

"That day, and the days that followed, were fabulous. We used the houseboat to explore a myriad of coves and inlets. Sometimes we pulled into shore and climbed as high as we could to look over the lake and surrounding countryside. Other times we beached on an island and the kids played pirate.

"There was fishing, of course, and the children also boarded our inflatable raft and rowed around the boat, across to the shore and up to the other boats that came by frequently. Sometimes we'd pull into one of the shore campgrounds and have a weiner roast. Other times we'd ground near another boat and both families would get together and compare notes while the kids played.

"At night we'd either pull up alongside other families and spend a long, fun-filled evening on shore around a big campfire, or tuck the boat away up some secluded cove where we could enjoy complete privacy.

"By the end of two weeks we were all brown, relaxed and completely convinced that this was the only way to spend a vacation."

It's possible to cruise on a houseboat for an indefinite period: two weeks, six months or more. Many families now spend the entire summer traveling our country's many waterways. The only imperative in most modern houseboats is to pull in and stock up on fuel and groceries at regular intervals.

The decision as to where to go on a houseboat vacation and for how long depends mainly on where you live, how close you are to the nearest body of water and what kind of an area you wish to cruise in. A geographical breakdown of major houseboating areas in the United States designed to help you plan the best trip for you is given in the following chapter.

No matter what kind of a houseboat vacation you are looking for, it is available today. No doubt about it, houseboating as a family activity has literally exploded onto the scene.

CHAPTER TWO

Where Is Houseboating Country?

Just where in the United States can you go houseboating? The answer is just about anyplace. As we have seen, all that you need for a successful excursion afloat is a large enough body of water to permit some casual cruising and exploration. This can be found in abundance throughout the nation.

Some of the more seaworthy cruiser-type houseboats cruise both oceans and the Great Lakes; these areas, however, are too rough for many houseboats. The majority of houseboat traffic travels our nation's vast river systems with their miles and miles of connecting waterways and the larger lakes. Important houseboating centers are scattered throughout this network, from California to Florida.

Let's take time out to examine houseboating country, area by area, with an eye to exploring the possibilities nearest to you.

The Northeast

Houseboating is relatively new to the East as a whole, but there is tremendous potential here. New England's scenic Lake Champlain, for example, is dotted with excellent marinas over its entire surface and provides access into Canada and the St. Lawrence River-Thousand Islands area. From Sorel, Quebec, at the mouth of the Richelieu River to Cape Vincent on Lake Ontario, the St. Lawrence River offers 234 miles of tremendous boating. The river is fairly broad for the first 46 miles upstream from

Sorel, and you will see many oceangoing vessels. At Montreal you enter the St. Lawrence Seaway and pass through seven large locks. It is also possible to enter the Ottawa River near here and cruise to Ottawa.

Between Brockville, Ontario, and Cape Vincent, New York, you will be cruising through the Thousand Islands region (see map p. 36), one of the most famous boating areas in the United States. Along this stretch of water are about 1700 emerald-green islands which crowd in clusters and strands along the river. Seen from the air, this sight is fabulous. One of the major attractions in this section is unfinished Boldt Castle, a bereaved millionaire's dream house. Throughout the area there are numerous parks and facilities on both sides of the river.

The entire length of the river between Kingston and Brockville, including some offshore islands, is dotted with a chain of recreational areas known as the St. Lawrence Islands National Park. The mainland parks are accessible from the Thousand Islands Parkway, others only by boat. This continuous chain of parklands offers camping, boating, picnic, playground and swimming facilities. The New York State parks in this area also provide a wide variety of facilities. Wellesley Island boasts a nine-hole golf course, and at Robert Moses State Park it's possible to examine the St. Lawrence Power and Seaway projects closely.

Other New England areas on the rise include the Connecticut River, New Hamp-

The New York Barge Canal System is one of the major houseboating areas in the nation. Historic Mohawk Valley.

One of the many beautiful areas in New York State.

shire's forested 72-square-mile Lake Winnipesaukee, and a strip of the New Hampshire seacoast area, including the Piscataqua River and Great Bay. And don't overlook little Rhode Island whose Narragansett Bay (see map p. 37) boasts one of the largest and most varied saltwater recreation areas in all New England. Narragansett Bay itself extends 28 miles inland with the Providence, Seekonk and Sakonnet rivers being really saltwater arms of the bay. It is irregularly shaped with many smaller arms including Greenwich and Mount Hope bays which will also be of interest to houseboaters. Some of the islands in the bay have high rocky cliffs which rise in many places behind the island beaches.

Farther north, in Maine, houseboating surprisingly enough has not yet come into its own, despite the area's more than 3500 miles of dramatic coastline and 2500 lakes crying for exploration. Maine's coastal waters offer excellent houseboating for the more seaworthy type of craft; boaters are never more than a short run from a safe harbor, and they enjoy the protection of hundreds of offshore islands. Some of the state's inland waters, including Grand and Moosehead lakes, also offer attractive cruising possibilities. Moosehead is a majestic lake, forty miles long and twenty miles wide, ringed by beautiful timbered mountains and sprinkled with many large and small islands, sheltered inlets and coves.

To the south, in New York State, lies houseboating country at its best. The State Barge Canal System is one of the major houseboating areas in the nation and can be cruised for miles, with side trips to such spots as the Finger Lakes and Lake Champlain (see map p. 38). This remarkable network provides convenient linkage for the state's natural water facilities as well as feeding into a virtual labyrinth of canals and waterways that offer easy access to the Canadian wilderness.

There are four basic divisions of the State Barge Canal System: the Erie, the Champlain, the Oswego, and the Cayuga-Seneca canals.

The Erie Canal stretches 348 miles from Waterford near Troy through thirty-four locks to Tonawanda, New York, on the Niagara River. First, it runs up the Mohawk River to Frankfort, continues as an artificial land cut to New London, then through Wood Creek, Oneida Lake, Oneida River, Seneca River and Clyde River to Lyons. From Lyons to Lockport the Erie Canal is an artificial land cut channel often located higher than the adjacent countryside. The route traverses a wide variety of scenery with a number of marina facilities along the way.

The Oswego Canal which leaves the Erie Canal at Three Rivers proceeds north 24 miles through seven locks to the Port of Oswego and Lake Ontario. From here it's possible to continue along the lake to the St. Lawrence River or to Lake Erie through the Welland Canal.

The Cayuga-Seneca Canal leaves the Erie Canal near Montezuma. Houseboaters may cruise 42 miles to Ithaca through the first lock of the Cayuga-Seneca Canal and Cayuga Lake; or 52 miles to Watkins Glen by way of all four locks of the Cayuga-Seneca Canal. These long narrow lakes are extremely beautiful and popular with boaters. Of special interest are the Painted Rocks on Seneca Lake's east shore palisades and the underground grottos, walkways and waterfalls at Watkins Glen.

The Champlain Canal extends 60 miles from Waterford near Troy through eleven locks to Whitehall at the southern tip of Lake Champlain. From here it's then possible to proceed through Lake Champlain to the Canadian border. This lake, 120 miles long and covering 435 square miles, is shared by both New York and Vermont.

Partridge Harbor, two miles north of Westport, New York, offers a fine secluded anchorage. At Burton Island (near St. Albans Bay, Vermont) you'll find a 300-acre island which offers the houseboater a choice of sleeping aboard or staying ashore in a lean-to, campsite or cabin rented from Vermont's Department of Forests and Parks.

Cruising up Lake Champlain the houseboater passes such prominent landmarks as the

Four Brothers, South Hero, Valcour and Cumberland Head.

From the Canadian border north, the navigable channels are regulated by Canada. It's possible from the border to continue north 76 miles through eleven locks up the Richelieu River and Chambly Canal to Sorel. From there houseboaters can cruise the many miles of Canadian waters or proceed past Montreal and the Thousand Islands area to Lake Ontario. Pleasure craft may enter Canada for a period of up to twelve months under a permit obtainable from Canadian Customs at the port of entry. Information on Canadian canals is available from the Canals Division, Department of Transport, Ottawa, Ontario, Canada.

In addition to the State Barge Canal System, Federal waterways connect both ends of the Erie Canal. At the western end, it's possible to houseboat all the way down the Hudson from near Troy to New York City. At the easterly end, the Federal Government has improved the Niagara River from Tonawanda to Buffalo. All canals are toll free and no permits are needed. A map of the New York State Barge Canal System and Connecting Waterways is available free from the Waterways Maintenance Subdivision, State Department of Transportation, 1220 Washington Avenue, Albany, New York 12226.

Currently also, the New York State Office of Parks and Recreation in cooperation with the Department of Transportation is beginning to develop recreational facilities along the canals. These will include trailways and canal lock parks. In addition, marine facilities along the canal continue to be expanded and improved regularly.

Another excellent houseboating area that lies within New York State borders Long Island Sound (see map p. 39). Some 110 miles long and 20 miles wide, it is considered one of the leading pleasure boat centers of the United States. You can explore both the Long Island and the Connecticut shores, or swing around the end of the island into Great Peconic Bay. There is also good cruising along the Fire Island National Seashore.

Also in New York, thirty-six-mile-long Lake George located in the Adirondack Mountains is one of the state's most popular summer resorts offering some houseboating possibilities. There are excellent facilities here and tremendous views of the surrounding mountains from every part of the lake.

Pennsylvania is another eastern state that offers attractive possibilities to the houseboater, particularly along the Ohio, Allegheny, Delaware and Susquehanna rivers. The Susquehanna is of special interest. It has been sectioned into three widely used, well-developed pleasure boating areas—Conowingo Lake, Lake Aldred and Lake Clarke—through the creation of three power dams in Pennsylvania and Maryland.

The Pennsylvania and New York shores of Lake Erie also offer facilities galore combined with interesting possibilities for exploration. Nearby Lake Wallenpaupack, Pennsylvania's largest lake in the lake region of the Poconos, provides enjoyable cruising on a smaller scale. It is also possible to houseboat Delaware Bay (see map p. 42) for many miles. There are few bays and inlets on Delaware Bay, however, and most of the shoreline is smooth and marshy.

Last but not least, West Virginia offers attractive houseboating possibilities along the Ohio River, the Little Kanawha River starting at Parkersburg, the Kanawha River beginning at Point Pleasant, the Elk River starting at Charleston, and part of the Monongahela River. Waterborne travelers exploring these routes will be rewarded with some extremely picturesque scenery.

The South

Let's begin with Florida, because when it comes to houseboating, Florida is in a class all its own. This vacation state may well be the houseboat center of the world. It boasts a total of eight major houseboat cruising areas that offer visitors thousands of miles of waterways and days on end of family cruising (see map p. 43).

16

Florida's meandering waterways cry out for exploration.

Houseboaters in the Sunshine State have the choice of some or all of the following possibilities:

(1) A trip along the Caloosahatchee River, navigable all the way to Lake Okeechobee. The scenic islands of Sanibel, La Costa and others reached from Fort Myers through the mouth of the Caloosahatchee River are noted for their fishing and their beauty. Sanibel and Captiva offer one of the finest hunting grounds for shell collectors in North America.

(2) A tour of the Ten Thousand Islands area of which Marco Island is the largest and best known. The entire area is known as a paradise for sport fishermen and birdwatchers. Flamingo, headquarters for the Everglades National Park, lies southeast of the Thousand Islands and can be easily reached from there by houseboat. It is fully equipped with a marina, campgrounds and visitor accommodations.

(3) A visit to the Florida Keys, through the calm, shallow waters of Florida Bay. The over 600 square miles of island-dotted waters that make up the Florida Keys area are clearly marked, and the tiny palm-fringed islands are linked with bridges. Fishing is good and there are excellent facilities all the way to Key West. Be sure to obtain navigational charts before attempting to cruise. The Straits of Florida on the Atlantic side of the Keys are open water, potentially dangerous to houseboaters.

(4) A voyage down the Indian River (part of the Atlantic Intracoastal Waterway), to the mouth of the St. Lucie River near Stuart. From here the St. Lucie Canal leads into Lake Okeechobee. The northern part of this cruise begins within sight of the space center at Cape

The Intracoastal Waterway at Fort Lauderdale, often called the "Venice of America".

Houseboating in the Everglades.

Kennedy, then winds down the long narrow lagoon known as Indian River. The area from Vero Beach south is called the Gold Coast and from the Indian River it is possible to cruise all the way south to Miami. Stately mansions and sweeping estates dot the shore from Jupiter lighthouse to Miami Beach.

(5) Water exploration along the Kissimmee River Valley Waterway. Houseboat rentals are available at the top of Lake Tohopekaliga. The cruise route passes through Lake Tohopekaliga, Lake Cypress, Lake Hatchineha, Lake Kissimmee via the Kissimmee River and on into Lake Okeechobee. The lakes offer good fishing, with fish camps and marinas conveniently located for houseboaters. Navigational charts can be obtained from the Kissimmee Chamber of Commerce, Kissimmee, Fla., 32741. The Kissimmee cruise samples some real Florida backcountry.

(6) A cruise down the broad St. John's River from Sanford on Lake Monroe north to Jacksonville. The St. John's River, famous for its bass fishing, is the continent's only major north-flowing river. Known as the "Nile of America," it opens into several large lakes between Sanford and Jacksonville.

(7) The opportunity to travel way down upon the Suwannee River, navigable from Bradford southward to the Gulf of Mexico. A feature of the trip is the numerous sparkling streams that gush from crystal springs into the river. Many of the springs are developed as parks, campgrounds or picnic-swimming areas. The Stephen Foster Memorial borders the river at White Springs.

(8) A river adventure along the Apalachicola, through beautiful thick forest land, to its confluence with the Chattahoochee at Lake Seminole.

Taken as a whole, these eight areas plus the Intracoastal Waterway discussed later in this chapter make Florida a real houseboater's paradise.

The rest of the South offers excellent houseboating as well. This is largely thanks to its vast TVA reservoir system (see map pp. 48-49) with forty-one reservoirs in or bordering seven states—Alabama, Georgia, Kentucky, Mississippi, North Carolina, Tennessee and Virginia.

These provide 600,000 acres of water surface, 11,000 miles of shoreline on the Tennessee River alone. Dams along the Tennessee are equipped with locks, allowing you to cruise for over 600 uninterrupted miles. Dams on the tributary streams are not locked, however, except for Melton Hill Dam on the Clinch River between Harriman and Knoxville.

Another scenic run made possible by the lock system is a trip down 184-mile-long Kentucky Lake and into the Ohio River at Paducah. From here you can continue on to join the Mississippi at Cairo, Illinois.

All of the lakes in the TVA system have conveniently located marinas, stores and overnight accommodations. Many areas also offer good public recreational facilities.

The run from Paducah to Knoxville can be made in about a week, but two to three weeks is really needed to do justice to the trip. Along this stretch, houseboaters will pass through a total of nine reservoirs. Kentucky Lake, twenty-two miles upstream from Paducah, offers a fascinating variety of sights varying from rich pasture lands to rock cliffs rising high above the water. Along the 184-mile-long lake lies the huge Land Between the Lakes, the Tennessee National Wildlife Refuge and the Shiloh National Military Park (mile 198).

Fifty-three-mile-long Pickwick Lake, behind Pickwick Dam, carries the houseboater through a short stretch of Tennessee, and northeastern Mississippi into northern Alabama. Wilson Dam, backing up Wilson Lake, has been designated a national historic landmark. A large industrial complex, including TVA's National Fertilizer Development Center, has grown up in the dam area. Wheeler Lake, stretching 74 miles upstream, boasts Joe Wheeler State Park, the Brown's Ferry Nuclear Plant and Wheeler National Wildlife Refuge along the lake's shores.

The TVA lakes are widely used for recreation. This is Wheeler Lake.

From Guntersville Dam on Guntersville Lake it is a 76-mile run up the reservoir to Nickajack Dam, cruising past giant Widows Creek Stream Plant and Russell Cave National Monument. Guntersville, a thriving port city on Guntersville Lake, offers some of the most complete water-oriented recreation facilities and services on the waterway.

Probably some of the most spectacular scenery on the cruise can be found on 46-mile-long Nickajack Lake. Here houseboaters cruise through high-cliffed areas such as Skillet Gap, Grindstone Ridge and Raccoon Mountain as well as passing heavily industrialized Chattanooga, Tennessee.

The remaining lakes before reaching Knoxville, Chickamauga, Watts Bar and Fort Loudoun also offer excellent cruising and enjoyable water exploring.

In addition to the mainstream cruising, the TVA's landlocked reservoirs boast some tremendous boating opportunities. Most are quite large, offering wide expanses of water and numerous secluded coves. These include Fontana Lake on the Little Tennessee River, Hiwassee and Chatuge lakes on the Hiwassee

River, Nottely Lake on the Nottely River, Parksville Lake on the Ocoee River, Blue Ridge Lake on the Toccoa River, Norris Lake with arms on the Clinch and Powell rivers, Douglas Lake on the French Broad River, Davy Crockett Lake on the Nolichucky River, Fort Patrick Henry Lake and South Holston Lake on the southern fork of Holston River, Cherokee Lake on the Holston River, Boone Lake with arms on the southern fork of the Holston River and Watauga River and Watauga Lake on the Watauga River. All can be houseboated. Probably the most spectacular of all these landlocked TVA lakes is 29-mile-long Fontana Lake in North Carolina nestled among the breathtaking "misty" peaks of the Great Smokies and Nantahalas. The dam here is the highest in the eastern United States, 480 feet, and attracts millions of visitors.

In addition to the TVA system, houseboaters can also cruise much of the Cumberland. This is due to the handiwork of the U.S. Corps of Engineers which impounded the Cumberland in 1966 and created handsome Lake Barkley.

The Corps of Engineers is also responsible

for the creation of scenic Lake Cumberland, 200 miles east of Lake Barkley. Between the two lie over 300 miles of 9-foot navigable waters and three other headwater reservoirs.

Lake Barkley, named after the late vice-president from Kentucky, extends 118 miles upstream to Cheatham Lock near Nashville. Running some 40 miles along the right shoreline is the Land Between the Lakes, a 170,000-acre demonstration project in outdoor recreation and environmental education being developed by the TVA. This land actually lies between Lake Barkley and the TVA Kentucky Reservoir. There are a number of campgrounds here and a conservation education center located near the middle of the Land Between the Lakes on Lake Barkley. Visitors to the reception facility station center here are directed to attractions within the area including hiking trails that lead to various points of interest. Between Lake Barkley and Lake Cumberland, there are three locks: Cheatham Lock 148.7 miles from Lake Barkley; Old Hickory Lock, 216.9 miles; and Cordell Hull Lock, 313.5 miles. Old Hickory Lake is a 22,500-acre lake lying in an area rich in past Indian culture. Recreation areas around Old Hickory Lake range in size from 30 to 150 acres. There is a permanent population of over 500 Canadian geese on this lake and nearby there are ducks, mourning doves, rabbits, quail, squirrels and a few deer in the upper reaches of the lake. Lake Cumberland, at the upper end of the chain, is in the foothills of the Cumberland Mts. World-famous Cumberland Falls, often called the Niagara of the South, is located at the upstream end of the lake. Here Cumberland Falls boasts one of only two moon bows in the world that may be seen during full moon. Recreation areas here range in size from two acres to more than 200. The lake itself runs for about 50 miles on the Cumberland River providing unlimited cruising opportunities. The three headwater lakes in this project are: J. Percy Priest Lake, Center Hill Lake, and Dale Hollow Lake. All lie just a few miles south of the main stream and are beautiful lakes in their own right. Dale Hollow Lake is large and sprawling with many fingers to provide excellent houseboat exploring.

Here are a few suggestions on how to utilize this extensive water network to enjoy mile after mile of unbroken cruising:

Step onto your houseboat at Carthage, Tennessee. Follow the Cumberland River westward as far as Lake Barkley. At Lake Barkley you can cruise up the Ohio and Mississippi rivers via Paducah, or you can cross over from Lake Barkley through the 1¾-mile interconnecting canal into Kentucky Lake, head southward along Kentucky Lake and boat right into the Tennessee River. If you're hungry for more, continue southward on the Tennessee at Chattanooga, and still following the Tennessee go all the way down to Knoxville.

For those with the time, another spectacular run through the South can be enjoyed by utilizing the East Coast's Intracoastal Waterway with an assist from Chesapeake Bay. This will enable you to houseboat all the way from Baltimore, Maryland, to Miami, Florida. The inland waterway begins on the south branch of the Elizabeth River in Virginia and heads down through North Carolina, South Carolina, Georgia and Florida. Along the way you will pass through Pamilco Sound, Charleston Harbor, Cumberland Sound and other scenic areas. In the Palm Beach, Fort Lauderdale and Miami areas the canal is lined with handsome mansions and real estate developments.

Spacious Chesapeake Bay itself, with its 3000 miles of shoreline, can get a little rough at times, but this does not discourage numerous houseboats from plying its waters as well as frequenting adjoining river areas. Running 200 miles from the coast of Virginia, the bay itself is actually a long narrow arm (4 to 40 miles wide) of the Atlantic Ocean that divides the state of Maryland into two parts. The shore of the bay is cut by many smaller bays and a number of wide-mouth rivers including the James, York, Rappahannock, Potomac and others (see map p. 42).

Still another excellent houseboating area in the South is the Roanoke River Basin complex. Stretching through Virginia and North Carolina, the 380-mile Roanoke River has been transformed by the U.S. Corps of Engineers into a huge, almost continuous body of water separated by dams and boasting over 18,000 miles of shoreline.

Eleven lakes are included in the projected system plan: seven in Virginia, one in North Carolina and three on the Virginia-North Carolina border. Each has a character and beauty of its own. Roanoke Rapids Lake is a beautiful body of water surrounded by sandy lowlands that extend upstream to the back of Gaston Dam at Gaston, North Carolina. Next on the Roanoke River, Gaston Lake has 350 miles of extremely irregular shoreline with many sheltered coves. Here you'll find excellent catfish, largemouth bass, northern pike and striped bass weighing up to 30 pounds. John H. Kerr Reservoir on the Roanoke River is a 50,000-acre body of water with 800 miles of wooded shoreline and many coves. The southern prong of John H. Kerr Reservoir extends up the Dan River to South Boston, Virginia, and the northern prong extends on up the Roanoke River (called the Staunton River in this area) to Randolph. The upper reaches of John H. Kerr Reservoir are steep and wooded.

Leesville and Smith Mountain dams and lakes located in the Blue Ridge Mountains are extremely beautiful. Leesville Lake has a shoreline of 100 miles. Smith Mountain is about 40 miles long with 500 miles of cove-studded shoreline. The mountain scenery here is exquisite. Philpott Lake, a small lake 50 miles south of Smith Mountain Lake, boasts 100 miles of shoreline. It is surrounded by the foothills of the Blue Ridge Mountains and has many coves along its shoreline with steep wooded hills and rugged cliffs.

Alabama is another southern state with a variety of cruising possibilities. You can houseboat along the Chattahoochee River through three locks to Columbus, Georgia, exploring Lake Seminole and Lake Eufaula.

Another scenic cruise through Alabama can be taken by following the Alabama River through the William B. Dannelly Reservoir to Montgomery. Above this on the Coosa River lie a series of beautiful lakes with up-and-coming facilities. These include the Alabama Power Company lakes (see map pp. 46-47) of Mitchell, Jordan, Lay, Logan Martin and Weiss on the Coosa, plus Martin Lake on the Tallapoosa River and Lewis Smith on the Sipsey fork of the Warrior.

In Mississippi there is excellent houseboating on the headwater reservoirs of Grenada, Enid, Sardis and Arkabutla lakes, plus Ross Barnett Reservoir. Grenada Lake is an extremely impressive Y-shaped lake that extends up the Yalobusha River Valley, a distance of 22 miles, and up the Skuna River Valley, a distance of 19 miles. There are a number of facilities around the lake. Sartis Lake on the Little Tallahatchie extends up the river valley a distance over 30 miles and has approximately 90 square miles of surface area. The lake is extremely popular and attracts boating enthusiasts from all over Mississippi.

In Louisiana there is boating at Toledo Bend Reservoir shared with Texas, Bayou Bodeau Reservoir shared with Arkansas and some of the smaller lakes. Louisiana also offers the boater approximately 7500 miles of navigable inland waterways. The Sabine, Calcasieu, and Vermilion rivers and a number of others linked with some of the coastal lakes are navigable north some distance from the Gulf of Mexico and generally tie into the Intracoastal Waterway forming an involved water network. The Red, Ouachita and Atchafalaya rivers are discussed elsewhere in this chapter.

To the north, Kentucky offers the houseboater 200 miles of cruising through fourteen locks along the Kentucky River between Beattyville and the Ohio River. These locks are small and antiquated. The dams here keep the river navigable guaranteeing a minimum water depth in the main channel of at least 6 feet. However, it is narrow. Some of the sights to see along the river are Fort Booneborough with picnic facilities, a restaurant and a boat camping area. The park includes the site of the fort that became Kentucky's first incorporated township. Of additional interest are the Kentucky Palisades, sheer wall precipices that tower 300 feet or more above the river. Other attractive boating will be found on the Rough River Reservoir, Barren River Reservoir, Herrington Lake and some of the other lakes, rivers and reservoirs within the state.

Before leaving the South, a final look at the available facilities in the Georgia-North and South Carolina areas:

In Georgia, 35 miles northeast of Atlanta you can houseboat 47,000-acre Lake Sidney Lanier which has 700 miles of shoreline and a complex myriad of coves, bays and islands, plus charming Lake Allatoona, sheltered in the foothills of the Blue Ridge Mountains. Also you will discover good houseboating on Lake Sinclair and on the Georgia-North Carolina border in Clark Hill and Hartwell reservoirs.

Cruising areas in South Carolina include Lake Moultrie, Lake Marion, Lake Murray and Lake Greenwood, plus Lake Catawba on the North Carolina border.

Lake Moultrie and Lake Marion together contain over 110,000 acres. The two lakes, which have a shoreline of 150 miles, are connected by a 7½-mile diversion canal. There are many fishing camps and landings around the lake.

Lake Murray, an 850,000-acre reservoir 15 miles northwest of Columbia, South Carolina, has the distinction of being called one of the five best largemouth bass lakes in the United States. Numerous islands dot the lake, making it one of the most interesting houseboating areas in the state.

There is also good houseboating in North Carolina on Lake Norman, the state's largest lake, and High Rock Lake. There is additional cruising on the bays, rivers and sounds of all three states. The Roanoke River Reservoirs are discussed elsewhere in this chapter.

The Mississippi River System

The mighty Mississippi deserves a section all its own. This majestic waterway flows over 2000 miles from its source near the Canadian border to empty into the Gulf of Mexico. Along the way it offers long stretches of perfect houseboating water with lots to do and see. In theory you could boat 2000 miles or more from the upper river, but few houseboaters have attempted this ambitious feat.

In a more practical vein, the Mississippi offers a variety of excellent vacation jaunts. Almost all of its 500-odd islands on the upper river are suitable for camping, and most of the upper river shoreline, as seen from the water, appears as wilderness.

The U.S. government owns about 540 of the 650 miles of riverfront stretching from Minneapolis to St. Louis. Most is either dedicated to wildlife refuges or public use area. North of Rock Island, Illinois, the Upper Mississippi Wildlife Refuge maintains both shores and sand islands in a natural condition.

From Minneapolis all the way down to the Gulf of Mexico, some 1800 miles, Army engineers maintain a navigational channel 300 to 400 feet wide, with a minimum 9-foot flow. This is clearly marked along its entire length with red and black buoys. The engineers are also busy along the sector between St. Paul and St. Louis, with twenty-six lock and dam projects en route. Most of these are low-level constructions, engineered to maintain channel depth rather than for flood control, and each includes a large lock with easy passage. A final factor that ensures a relaxed cruise is the Mississippi's current—a languid 2 to 6 miles per hour, depending on the season.

In addition to exploring the river and its tributaries, houseboaters in the area can branch out into the vast Mississippi Navigational System, a unique complex that provides cruising second to none in the United States.

Some of this network's major arteries, starting at New Orleans and working north, include:

• The Gulf Intracoastal Waterway. (see map pp. 52-53), extending westward from New Orleans to the Mexican border and eastward 400 miles to Apalachee Bay, Florida. Its tranquil waters, maintained at a 12-foot depth, are sheltered from the turbulent gulf and punctuated with picturesque bayous, bays and lagoons. To the west it links the Mississippi River, through Algiers and Harvey locks, with Lake Charles, Louisiana, and Beaumont, Port Arthur, Galveston, Houston and Brownsville, Texas. Near Mobile it joins up with the Tombigbee-Black Warrior, Alabama, system through a series of locks and dams, providing access to Birmingham, Alabama.

• The Red, Black and Ouachita rivers provide cruising along a 9-foot minimum depth channel through several locks in Louisiana and Arkansas to Camden, Arkansas. Several reservoirs on the Ouachita and its tributaries have been created at Lake Ouachita, Lake Greeson and De Gray, Arkansas. Lake Ouachita located 10 miles northwest of Hot Springs, Arkansas, lies wholly within the Ouachita National Forest. Formed by Blakely Mountain Dam, the reservoir is 52 miles long, has 975 miles of shoreline and covers 48,300 acres. There are a number of recreational facilities on the lake including Three Sisters Springs State Park.

• The Red River is the southernmost of the main branches of the Mississippi, and joins the larger river 341 miles above the mouth. It's possible to cruise here from the Mississippi to above Shreveport, Louisiana.

• The Arkansas River stretching all the way from the Mississippi River to Tulsa, Oklahoma, thanks to the Arkansas River Plan (see map pp. 50-51), which is a stairway of seventeen locks and dams, twelve in Arkansas and five in Oklahoma. There are four mainstream reservoirs in this project: Dardanelle, Ozark, Robert S. Kerr and Webbers Falls. Dardanelle Lake is of particular interest. Spreading westward behind the Dardanelle Dam the lake is 50 miles long, has 315 miles of shoreline and spreads through Pope, Yell, Logan, Johnson and Franklin counties. The surrounding country is extremely beautiful and forested and the lake itself contains a number of bays and inlets for water exploring. The plan also includes the reservoirs of Keystone, Oologah, Tenkiller Ferry, Eufaula, Pensacola, Grand

Arkansas' Bull Shoals Lake from Bull Mountain Tower, overlooking the Bull Shoals dock and Crowe-Barnes area. Long winding fingers make for interesting houseboat exploring.

Lake o' the Cherokees, Fort Gibson, Wister, Blue Mountain and Nimrod. All are located in picturesque country and all are big enough to provide good houseboating.

• The White River affords houseboating all the way to Batesville, Arkansas. The upper reservoirs in this system including Greers Ferry Reservoir, Norfork Lake, Bull Shoals Lake, Table Rock Reservoir and Beaver Reservoir are all beautiful lakes lying in the Ozark and Boston Mountain Country. Greers Ferry Lake (see map p. 44) is a beautiful 40,000-acre lake nestled in the eastern foothills of the Ozarks. Sugarloaf Mountain, now an island in the lake, has a winding nature trail up the mountain and excellent views from the top. Bull Shoals Lake on the Missouri-Arkansas border provides probably the most spectacular houseboating in this area. The lake itself winds like a many-legged serpent for 80 miles among the forested hills of the two states and boasts well over a thousand miles of shoreline for houseboat exploring.

• The Ohio River, which joins the Mississippi at Cairo, Illinois. Houseboaters can follow the Ohio over 800 miles, with 90 miles of additional cruising up the Monongahela and a 72-mile jaunt up the Allegheny to Pittsburgh. Modernization of the Ohio's locks and dams is currently underway. The project calls for 19 high-level dams by 1975, creating a number of pools, each worthy of a houseboating vacation. Currently the Cincinnati Pool is extremely popular with houseboaters, providing 99 miles of open river, numerous marinas and excellent riverside restaurants.

Those tenacious enough to follow the Ohio along its entire length will be rewarded with a wide variety of scenery ranging from wide bottom land near the Mississippi to high scenic rock bluffs and mountainous terrain. Along the route lie cities including Wheeling, Huntington, Cincinnati, Madison and Louisville, each with a distinctive character. It's also possible to cut off the Ohio at the Green River and boat to Bowling Green, Kentucky, or to take the Kanawha River from the Ohio as far as Charleston, West Virginia.

• The Missouri, which will carry the houseboater from St. Louis to Sioux City, Iowa, as well as providing access to an attractive series of large houseboating reservoirs (see pp. 54-55).

• The Illinois River Waterway, which joins the Mississippi at Grafton, Illinois, and continues on to the Great Lakes at Chicago. Interesting stopovers along the waterway include Starved Rock and Buffalo Rock state parks.

The Midwest

Houseboaters way up north in Minnesota can profit from the Mississippi-St. Croix River complex. The St. Croix River branches off the Mississippi just south of Minneapolis-St. Paul and extends north along the Minnesota-Wisconsin border. There is great contrast between the St. Croix River and the Mississippi. Where the two part company above Minneapolis, water turns from a sickly color to the consistency of a bad chocolate, then into green. A few miles more up river the St. Croix becomes extremely beautiful with the surrounding hills and riverbanks covered in summer with gorgeous green foliage.

In addition, there is excellent cruising in the beautiful country along the Canadian border, boasting literally hundreds of jewel-like wilderness lakes (see map pp. 58-59). These include Lake of the Woods, Rainy Lake, Namakan Lake, Lac La Croix, Crooked Lake, Basswood Lake, Saganaga Lake, Birch Lake, Lake Vermillion and Crane Lake. Lake of the Woods is one of the most interesting lakes in this area. The lake is divided between Ontario, Manitoba

Isle Royale National Park in Lake Superior is good houseboating country.

and the state of Minnesota. It is roughly 65 miles long, 65 miles wide, covers an area of 1500 square miles and has a shoreline longer than Lake Superior's. Lake of the Woods boasts 12,000 islands and it's possible to houseboat for weeks without ever passing the same shoreline again. From here it's possible to cruise Rainy River past Ft. Frances and International Falls into Rainy Lake. This lake is a sprawling boulder-bound expanse of water speckled with islands with many channels in between. Cruising in the lake houseboaters usually pass through Canadian customs and cruise for most of the trip on either one side of the line or the other. All of the lakes are sparkling blue, with timbered shorelines and miles and miles of fingers and inlets. This area, with its many islands and inlets, offers houseboating exploration at its best with the possibility in many areas of a vacation on either side of the Minnesota-Canadian border. Also interesting in northern middle Minnesota are Winnebigoshish, and Leech lakes, the Cross Lake-Whitefish Chain and others.

In nearby Wisconsin, a popular cruising complex includes 137,000-acre Lake Winne-

bago, the Fox and Wolf rivers and an interconnecting chain of lakes. These offer a variety of attractive vacation routes. Below Winnebago you can follow the Fox River 39 miles to Green Bay along a navigable 6-foot-deep channel. Above the lake you can travel 28-odd miles to Eureka Dam. Or you can explore the Wolf River from Lake Winnebago for 47 miles, passing through or alongside a variety of lakes, including Lake Butte des Morts and Lake Poygan.

Among the Dairy State's other cruisable waterways, Wisconsin's spectacular Eagle River area is worthy of special mention. This houseboater's dream consists of a chain of twenty-seven heavily forested, navigable, interconnecting lakes.

Ohio is another midwestern state well endowed with cruising waters. These include the Maumee, Great Miami and Muskingum rivers, and 13,500-acre Grand Lake (St. Mary's), Ohio's largest inland lake.

Houseboat travel on the windswept Great Lakes is pretty well limited to seaworthy cruiser hull and catamaran houseboats, but there are a few notable exceptions. Among

Houseboating in South Dakota: the huge Oahe Reservoir.

these are Lake Superior's protected Green and Nipigon bays. Nipigon, in particular, offers true wilderness country, completely sheltered by an island chain more than 60 miles long.

Michigan, of course, is dominated by the Great Lakes and while these waters are not for all houseboats a number of cruiser hull types ply the waters of Lake Michigan, Lake Superior, Lake Huron and Lake Erie. River Queen Houseboats, for instance, regularly cruise into Lake Michigan from the plant at Douglas, Michigan. Houseboating is good on protected waters such as Grand Traverse Bay, Keweenaw Bay and similar areas.

Illinois offers houseboat rentals on Crab Orchard Lake with 124 miles of shoreline for exploring and additional houseboat cruising on some of the other reservoirs in the state. Indiana features houseboat cruising on 10,000-acre Monroe Lake, and Kansas boasts boating on both Milford and 15,800-acre Tuttle Creek reservoirs.

In Missouri, houseboating undoubtedly is at its best on Lake of the Ozarks (see map p. 57). Formed by the completion of Bagnell Dam on the Osage River in 1931, the lake literally winds its way back and forth among Central Missouri's Ozarks for about 130 miles. There are probably more commercial facilities on this lake than any other of comparable size in the United States. Houseboating is also good on Harry S. Truman Reservoir, 7800-acre Pomme de Terre, Wappapello Reservoir and some of the other smaller reservoirs within the state. Table Rock Reservoir, Bull Shoals and Norfork Lake have been mentioned elsewhere in this chapter.

Southward, Oklahoma has tremendous houseboating on its many manmade reservoirs. The majority have been developed in connection with the Arkansas River multiple purpose plan covered briefly under the Mississippi River section. Some of the outstanding lakes in this area are Eufaula, Keystone, Oologah, Tenkiller Ferry, Robert S. Kerr and Grand Lake o' the Cherokees. Lake Eufaula is a giant sprawling body of water with arms extending in many directions. Some of the lodges on this lake are outstanding. Grand Lake o' the Cherokees, covering 59,000 acres, spreads northward from the damsite on the Grand River 66 miles to Miami, Oklahoma. Many facilities are available along its 1300 mile shoreline. Lake Texoma is

27

Puget Sound is rapidly becoming a major houseboating area in the state of Washington. There are over 100 islands in the San Juan chain.

described elsewhere in this chapter.

Besides excellent midwest lakes, much houseboating in this area is dominated by the Mississippi River and its tributaries, as described elsewhere in this chapter. In Iowa, for example, it's possible to houseboat the Mississippi River completely up the eastern side of the state and the Missouri River most of the way up the western. In Illinois, boaters can cruise entirely around the eastern and southern part of the state on the Mississippi and Ohio rivers, and cut diagonally almost through the middle on the Illinois Waterway. In Missouri, it's possible to take a houseboat up the entire western side of the state on the Mississippi, then cut across the state through the middle on the Missouri River from St. Louis to Kansas City. Similarly, boaters can cruise along the southern boundaries of Indiana and Ohio on the Ohio River.

Further to the west, houseboaters can once again thank the Corps of Engineers for the creation of what amounts to a houseboating paradise along the Missouri River. As part of a multipurpose project designed to provide flood control, power and regulation of water flow, the engineers have dammed the Missouri from Gavins Point Dam, Nebraska, to Fort Peck Dam, Montana, putting North and South Dakota, Nebraska and eastern Montana onto the houseboating map.

South Dakota alone boasts four large lakes: Lewis and Clark Lake (33,000 acres) with its shores in Nebraska, 102,000-acre Lake Francis Case (see map p. 56), Lake Sharpe (58,800 acres) and Oahe Reservoir (376,000 acres), extending into North Dakota. Taken together these provide over 1000 square miles of water surface and 2350 miles of shoreline.

North Dakota and eastern Montana each have one additional large lake. North Dakota's Lake Sakakawea is huge—323,000 acres, harboring seventeen well-developed campgrounds. Fort Peck Reservoir, Montana, although slightly smaller (247,000 acres), guarantees interesting houseboat exploring in the "Big Sky" country.

The Missouri River has the added attraction of having once provided the principal passageway to our northern plains. The Lewis and Clark expedition passed along here in 1804-05, and the entire area is steeped in Indian and pioneer lore.

The Pacific Northwest

There was a time when Washington's tempestuous Puget Sound was not considered houseboating water. But today the deeper hull houseboats navigate here quite well. And it's well worth the effort. Puget Sound and Hood Canal, Washington, offer 2500 square miles of water and 5000 miles of stunning shoreline, with over 100 islands to explore in the San Juan group alone (see map p. 62).

Across the border in British Columbia, Sicamous claims the title of houseboat capital of Canada. Mara Lake and the Shuswap River offer calm waters, and Mara and Shuswap lakes provide 1000 miles of cruisable shoreline.

The Pacific Northwest also boasts fine boating on Lake Chelan in eastern Washington. This 50-mile lake is set among towering 7000 to 8000-foot peaks in an area the natives often call the Switzerland of America.

Nearby Franklin D. Roosevelt Lake (see map p. 63), above Grand Coulee Dam, has over 6000 miles of shoreline, stretching all the way up to Canada. There is a fascinating range of vegetation as you progress from one end of the lake to the other. Farther south, the Columbia River provides many miles of upriver cruising from the Pacific Ocean near Astoria, Oregon, with Washington on one side and Oregon on the other.

It's also possible to houseboat the Willamette River from Portland to Corvallis, Oregon. Below the locks at Oregon City, the Willamette resembles a broad canal and within Portland itself the river is quite urban. At Oregon City, five locks take about 45 minutes to pass through. From here to Corvallis, the Army Corps of Engineers maintains a dredged channel five feet deep.

California

Down the coast in California, houseboating has really come into its own. If there is any place comparable to Florida in terms of houseboating, it's the Sacramento-San Joaquin Delta (often called the Everglades of the West).

The Columbia River flows softly at the Oregon-Washington border.

Here at the junction of three rivers—the San Joaquin, Mokelumne and Sacramento—at the eastern edge of San Francisco Bay, you will find over 1000 miles of sloughs, cuts, reaches and breaks spreading mile after mile to the north and to the south. They form what amounts to 1500 square miles of houseboating heaven (see map p. 67).

The Delta, as we know it now, is actually manmade. In the days of the California 49'ers it was an inland everglade, but today it has been harnessed by a series of levees into low-level, 2 to 5-mile wide islands called tracts, which are used for agricultural purposes. This transformation has created a maze of waterways that provides some of the most unusual houseboating in the West.

The Delta area subdivides neatly into the Sacramento River section, the meandering San Joaquin River and the miles of waterways in between. Each offers a variety of touring possibilities. Houseboaters on the Sacramento will glide by a series of old towns as well as the Chinese community of Locke. Those traveling the San Joaquin will come up a deep-water ship channel carrying ocean freighters to Stockton and will have a chance to explore dozens of little wilderness islands. The area is well equipped with marinas ready to provide gasoline or a cup of coffee as well as some surprisingly sophisticated restaurants. Houseboat rentals are available at Richard's Yacht Sales, Bethel Island and other places throughout the Delta.

Northern California's Lake Shasta and Clair Engle (Trinity) Lake also offer excellent large-scale houseboating. Lake Shasta (see map p. 66), reached from the south through the town of Redding, was developed as an irrigation, flood and power project on the Sacramento River. It boasts 30,000 surface acres of water and 365 miles of shoreline. The lake is dotted with bays, inlets and islands ready to be explored and is equipped with a number of forest service campgrounds, some attainable only by water. There are a number of rental houseboat facilities in the area. Nearby, Clair Engle (Trinity) Lake offers much the same type of scenery, with over 422 miles of shoreline and

lake fingers that penetrate into beautiful, heavily timbered country.

North of San Francisco, Clear Lake (the largest lake lying wholly within the state boundaries) is another fine cruising spot, as is translucent Lake Tahoe. This is a beautiful oval-shaped glacial lake, 23 miles long and 12 miles wide, that lies in a mountain-ringed valley of the Sierra Nevada Range on the California-Nevada border. Perched at 6228 feet above sea level the lake has an average depth of about 1500 feet. There are numerous camps, homes and resorts around the lake. Lake Tahoe, of course, boasts gambling on the Nevada side, and the casinos at both the north and south ends of the lake offer big-name entertainment as a tantalizing diversion.

Houseboating in the southern part of the state is generally more rugged. Except for Long Beach Harbor, San Diego Bay and a few protected waterways, cruising takes place mainly off the coast. To navigate along the coastline or jaunt across to Santa Catalina Island requires a cruiser hull or one of the more seagoing catamarans. But business is booming here, with more boats available all the time.

The one exception to this offshore type of Southern California boating, other than the landlocked Salton Sea southeast of Palm Springs, is the 265-mile stretch of the Colorado River, running from Hoover Dam in Nevada to the Mexican border. Because of the dams you cannot cruise the entire system without a break, but many enthusiasts spend their entire vacations exploring Lake Havasu, created by the construction of Parker Dam on the Colorado. This 45-mile-long lake is lined with deep-set bays and picturesque coves, with well-developed recreational facilities in many areas. The 80-mile stretch of the Colorado River from Blythe Marina to Martinez Lake Marina on the Arizona side of the river provides interesting boating with an unusual cruise through the Topock Gorge wild area.

The Southwest

Houseboating in the Southwest varies

A visit to another planet: the Wahweap arm of Lake Powell.

tremendously from state to state. In Texas, as in Oklahoma (which has been covered in the section on the Mississippi), excellent houseboating is available on the large reservoirs designed for flood control. The bays along the gulf are also popular boating areas. There is much protected water and numerous sights to see in such areas as Corpus Christi Bay, Copano Bay, St. Charles Bay and others.

Texas' Red, Trinity, Brazos and Colorado rivers are the state's principal rivers with reservoirs. The Red River Basin, for example, boasts Lake of the Pines, Lake Texarkana, Lake Texoma, Caddo Lake and others (some to still be completed). Lake Texoma (see map p. 45) is one of the most popular recreational areas in Texas-Oklahoma, with 580 miles of shoreline. The lake itself offers many coves and a wide variety of recreational facilities. The 405-acre Eisenhower State Park, located a mile west of the south end of Denison Dam, has a large marina and is one of the finest camping and public use parks in Texas.

In Eastern Texas it is also possible to houseboat on Toledo Bend Reservoir, Sam Houston Reservoir, Lake Livingston, Falcon Reservoir, Lake Tawakoni and many others. In Western Texas, Amistad Reservoir and Lake Meredith are large enough to offer interesting houseboating.

In contrast to the peacefully located waters of Oklahoma and Texas, the states of Arizona and New Mexico boast some of the most rugged houseboating mountain country to be found. New Mexico's scenic lakes—Conchas, Ute, Navajo, Elephant Butte, Caballo and Alamogordo—although small by houseboating standards enjoy superb settings. Utah-Arizona's Lake Powell and Nevada-Arizona's Lake Mead are guaranteed to leave you breathless.

Lake Mead (see map p. 71), adjacent to Las Vegas, offers year-round vacationing. There are actually two lakes in the area—229-square-mile Lake Mead and 45-square mile Lake Mojave. One word of warning: The temperatures on Lake Mead rise above 110 degrees in July and August, but the weather is delightful from September through early December and again from February to May. The shores of Lake Mead offer exciting exploration for geologists, archaeologists and historians. There are good facilities here.

Lake Powell, 186 miles long, offers the houseboater 1800 miles of dramatic shoreline.

The marina at Rainbow Bridge, Glen Canyon.

The surrounding red-rock country is composed of multiple layers formed in ancient shallow seas. Earthquakes and volcanic eruptions helped shape the terrain a million years ago when the land was thrust upward in huge blocks. Then erosion sculptured the plains into fantastic shapes and designs. The result must be seen to be believed. There are five marinas on Lake Powell, spaced about 50 miles apart at Wahweap, Rainbow Bridge, Halls Crossing, Bullfrog Landing and Hite Landing. (Houseboat rentals are available at Wahweap marina.) (See map p. 70.)

The Rocky Mountain States

Despite this area's natural beauty, houseboating here is still in its infancy. You will find some of the nation's best, however, on lakes Coeur d'Alene, Pend Oreille and Priest in Idaho's panhandle.

This is beautiful, thickly timbered, primitive country offering total peace and relaxation.

Lake Coeur d'Alene has particularly attractive cruising thanks to river linkage with Lake Chatcolet, which allows boating from one lake to the other.

Houseboaters in next-door Montana can enjoy Flathead Lake. There are campgrounds on both sides of the lake plus one on the eastern side run by the Indians on the Flathead Indian Reservation. Thirty-five miles long, fed by nearby glaciers and hemmed in by rugged mountains, this lake is the largest freshwater lake in the West. On the east end of the lake, accessible only by boat, is a large Indian pictograph, about a thousand years old.

Another unique cruising area in the Rocky Mountain area is 90-mile-long Flaming Gorge Reservoir (see map p. 64) on the Utah-Wyoming border. Its spectacular shoreline ranges from the flat-rock stratum of the Wyoming area (one stratum on top of the other resembling the layers of a cake) to the Utah section, where colorful rocks that once lay flat have been bent upward and forced into grotesque positions by tremendous earth move-

From the picturesque to the dramatic, the world of houseboating offers something for every taste. Houseboating on the flamboyant Flaming Gorge Reservoir.

ments. A particular point of interest is the entrance to Flaming Gorge, where the Green River has chiseled its way through steeply tilted layers of brightly colored rocks.

In this flamboyant mountain-canyon setting, our tour of houseboating country has come to an end. For those wishing additional information on specific waters, a list of available documentation and where to obtain it is provided on Appendix pp. 188-189.

Year-Round Houseboating

Because houseboating has become such a popular family activity, with many households spending their entire vacation on the water, the summer months of June, July and August are prime houseboating time. During this period of the year temperatures are comfortably high and the water agreeably warm. But this does not mean that the other seasons should be overlooked. In spring, for example, when the air is slightly cooler, fishing is often better and the weather is generally more pleasant for onshore activities. And in autumn, cruisers will be rewarded with a panorama of breathtaking colors.

In the fall, houseboating often takes on a new dimension. The tendency today in areas like the San Joaquin Delta is to use the houseboat as a base camp for duck hunting rather than a means of cruising. The houseboat can be easily moved to follow the birds. In addition, in California, Florida and other southern areas, houseboaters are on the water all winter long.

An added vacation plus in both spring, fall and winter is the lack of crowding along the waterways and the ease of arranging houseboat rentals. But no matter what time of year you want to go houseboating, you will find many rental houseboats available in all areas. Where to find these rentals and how to select the right rental houseboat for you is the subject of the next chapter.

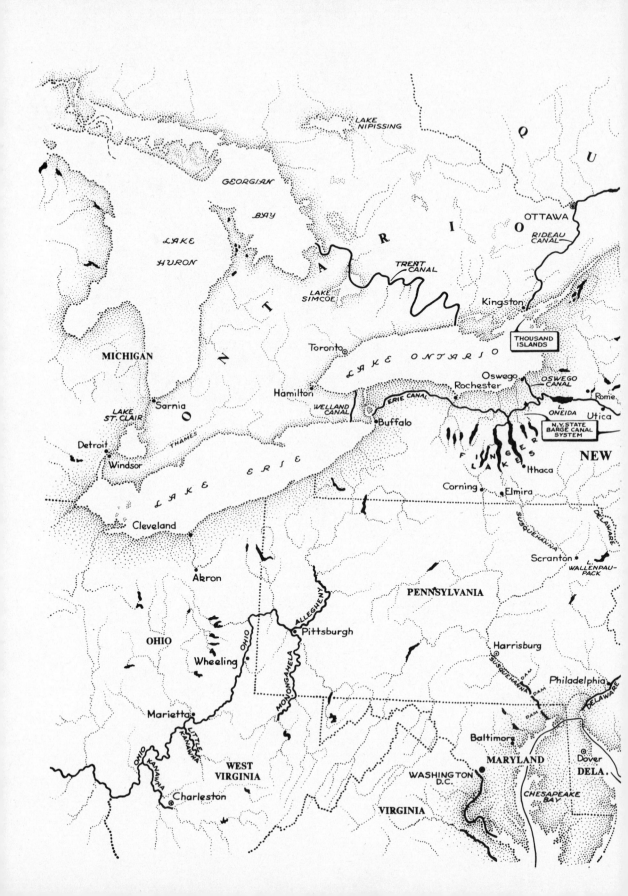

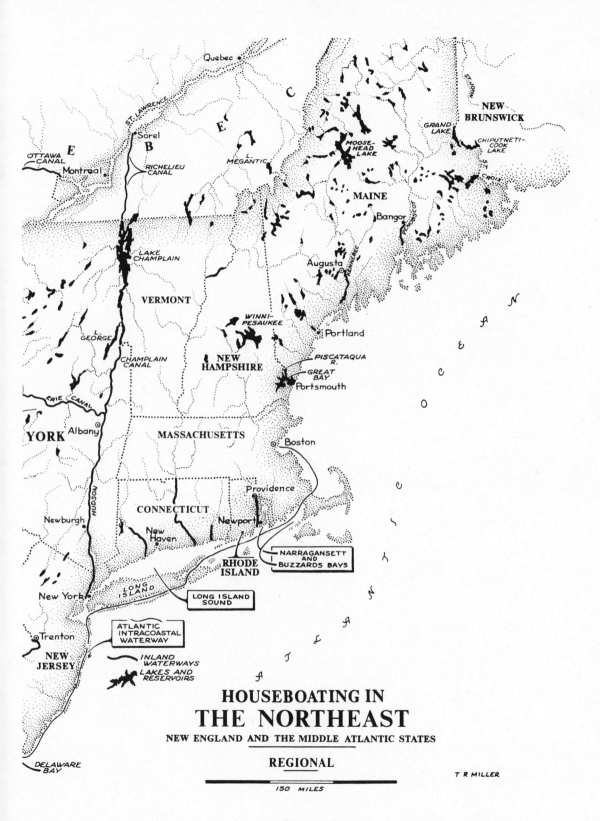

HOUSEBOATING IN
THE NORTHEAST
NEW ENGLAND AND THE MIDDLE ATLANTIC STATES

REGIONAL

150 MILES

T R MILLER

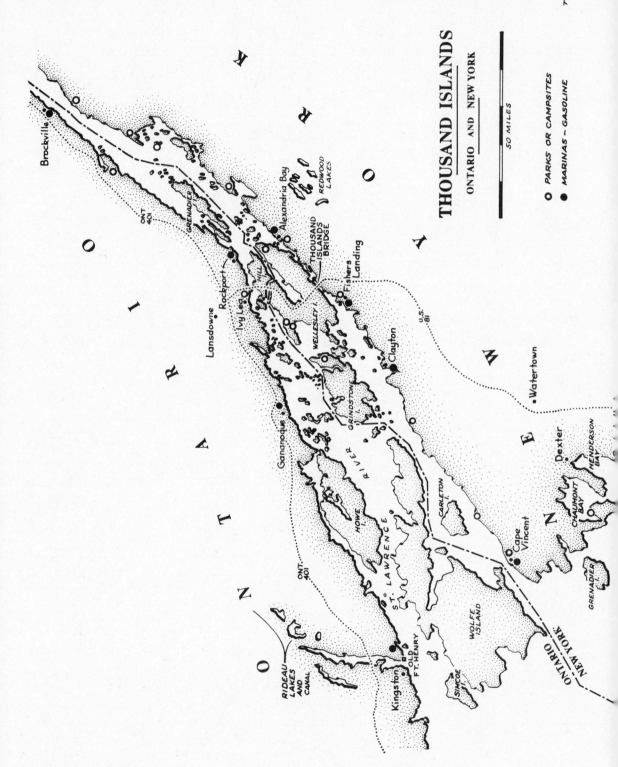

THOUSAND ISLANDS

ONTARIO AND NEW YORK

50 MILES

○ PARKS OR CAMPSITES

● MARINAS — GASOLINE

Brockville

ONT. 401

GRENADIER I.

Alexandria Bay

REDWOOD LAKES

THOUSAND ISLANDS BRIDGE

Rockport

Lansdowne

Ivy Lea

HILL

WELLESLEY I.

Fishers Landing

U.S. 81

Clayton

GRINDSTONE I.

Gananoque

HOWE ISLAND

ST. LAWRENCE RIVER

CARLETON I.

Watertown

Dexter

HENDERSON BAY

CHAUMONT BAY

Cape Vincent

GRENADIER I.

ONT. 401

RIDEAU LAKES AND CANAL

OLD FT. HENRY

WOLFE ISLAND

SIMCOE I.

Kingston

ONTARIO

NEW YORK

TRM

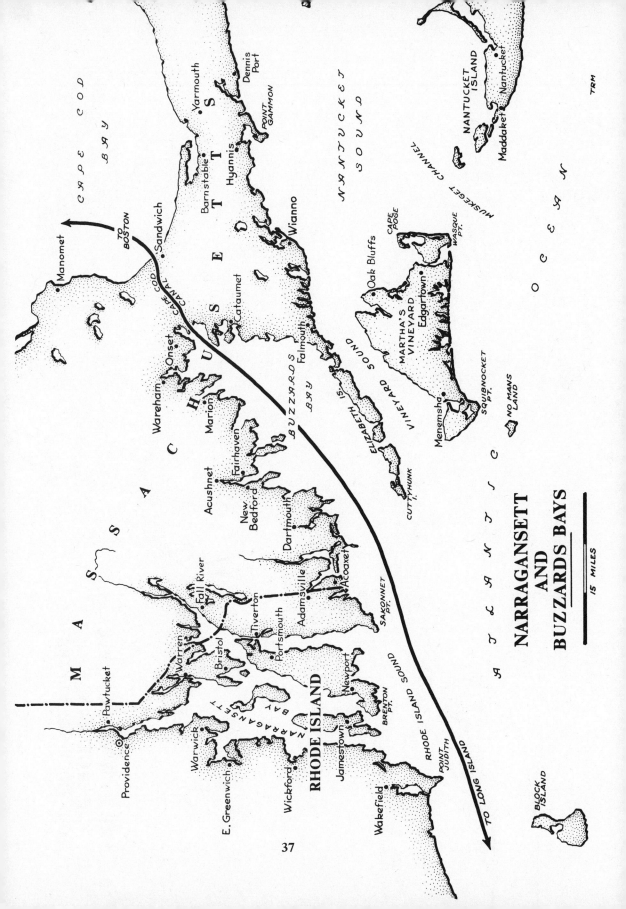

NARRAGANSETT
AND
BUZZARDS BAYS

15 MILES

37

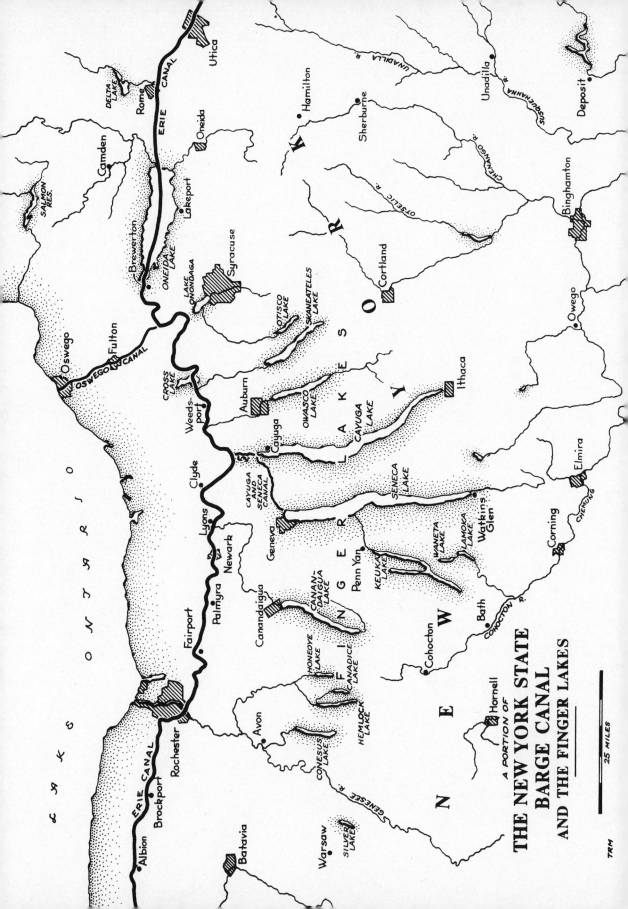

THE NEW YORK STATE
BARGE CANAL
AND THE FINGER LAKES

A PORTION OF

25 MILES

LAKE ONTARIO

ERIE CANAL

OSWEGO CANAL

NEW YORK

FINGER LAKES

Albion
Brockport
Rochester
Fairport
Palmyra
Newark
Lyons
Clyde
Weedsport
Oswego
Fulton
Brewerton
Camden
Rome
DELTA LAKE
Utica
Oneida
Lakeport
ONEIDA LAKE
Syracuse
LAKE ONONDAGA
CROSS LAKE
SALMON RES.
Hamilton
Sherburne
Unadilla
Deposit
Binghamton
Cortland
Owego
Elmira
Corning
Bath
Cohocton
COHOCTON R.
CHEMUNG
Hornell
Warsaw
Batavia
Avon
SILVER LAKE
GENESEE R.
CONESUS LAKE
HEMLOCK LAKE
CANADICE LAKE
HONEOYE LAKE
Canandaigua
CANANDAIGUA LAKE
Geneva
Penn Yan
KEUKA LAKE
WANETA LAKE
LAMOKA LAKE
Watkins Glen
SENECA LAKE
CAYUGA LAKE
Ithaca
Cayuga
CAYUGA AND SENECA CANAL
Auburn
OWASCO LAKE
SKANEATELES LAKE
OTISCO LAKE
UNADILLA R.
SUSQUEHANNA R.
CHENANGO R.
OTSELIC R.
TRM

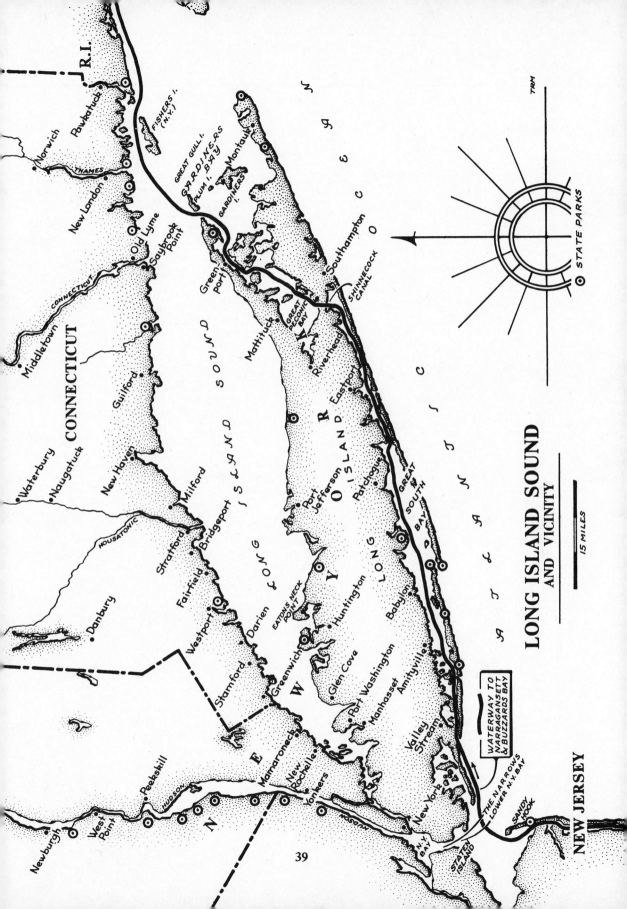

LONG ISLAND SOUND
AND VICINITY

15 MILES

⊙ STATE PARKS

TRM

R.I.

CONNECTICUT

Norwich
Pawkatuck
Middletown
Waterbury
Naugatuck
Danbury
New London
New Haven
Old Lyme
Saybrook Point
Guilford
Milford
Stratford
Bridgeport
Fairfield
Westport
Darien
Stamford
Greenwich
Mamaroneck
New Rochelle
Yonkers
Peekskill
West Point
Newburgh

THAMES
CONNECTICUT
HOUSATONIC
HUDSON

FISHERS I. (N.Y.)
GREAT GULL I.
GARDINERS BAY
PLUM I.
GARDINERS I.
Montauk
Greenport
Mattituck
GREAT PECONIC BAY
Riverhead
Eastport
Southampton
SHINNECOCK CANAL

LONG ISLAND SOUND

LONG ISLAND

Port Jefferson
Patchogue
EATONS NECK POINT
Huntington
Babylon
GREAT SOUTH BAY
Glen Cove
Port Washington
Manhasset
Amityville
Valley Stream
New York

N E W Y O R K

WATERWAY TO NARRAGANSETT & BUZZARDS BAY

THE NARROWS
LOWER N.Y. BAY
N.Y. BAY
STATEN ISLAND
SANDY HOOK

NEW JERSEY

A T L A N T I C   O C E A N

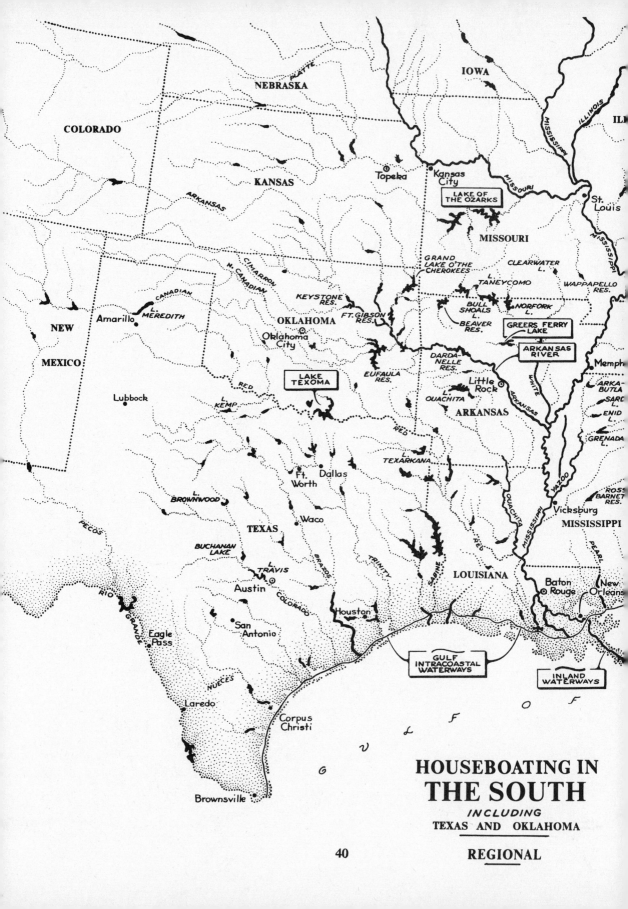

HOUSEBOATING IN
THE SOUTH
INCLUDING
TEXAS AND OKLAHOMA

REGIONAL

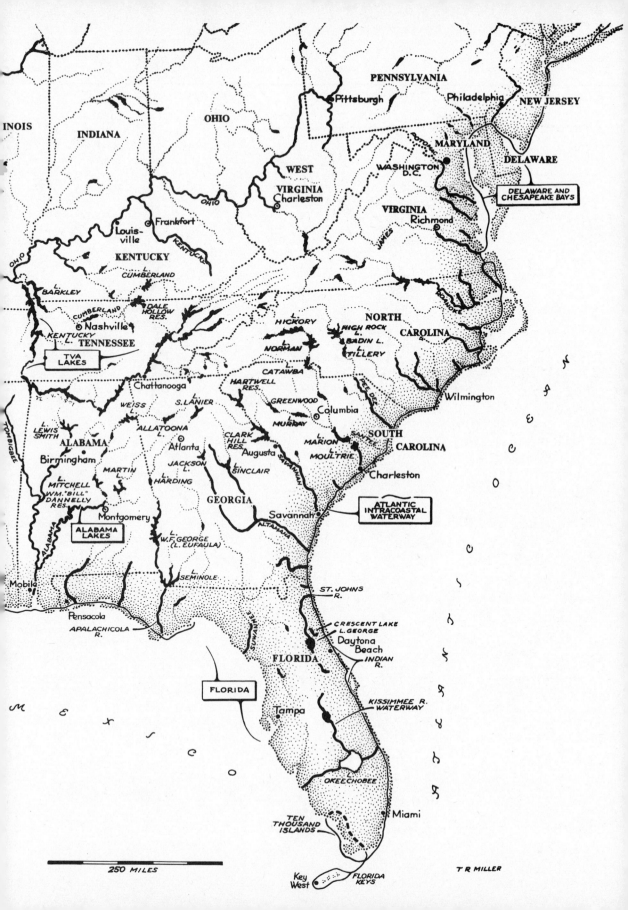

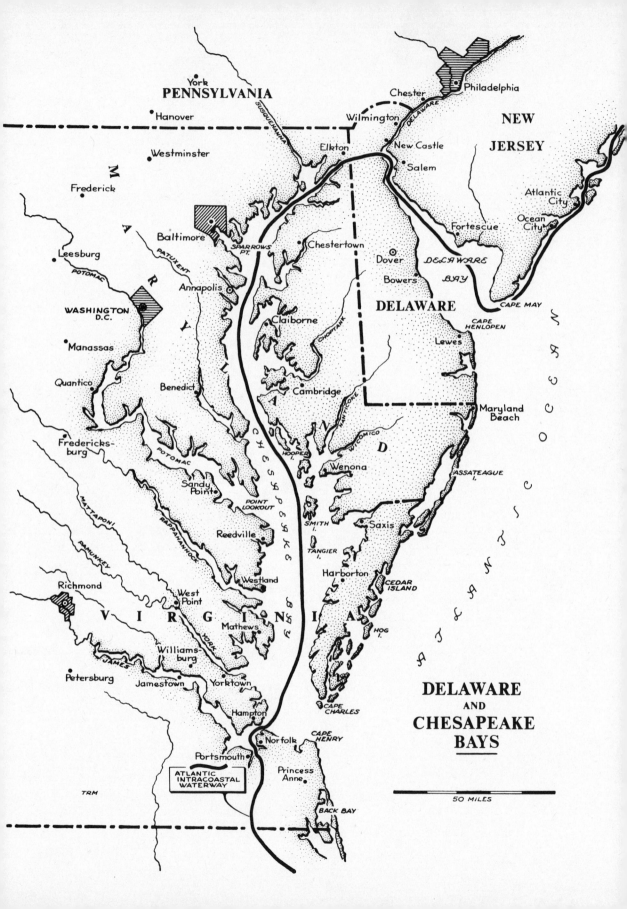

DELAWARE
AND
CHESAPEAKE
BAYS

GEORGIA

LAKE SEMINOLE

F

Tallahassee

L

⑧ APALACHICOLA RIVER

CAPE ST. GEORGE

GULF INTRACOASTAL WATERWAY

APALACHEE BAY

PINE POINT

⑦ SUWANNEE RIVER

⑥ ST. JOHNS RIVER

LAKE GEORGE

Saint Marys

MARYS

Jacksonville

St. Augustine

CRESCENT LAKE

Daytona Beach

R

Orlando

CAPE CANAVERAL

④ INDIAN RIVER (INTRACOASTAL WATERWAY)

ST. LUCIE CANAL

⑤ KISSIMMEE RIVER VALLEY WATERWAY

LAKE KISSIMMEE

Tampa

St. Petersburg

TAMPA BAY

Sebring

Sarasota

I

LAKE OKEECHOBEE

ST. LUCIE CANAL

West Palm Beach

① CALOOSA-HATCHIE RIVER

Naples

Fort Lauderdale

THE EVERGLADES

Miami

Miami Beach

HOUSEBOATING IN

FLORIDA

② TEN THOUSAND ISLANDS AREA EVERGLADES NATIONAL PARK

EVERGLADES NATIONAL PARK

50 MILES

INLAND WATERWAYS

INTRACOASTAL WATERWAYS

CIRCLED NUMBERS REFER TO THE CRUISES DESCRIBED ON PAGES 17 AND 19.

Key West

③ FLORIDA KEYS

TRM

GREERS FERRY LAKE

ARKANSAS

5 MILES

KEY

PUBLIC USE AREA

T R MILLER

Drasco

ARK 92

AFTER CREEK

Tumbling Shoals

OLD HIGHWAY 25

DAM

ARK 25

SWINGING BRIDGE

LITTLE RED

HEBER SPRINGS TO SEARCY 31 MI.

S

A

Brownsville

DEVIL'S FORK OF LITTLE RED R.

Heber Springs

ARK 25

S

CHEROKEE

SHILOH

EDEN ISLE

STARK POINT

Pearson

ARK 16

HEBER SPRINGS TO LITTLE ROCK 71 MI.

N

COVE CREEK

MILLERS POINT

A

MILL CREEK

MIDDLE FORK OF LITTLE RED R.

GREERS FERRY

DEVIL'S FORK

NARROWS

ARK 16

SALT CR.

ARK 16

Edgemont

MILL CREEK

ARK 92

K

ARK 16

SUGAR LOAF MT. (I.)

SUGAR LOAF

Shirley

ARCHEY CR.

VAN BUREN

SOUTH FORK

STEVENS PT.

ARK 330

Eglantine

THOMPSON CR.

SOUTH FORK OF LITTLE RED R.

ARK 92

R

Morganton

CHOCTAW

A

CLINTON TO MARSHALL 28 MI.

U.S. 65

Clinton

CHOCTAW TO MORRILTON 35 MI.

Choctaw

Bee Branch

U.S. 65

BEE BRANCH TO LITTLE ROCK 69 MI.

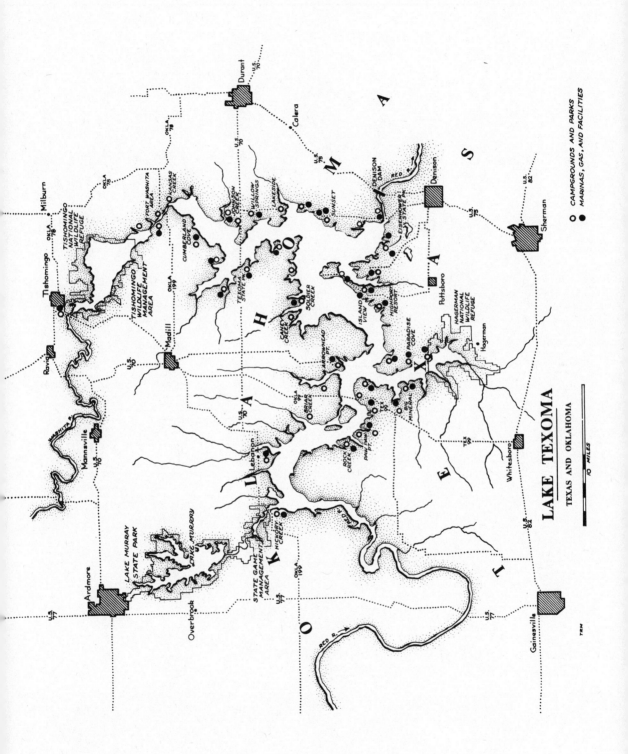

LAKE TEXOMA

TEXAS AND OKLAHOMA

○ CAMPGROUNDS AND PARKS
● MARINAS, GAS, AND FACILITIES

10 MILES

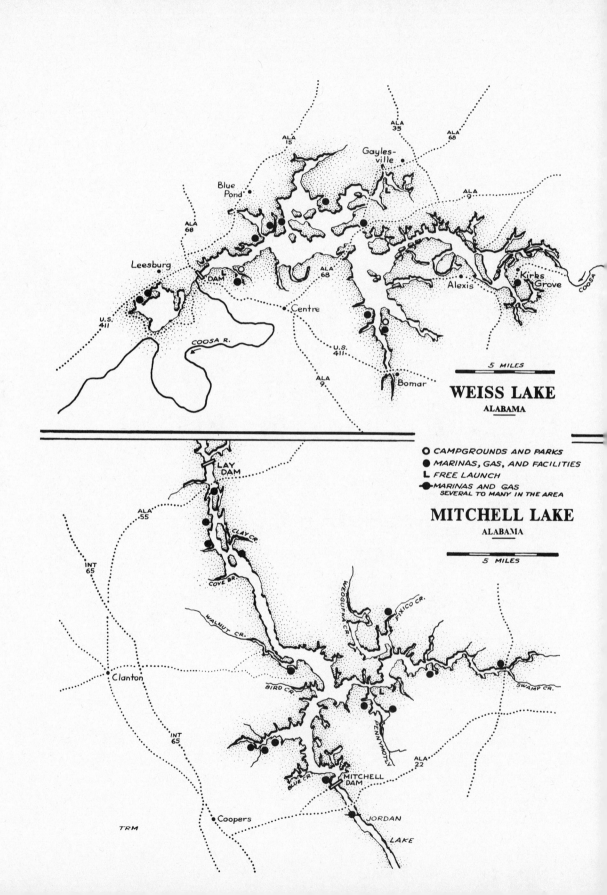

WEISS LAKE
ALABAMA

COOSA
ALA 35
ALA 68
Gayles-ville
Blue Pond
ALA 15
ALA 9
Kirks Grove
ALA 68
Leesburg
DAM
Alexis
ALA 68
COOSA
U.S. 411
Centre
COOSA R.
U.S. 411
ALA 9
Bomar
5 MILES

○ CAMPGROUNDS AND PARKS
● MARINAS, GAS, AND FACILITIES
L FREE LAUNCH
●—● MARINAS AND GAS
SEVERAL TO MANY IN THE AREA

MITCHELL LAKE
ALABAMA

5 MILES

LAY DAM
ALA 55
CLAY CR.
INT 65
COVE BR.
WALNUT CR.
WEOGUFKA CR.
FIXICO CR.
Clanton
BIRD CR.
SWAMP CR.
L
INT 65
PENNYMOTH
ALA 22
MITCHELL DAM
CR.
Coopers
JORDAN
TRM
LAKE

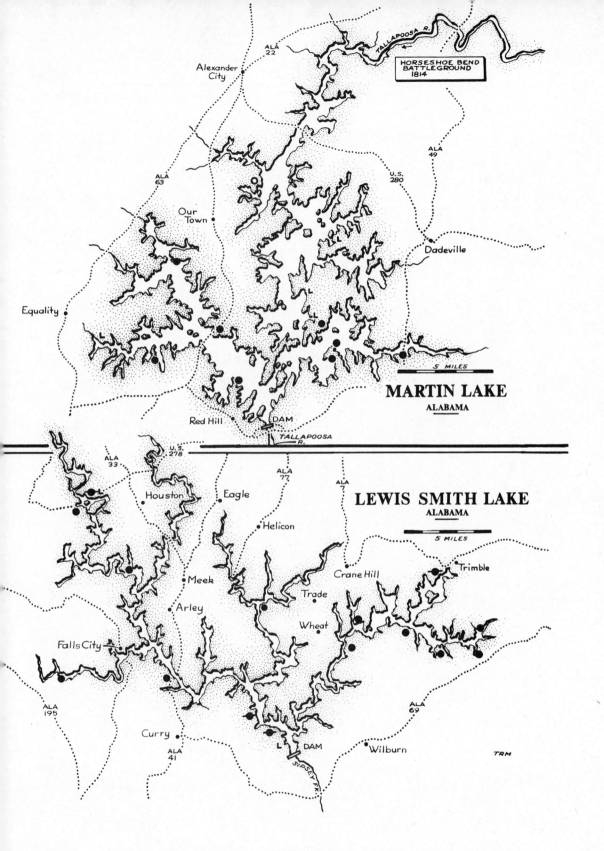

ALA 22

Alexander City

HORSESHOE BEND
BATTLEGROUND
1814

TALLAPOOSA R.

ALA 49

U.S. 280

ALA 63

Our Town

Dadeville

Equality

L

L

MARTIN LAKE
ALABAMA

5 MILES

Red Hill

DAM

TALLAPOOSA R.

ALA 33

U.S. 278

ALA 77

ALA 7

LEWIS SMITH LAKE
ALABAMA

Houston

Eagle

Helicon

5 MILES

Meek

Crane Hill

Trimble

Arley

Trade

Wheat

Falls City

Curry

L

DAM

Wilburn

ALA 195

ALA 69

ALA 41

SIPSEY FK.

TRM

47

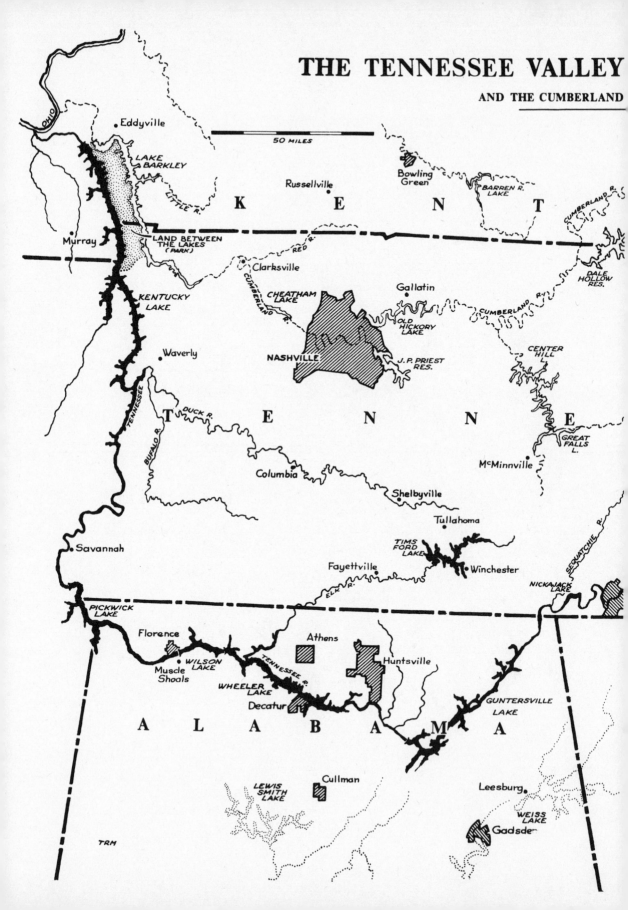

THE TENNESSEE VALLEY
AND THE CUMBERLAND

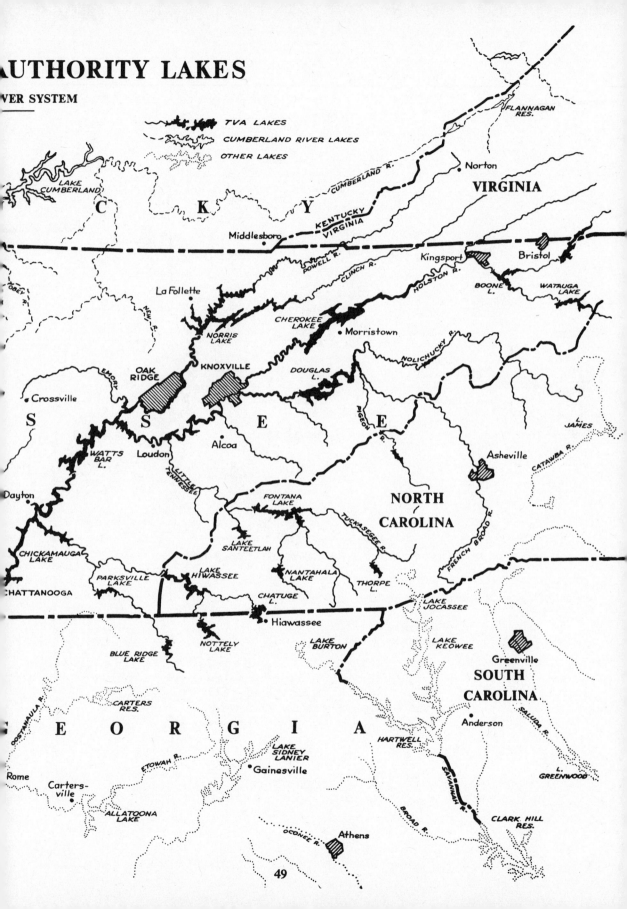

AUTHORITY LAKES

VER SYSTEM

TVA LAKES
CUMBERLAND RIVER LAKES
OTHER LAKES

FLANNAGAN RES.

Norton

VIRGINIA

LAKE CUMBERLAND

C K Y

KENTUCKY
VIRGINIA

Middlesboro

CUMBERLAND R.

POWELL R.

CLINCH R.

HOLSTON R.

Kingsport

Bristol

BOONE L.

WATAUGA LAKE

OBEY R.

NEW R.

La Follette

NORRIS LAKE

CHEROKEE LAKE

Morristown

NOLICHUCKY R.

EMORY R.

OAK RIDGE

KNOXVILLE

DOUGLAS L.

L. JAMES

Crossville

S

S

E

E

E

PIGEON R.

Asheville

CATAWBA R.

Alcoa

WATTS BAR L.

Loudon

LITTLE TENNESSEE

FONTANA LAKE

TUCKASEGEE R.

NORTH CAROLINA

FRENCH BROAD R.

Dayton

CHICKAMAUGA LAKE

PARKSVILLE LAKE

LAKE HIWASSEE

LAKE SANTEETLAH

NANTAHALA LAKE

THORPE L.

LAKE JOCASSEE

CHATTANOOGA

CHATUGE L.

Hiawassee

LAKE BURTON

LAKE KEOWEE

Greenville

SOUTH CAROLINA

BLUE RIDGE LAKE

NOTTELY LAKE

OOSTANAULA R.

CARTERS RES.

E O R G I A

Anderson

SALUDA R.

Rome

Cartersville

ETOWAH R.

LAKE SIDNEY LANIER

Gainesville

HARTWELL RES.

SAVANNAH R.

L. GREENWOOD

ALLATOONA LAKE

OCONEE R.

BROAD R.

Athens

CLARK HILL RES.

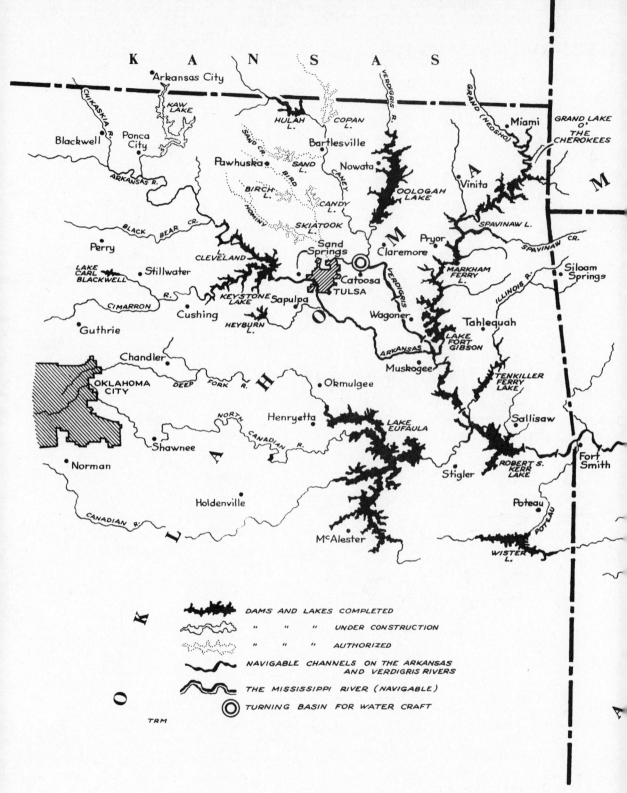

KANSAS

Arkansas City

Blackwell

Ponca City

KAW LAKE

CHIKASKIA R.

HULAH L.

COPAN L.

VERDIGRIS R.

GRAND (NEOSHO)

Miami

GRAND LAKE O' THE CHEROKEES

M

Pawhuska

Bartlesville

Nowata

SAND CR.

SAND L.

CANEY

OOLOGAH LAKE

Vinita

A

ARKANSAS R.

BIRCH L.

BIRD

SAND

CANDY

OOLOGAH LAKE

SPAVINAW L.

Perry

BLACK BEAR CR.

MO MINY

SKIATOOK L.

Sand Springs

M

Pryor

MARKHAM FERRY L.

SPAVINAW CR.

Siloam Springs

LAKE CARL BLACKWELL

Stillwater

CLEVELAND

L. CLEVELAND

Claremore

Catoosa

TULSA

VERDIGRIS R.

Cushing

CIMARRON R.

KEYSTONE LAKE

Sapulpa

O

Wagoner

ILLINOIS R.

Tahlequah

Guthrie

HEYBURN L.

LAKE FORT GIBSON

ARKANSAS

Chandler

DEEP FORK R.

H

Okmulgee

Muskogee

TENKILLER FERRY LAKE

OKLAHOMA CITY

Henryetta

NORTH CANADIAN R.

LAKE EUFAULA

Sallisaw

Norman

Shawnee

A

Fort Smith

Holdenville

ROBERT S. KERR LAKE

Stigler

CANADIAN R.

McAlester

Poteau

POTEAU

WISTER L.

K

L

O

TRM

A

DAMS AND LAKES COMPLETED

" " " UNDER CONSTRUCTION

" " " AUTHORIZED

NAVIGABLE CHANNELS ON THE ARKANSAS AND VERDIGRIS RIVERS

THE MISSISSIPPI RIVER (NAVIGABLE)

TURNING BASIN FOR WATER CRAFT

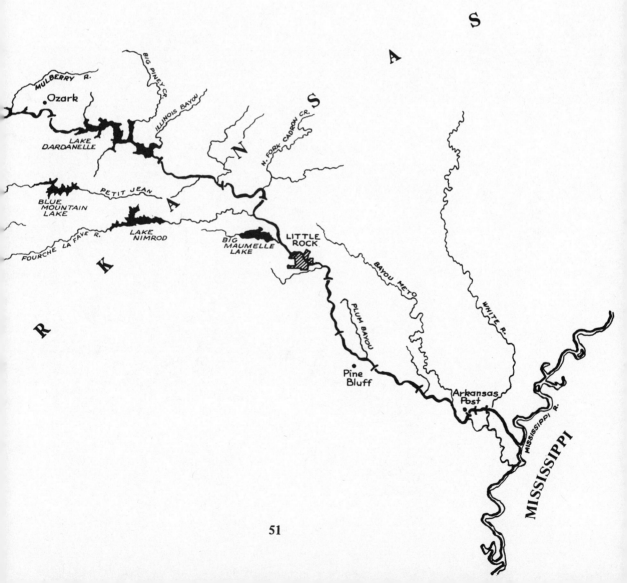

ARKANSAS RIVER, TRIBUTARIES, AND LAKES

OKLAHOMA AND ARKANSAS

50 MILES

M I S S O U R I

A S

MULBERRY R.

BIG PINEY CR.

Ozark

ILLINOIS BAYOU

LAKE DARDANELLE

N. FORK CADRON CR.

A N S

PETIT JEAN

BLUE MOUNTAIN LAKE

FOURCHE LA FAVE R.

LAKE NIMROD

BIG MAUMELLE LAKE

LITTLE ROCK

R K A

BAYOU METO

WHITE R.

PLUM BAYOU

Pine Bluff

Arkansas Post

MISSISSIPPI R.

MISSISSIPPI

R

TRM

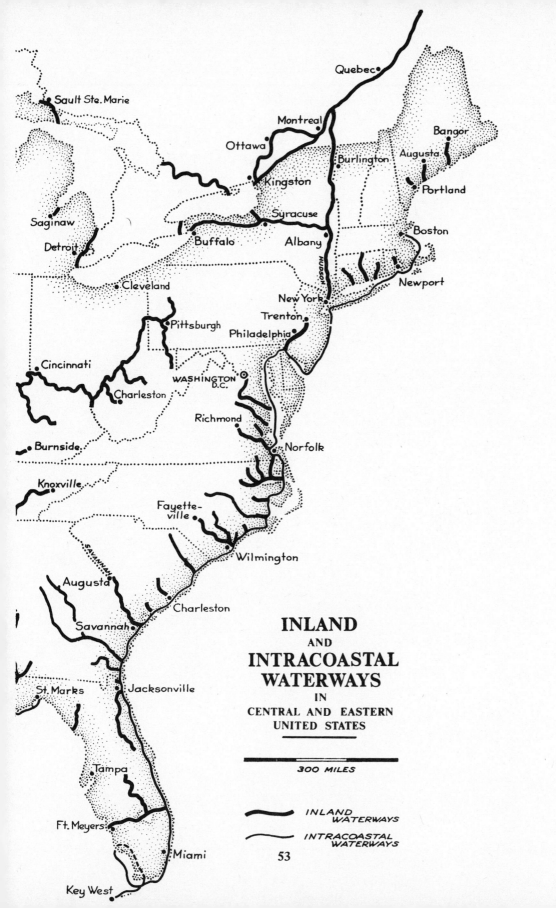

INLAND
AND
INTRACOASTAL
WATERWAYS
IN
CENTRAL AND EASTERN
UNITED STATES

300 MILES

———— *INLAND WATERWAYS*

~~~~ *INTRACOASTAL WATERWAYS*

53

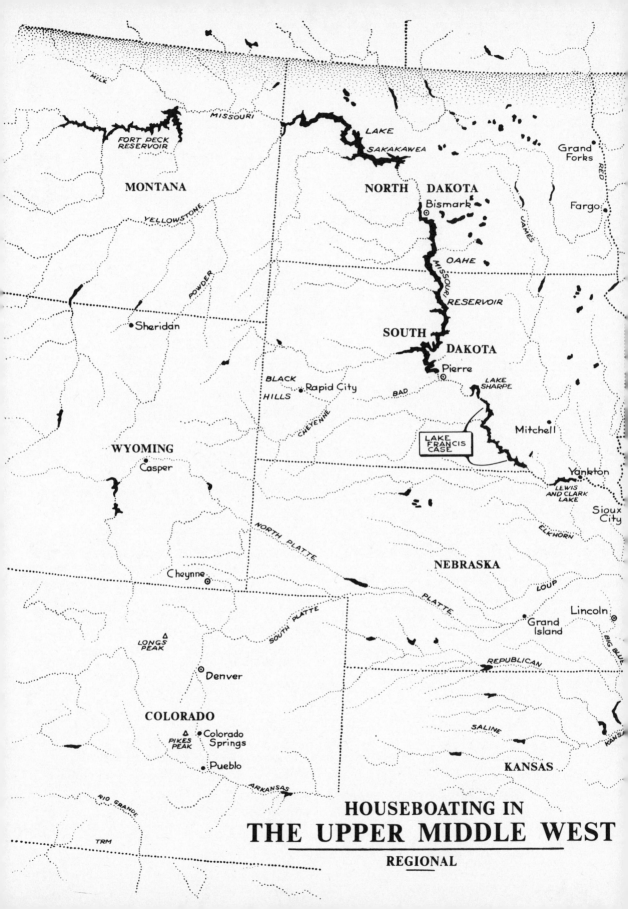

HOUSEBOATING IN
THE UPPER MIDDLE WEST
REGIONAL

LAKE OF
THE WOODS

RAINY L.

NAMAKAN L.
LAC LA CROIX
CROOKED L.
BASSWOOD L.
SAGANAGA L.

NIPIGON
BAY

ONTARIO

THE
D LAKES

NORTHERN
MINNESOTA
LAKES

BIRCH
LAKE

VERMILION
LAKE

LAKE SUPERIOR

Sault
Ste. Marie

LAKE
TASCA

LEECH
LAKE

WHITE FISH
LAKE

Duluth

M

MINNESOTA

MILLE
LACS
LAKE

ST. CROIX

EAGLE
RIVER
AREA

C

H

Minneapolis

St. Paul

Eau Claire

WISCONSIN

Green Bay

I

MINNESOTA

MISSISSIPPI

FOX

LAKE
WINNEBAGO

LAKE

G

Spirit Lake

Mason
City

WISCONSIN

Madison

MICHIGAN

Milwaukee

Grand
Rapids

A

Beloit

N

Dubuque

IOWA

Cedar
Rapids

CEDAR

Chicago

Des Moines

Joliet

Ft. Wayne

Omaha

Ottumwa

Rock
Island

ILLINOIS

Peoria

INDIANA

Indianapolis

Keokuk

CHARITON

ILLINOIS

Springfield

Terre Haute

St. Joseph

GRAND

Quincy

MISSOURI

MISSISSIPPI

Kansas
City

MISSOURI

Topeka

Jefferson
City

St. Louis

Louisville

OHIO

Evansville

WABASH

LAKE OF
THE OZARKS

KENTUCKY

250 MILES

OHIO

NAVIGABLE INLAND WATERWAYS

55

LAKE
FRANCIS CASE

SOUTH DAKOTA

15 MILES

O CAMPGROUNDS
● FACILITIES AND GAS
L LAUNCHING RAMPS

Ft. Thompson
Lower Brule
BIG BEND DAM
S.D. 47
Reliance
U.S. 16
Oacoma
Chamberlain
Pukwana
WHITE R.
RED LAKE
Ola
Eagle
BULL CR.
Iona
Academy
S.D. 47
Dixon
OL
Platte
U.S. 281
Armour
S.D. 50
Dallas
Gregory
Geddes
U.S. 18
LAKE ANDES
Burke
WHETSTONE CR.
PONCA CR.
L
U.S. 50
U.S. 281
U.S. 18
Herrick
St.Charles
U.S. 18
Bonesteel
Fairfax
FT. RANDALL DAM
U.S. 281
MISSOURI R.

SOUTH DAKOTA
NEBRASKA
U.S. 18
Mart.

TRM

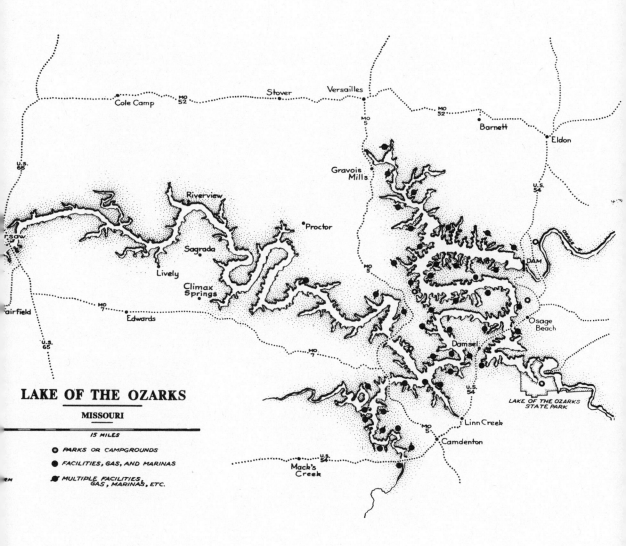

LAKE OF THE OZARKS

MISSOURI

15 MILES

⊙ PARKS OR CAMPGROUNDS

● FACILITIES, GAS, AND MARINAS

▰ MULTIPLE FACILITIES
GAS, MARINAS, ETC.

Cole Camp

MO 52

Stover

Versailles

MO 5

MO 52

Barnett

Eldon

U.S. 65

Gravois Mills

U.S. 54

Riverview

Proctor

rsaw

Sagrada

Lively

Climax Springs

MO 5

DAM

airfield

MO 7

Edwards

Osage Beach

U.S. 65

Damsel

MO 7

U.S. 54

LAKE OF THE OZARKS STATE PARK

Linn Creek

MO 5

Camdenton

Mack's Creek

U.S. 54

RM

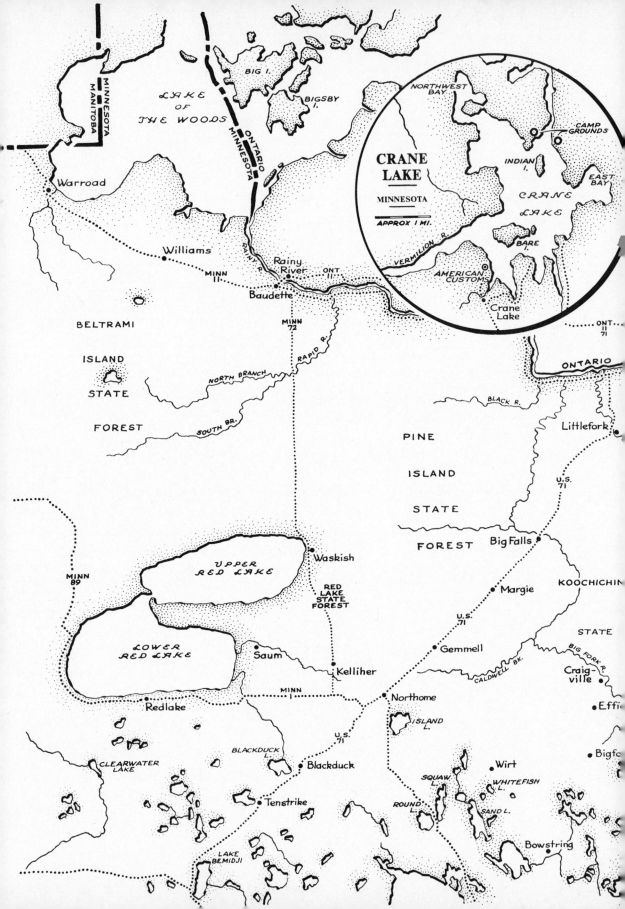

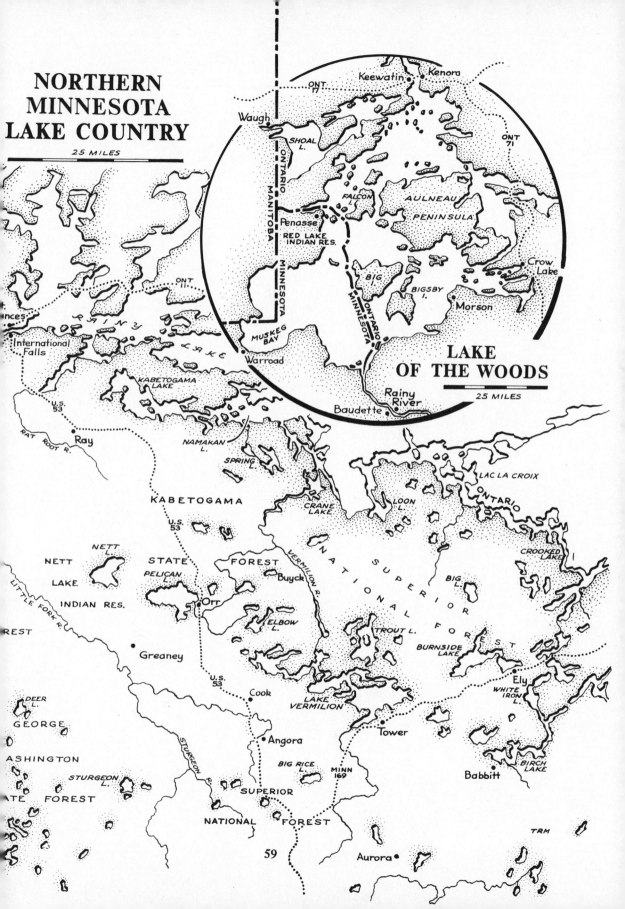

NORTHERN MINNESOTA LAKE COUNTRY

25 MILES

Waugh

ONT. 17

Keewatin

Kenora

SHOAL L.

ONTARIO

MANITOBA

MINNESOTA

ONT. 71

FALCON

AULNEAU PENINSULA

Penasse

RED LAKE INDIAN RES.

BIG I.

BIGSBY I.

Crow Lake

Morson

ONT 11

RAINY LAKE

MUSKEG BAY

MINNESOTA

ONTARIO

nces

International Falls

Warroad

Baudette

Rainy River

LAKE OF THE WOODS

25 MILES

U.S. 53

RAT ROOT R.

Ray

KABETOGAMA LAKE

NAMAKAN L.

SPRING

LAC LA CROIX

ONTARIO

KABETOGAMA

U.S. 53

CRANE LAKE

LOON L.

NETT L.

NETT LAKE

INDIAN RES.

STATE

PELICAN L.

FOREST

Orr

Buyck

VERMILION R.

NATIONAL

SUPERIOR

CROOKED LAKE

BIG L.

LITTLE FORK R.

ELBOW L.

TROUT L.

BURNSIDE LAKE

FOREST

Greaney

U.S. 53

Cook

LAKE VERMILION

Ely

WHITE IRON L.

REST

DEER L.

GEORGE

ASHINGTON

Angora

BIG RICE L.

Tower

BIRCH LAKE

Babbitt

STURGEON R.

STURGEON L.

SUPERIOR

MINN 169

TE FOREST

NATIONAL

FOREST

TRM

Aurora

59

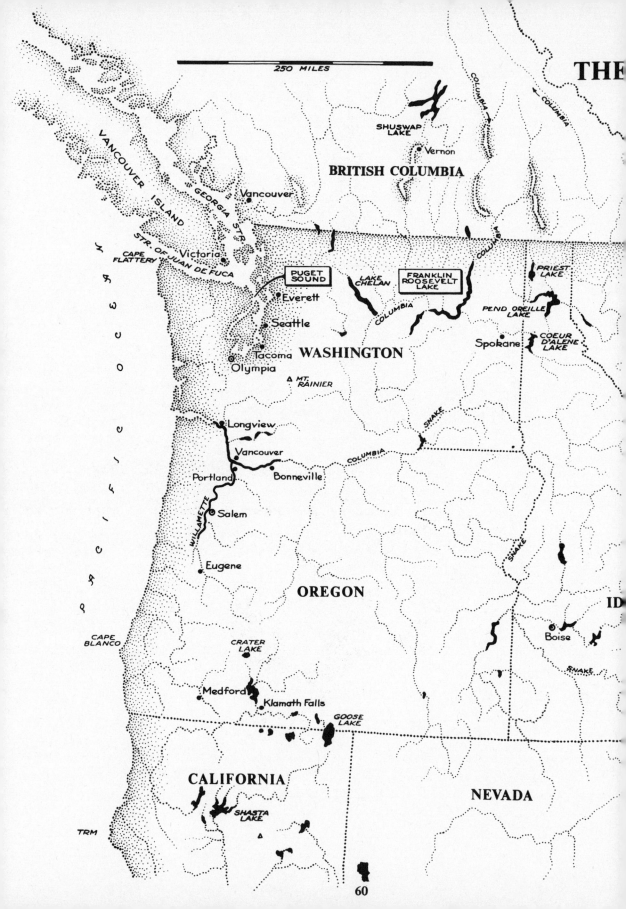

250 MILES

THE

COLUMBIA

COLUMBIA

SHUSWAP
LAKE

Vernon

BRITISH COLUMBIA

VANCOUVER ISLAND

GEORGIA STR.

Vancouver

COLUMBIA

Victoria

CAPE
FLATTERY

STR. OF JUAN DE FUCA

PUGET
SOUND

LAKE
CHELAN

FRANKLIN
ROOSEVELT
LAKE

PRIEST
LAKE

Everett

COLUMBIA

PEND OREILLE
LAKE

Seattle

Spokane

COEUR
D'ALENE
LAKE

Tacoma

WASHINGTON

Olympia

△ MT.
RAINIER

SNAKE

Longview

Vancouver

COLUMBIA

Portland

Bonneville

WILLAMETTE

Salem

SNAKE

Eugene

OREGON

ID

CAPE
BLANCO

Boise

CRATER
LAKE

SNAKE

Medford

Klamath Falls

GOOSE
LAKE

CALIFORNIA

NEVADA

SHASTA
LAKE

△

TRM

PACIFIC OCEAN

60

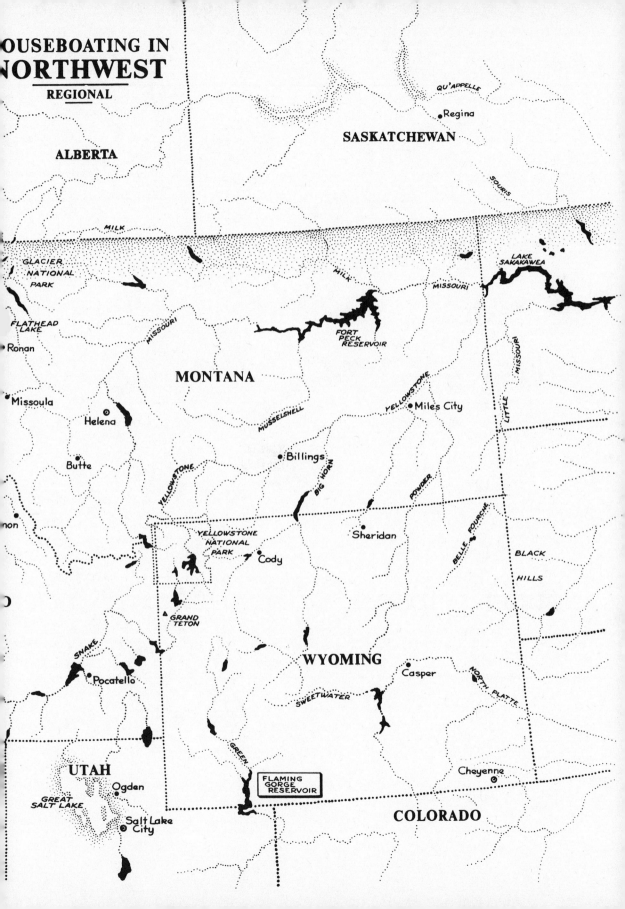

QU'APPELLE

Regina

SASKATCHEWAN

ALBERTA

SOURIS

MILK

GLACIER
NATIONAL
PARK

LAKE
SAKAKAWEA

MILK

MISSOURI

FLATHEAD
LAKE

Ronan

MISSOURI

FORT
PECK
RESERVOIR

MONTANA

Missoula

LITTLE MISSOURI

MUSSELSHELL

YELLOWSTONE

Miles City

Helena

Butte

Billings

BIG HORN

POWDER

YELLOWSTONE

Sheridan

BELLE FOURCHE

non

YELLOWSTONE
NATIONAL
PARK

Cody

BLACK

HILLS

GRAND
TETON

O

SNAKE

WYOMING

Casper

Pocatello

SWEETWATER

NORTH PLATTE

GREEN

UTAH

Ogden

Cheyenne

FLAMING
GORGE
RESERVOIR

GREAT
SALT LAKE

Salt Lake
City

COLORADO

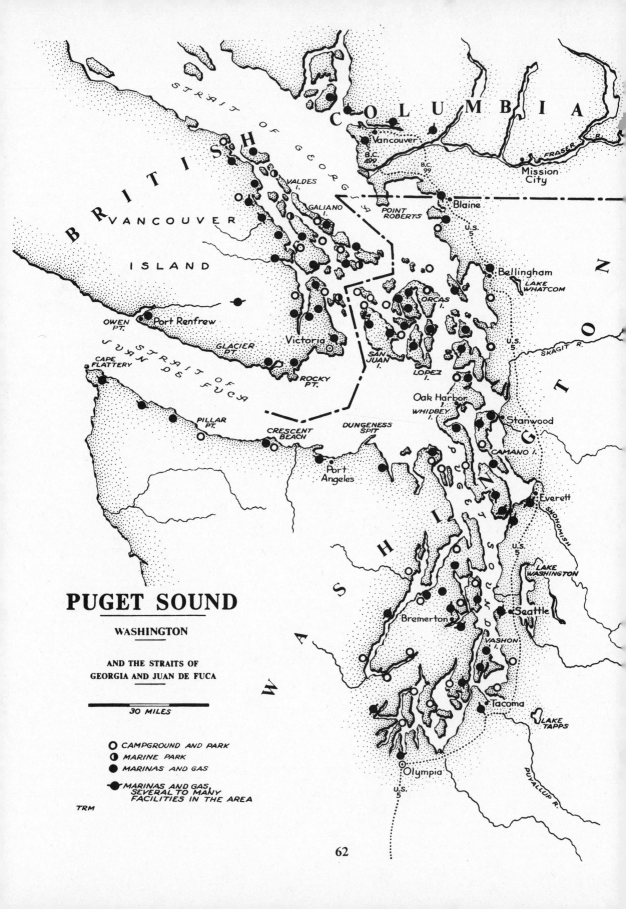

PUGET SOUND

WASHINGTON

AND THE STRAITS OF
GEORGIA AND JUAN DE FUCA

30 MILES

○ CAMPGROUND AND PARK
◐ MARINE PARK
● MARINAS AND GAS
◖ MARINAS AND GAS,
SEVERAL TO MANY
FACILITIES IN THE AREA

TRM

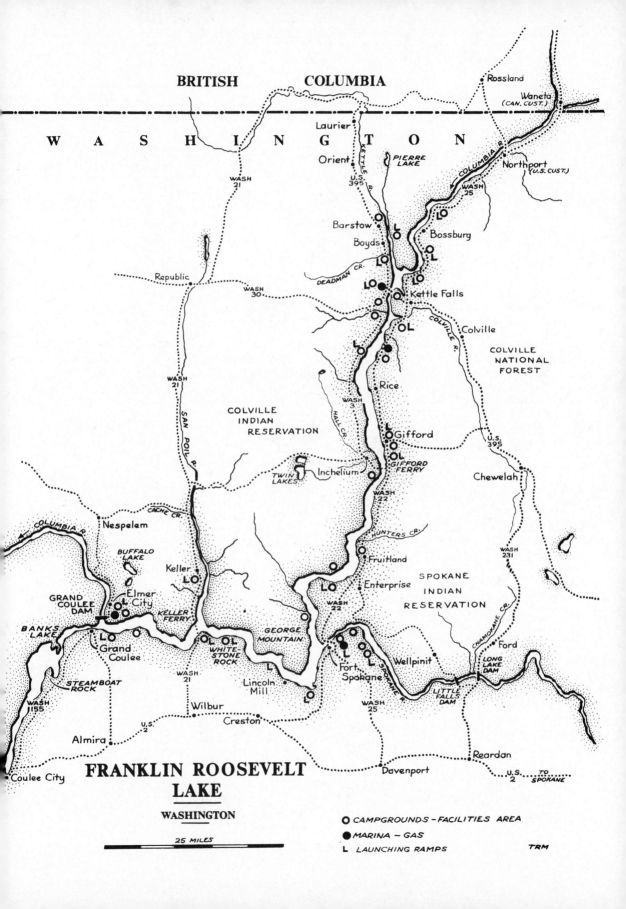

BRITISH COLUMBIA

WASHINGTON

Rossland

Waneta
(CAN. CUST.)

Laurier

Orient

PIERRE
LAKE

Northport
(U.S. CUST.)

WASH
21

KETTLE R.

U.S.
395

COLUMBIA R.

WASH
25

Barstow

LO

LO

Boyds

Bossburg

LO

Republic

WASH
30

DEADMAN CR.

LO

Kettle Falls

LO

COLVILLE R.

Colville

COLVILLE
NATIONAL
FOREST

WASH
21

SAN POIL R.

COLVILLE
INDIAN
RESERVATION

LO

L

Rice

WASH
3

HALL CR.

L

Gifford

LO

TWIN
LAKES

Inchelium

GIFFORD
FERRY

Chewelah

U.S.
395

WASH
22

CACHE CR.

Nespelem

BUFFALO
LAKE

Keller

LO

HUNTERS CR.

Fruitland

SPOKANE
INDIAN
RESERVATION

WASH
231

COLUMBIA R.

GRAND
COULEE DAM

Elmer
City

L

KELLER
FERRY

LO

Enterprise

LO

WASH
22

Ford

CHAMOKANE CR.

BANKS
LAKE

Grand
Coulee

LO

LO L

WHITE-
STONE
ROCK

GEORGE
MOUNTAIN

L

Fort
Spokane

L

LO

Wellpinit

LONG
LAKE
DAM

STEAMBOAT
ROCK

WASH
21

Lincoln
Mill

SPOKANE R.

LITTLE
FALLS
DAM

WASH
155

Wilbur

LO

WASH
25

U.S.
2

Creston

Almira

Reardan

Coulee City

Davenport

U.S.
2

TO
SPOKANE

FRANKLIN ROOSEVELT
LAKE

WASHINGTON

○ CAMPGROUNDS - FACILITIES AREA

● MARINA - GAS

L LAUNCHING RAMPS

25 MILES

TRM

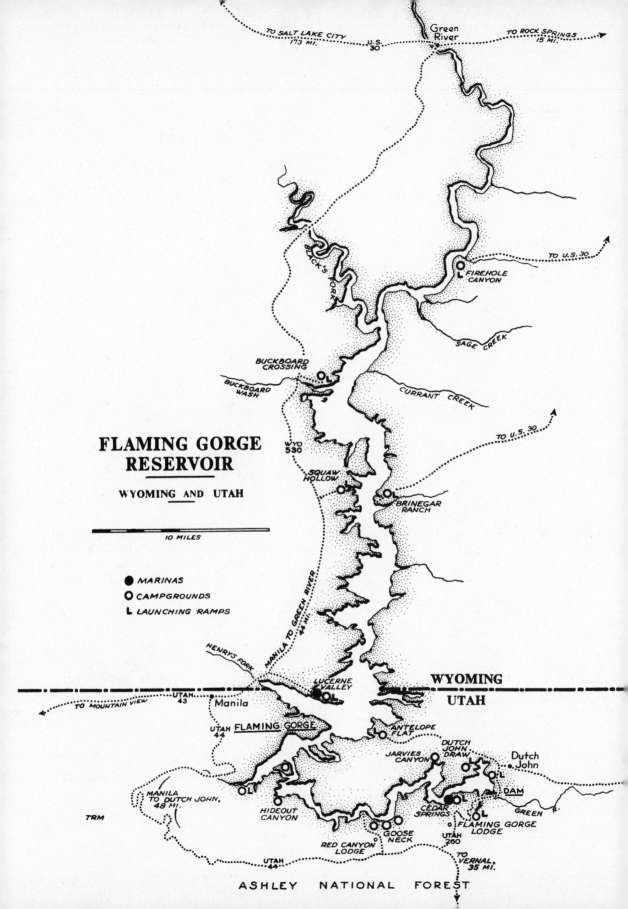

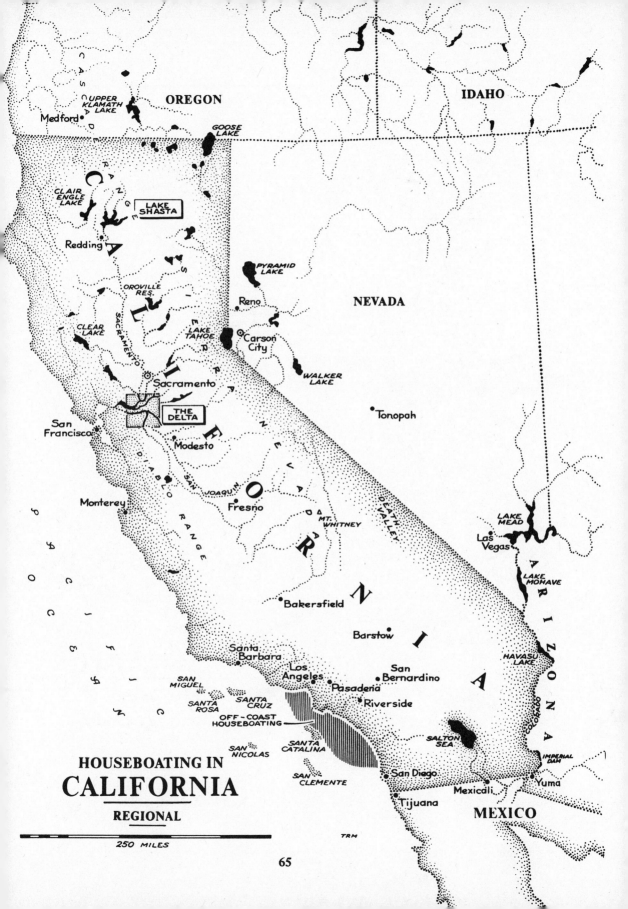

HOUSEBOATING IN
CALIFORNIA
REGIONAL

250 MILES

LAKE SHASTA

CALIFORNIA

5 MILES

○ CAMPGROUNDS AND PARKS
● MARINAS AND GAS
L LAUNCHING RAMPS

TRM

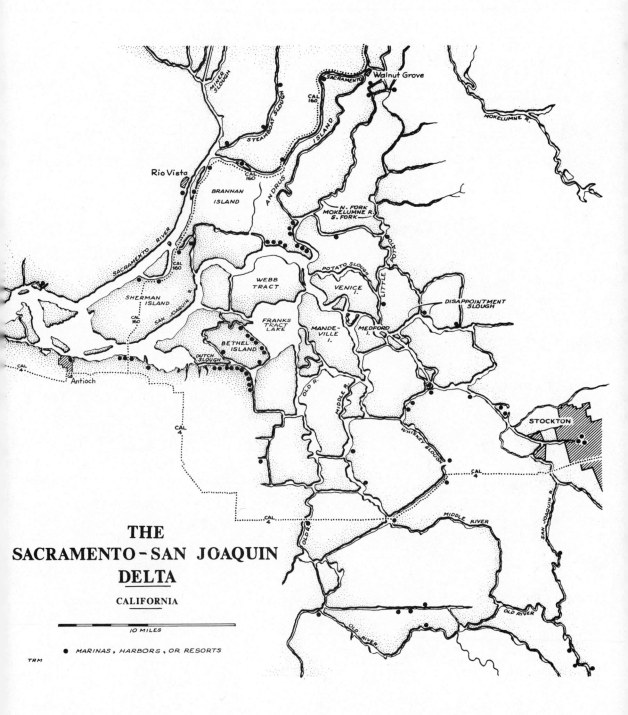

THE
SACRAMENTO - SAN JOAQUIN
DELTA

CALIFORNIA

10 MILES

● MARINAS, HARBORS, OR RESORTS

TRM

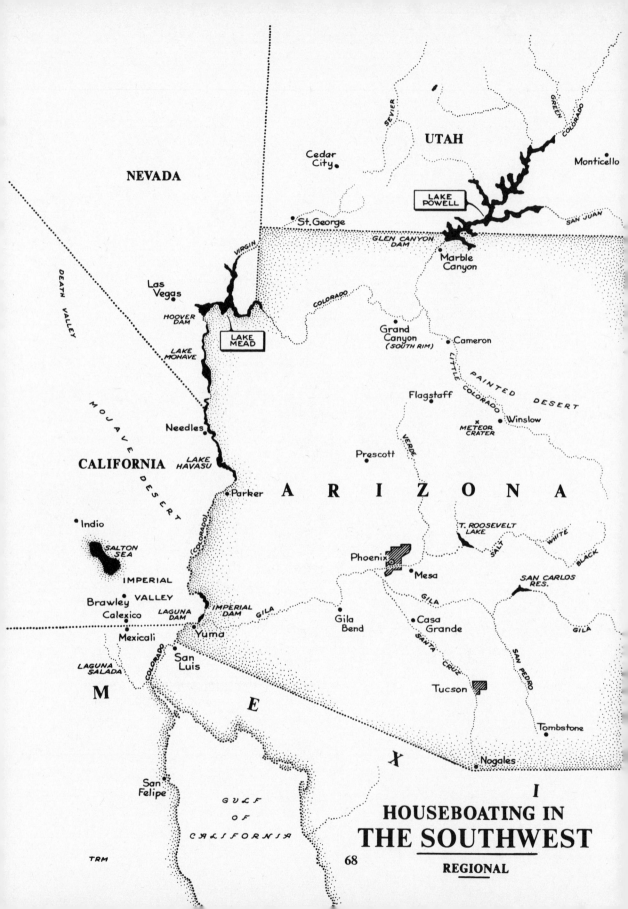

NEVADA

UTAH

Cedar
City•

•Monticello

SEVIER

GREEN

COLORADO

LAKE
POWELL

•St.George

SAN JUAN

*GLEN CANYON
DAM*

Las
Vegas•

VIRGIN

Marble
Canyon•

*DEATH
VALLEY*

*HOOVER
DAM*

LAKE
MEAD

COLORADO

Grand
Canyon
(SOUTH RIM)

•Cameron

LITTLE COLORADO

PAINTED   DESERT

*LAKE
MOHAVE*

Flagstaff•

Winslow•

×
*METEOR
CRATER*

Needles•

MOJAVE

*LAKE
HAVASU*

CALIFORNIA

Prescott•

VERDE

A R I Z O N A

DESERT

•Indio

•Parker

*T. ROOSEVELT
LAKE*

*SALTON
SEA*

(COLORADO)

Phoenix

WHITE

SALT

BLACK

IMPERIAL

•Mesa

*SAN CARLOS
RES.*

Brawley•

VALLEY

GILA

Calexico•

*LAGUNA
DAM*

*IMPERIAL
DAM*

GILA

Gila
Bend•

•Casa
Grande

•Mexicali

Yuma•

GILA

SAN PEDRO

SANTA CRUZ

*LAGUNA
SALADA*

COLORADO

San
Luis•

M

E

Tucson

X

San
Felipe•

*GULF
OF
CALIFORNIA*

•Tombstone

Nogales•

I

HOUSEBOATING IN
THE SOUTHWEST
REGIONAL

TRM

68

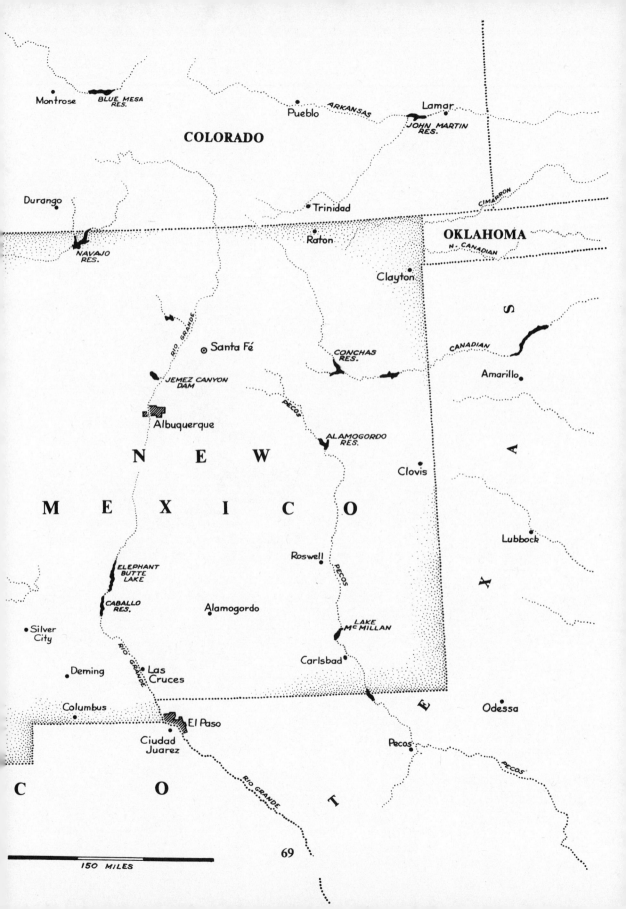

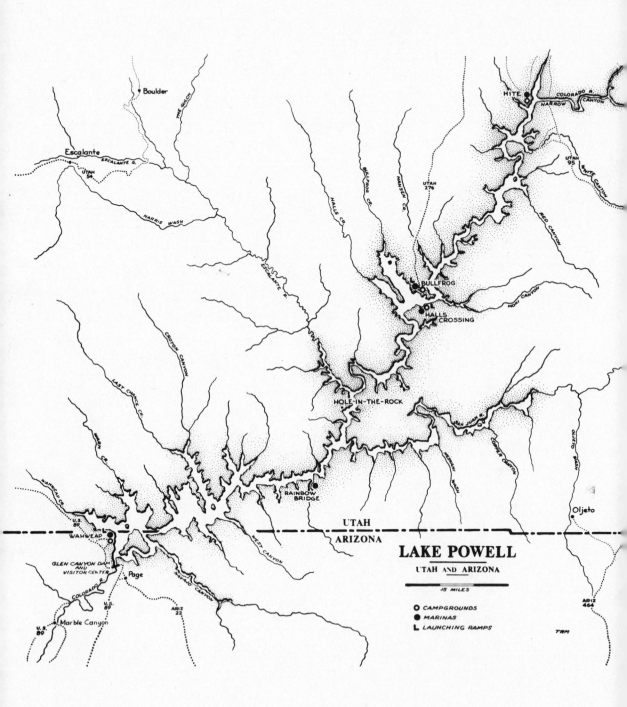

LAKE POWELL

UTAH AND ARIZONA

15 MILES

○ CAMPGROUNDS
● MARINAS
L LAUNCHING RAMPS

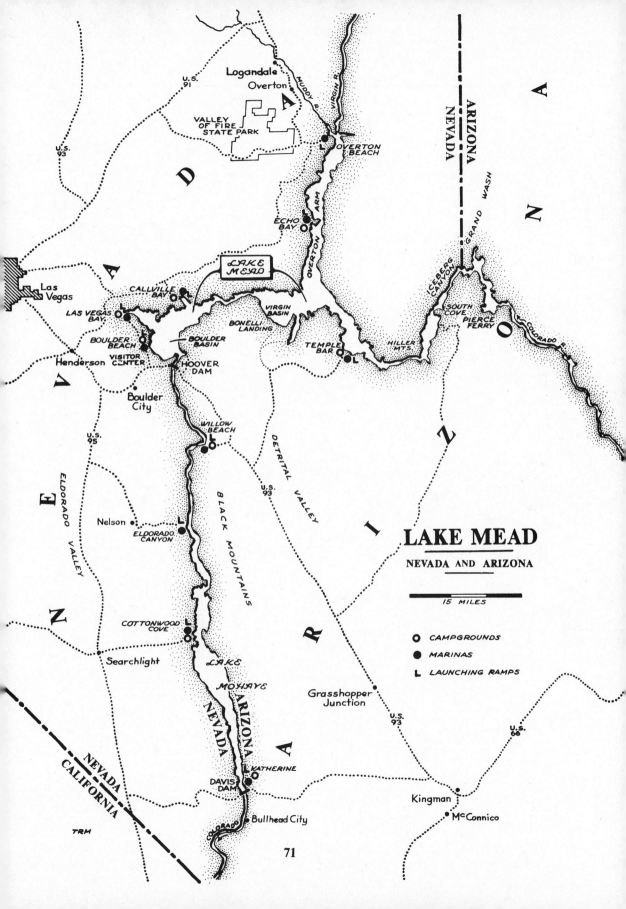

Logandale
Overton
VALLEY OF FIRE STATE PARK
N A D A
U.S. 91
U.S. 93
MUDDY R.
VIRGIN R.
OVERTON BEACH
ECHO BAY
OVERTON ARM
LAKE MEAD
CALLVILLE BAY
Las Vegas
LAS VEGAS BAY
VIRGIN BASIN
BONELLI LANDING
BOULDER BEACH
BOULDER BASIN
VISITOR CENTER
Henderson
HOOVER DAM
TEMPLE BAR
HILLER MTS.
ICEBERG CANYON
SOUTH COVE
PIERCE FERRY
GRAND WASH
COLORADO R.
ARIZONA
NEVADA
Boulder City
WILLOW BEACH
DETRITAL VALLEY
U.S. 95
U.S. 93
BLACK MOUNTAINS
Nelson
ELDORADO CANYON
ELDORADO VALLEY
N E V A D A
R I Z O N A

LAKE MEAD
NEVADA AND ARIZONA
15 MILES

○ CAMPGROUNDS
● MARINAS
L LAUNCHING RAMPS

COTTONWOOD COVE
Searchlight
LAKE MOHAVE
NEVADA
ARIZONA
Grasshopper Junction
U.S. 93
U.S. 66
KATHERINE
DAVIS DAM
NEVADA
CALIFORNIA
Kingman
McConnico
COLORADO R.
Bullhead City
TRM

CHAPTER THREE

Surveying the Houseboat Rental Scene

A carful of eager vacationers recently pulled up at a houseboat marina on California's Sacramento-San Joaquin Delta ready to embark on a two-week family adventure. About an hour later, after a careful checkout of their rental unit, they were under way.

Once afloat, the vacationers discovered to their amazement that a hefty part of the water traffic around them was comprised of houseboats. They were further surprised to learn that two-thirds of these were rental units like their own. Many of the families they encountered hailed from distant parts of the country. Some were renting for the second or third time.

During their two-week cruise the vacationers were treated to animated accounts of boating on Minnesota's Rainy Lake, the Columbia River, the Thousand Islands and other colorful spots. They were introduced to such catch names as "Boatel," "Leisure Craft" "River Queen" and "Seagoing," common names for rental units. As they continued chatting with fellow navigators, it became obvious that wherever there are good cruising waters, a houseboat rental can be found nearby. Some of the families they met were planning to harness these facilities to literally water explore their way across the United States.

You too may choose to embark on your maiden voyage in a rental unit. As you begin to plan your trip you are likely to find yourself faced with a bewildering number of attractive possibilities. The following survey of the houseboat rental scene is designed to help you arrive at the best vacation solution for you.

Where to Rent

There is no such thing as a "typical" rental operation. Rent-A-Cruise of America, in Springfield, Missouri, for example, franchises rentals at over 100 locations ranging from the West Coast to the Virgin Islands. The basic adventure of dealing with a franchise operation such as this is that it sets high standards of upkeep, service and equipment.

Another kind of operation is exemplified by Holiday Flotels, at Lake Shasta, California. Here you will find twenty or more rental units operating from a dock. On-the-spot facilities include electricity, water and gas pumps. The operator also carries a large stock of spare parts for his boats and motors to ensure quick repairs in case of breakdown.

In a slightly different vein, Richard's Yacht Center, across from Bethel Island in California's Delta country, rents River Queens (steel-hull houseboats) from a covered moorage stretched out about 600 feet along the bank of Dutch Slough. New boats can be purchased here as well, and the marina is equipped with complete repair facilities to keep rental units in tip-top condition.

In fact, wherever you rent your boat you will find one of the operator's major concerns during the season is the refurbishing of newly returned houseboats for the next customer. When a boat comes back to port after a week or two on the water, it is more than likely to show signs of wear and tear, ranging from spots on the carpet to minor mechanical damage. These

A typical rental marina.

receive immediate attention before being sent back out.

In some cases the damage is far from minor. One operator still talks about the vacationer who limped back into harbor minus much of the "house" part of his boat. Two days out, he'd met up with a bridge.

Occasionally operators are plagued by unscrupulous clients who try to conceal any damage they may have done. To avoid headaches later on, the operator therefore tends to go over the unit immediately on its return. Most concerns carry insurance, but since such policies nearly always have a deductible clause, any or all of the deposit may be kept in case of extensive damage.

Operators profit from off-season months to give their houseboats a thorough overhauling. Usually the units are hoisted out of the water. Steel-hull houseboats are thoroughly cleaned with a high-pressure hose, dents are knocked out, spots are scraped smooth and repainted with several coats of paint and the entire boat may be given a coat of antifouling body paint. The condition of safety railings and other important accessories is checked out as well. Needed engine repairs are made.

A comprehensive listing of rental facilities throughout the United States will be found on Appendix pp. 189-193. For additional up-to-the-minute information write for the Recreation Rental Guide, *Family Houseboating*, PO Box 500, Calabasas, Calif. 91302; $1.00.

How Much Will Your Vacation Cost?

The cost of a houseboat vacation depends on a number of factors: the type of boat you rent, the time of year and in some cases the number of passengers involved.

Quoting prices in a flexible economy is always a tricky matter, but let's begin with an approximate figure of $150 to $500 a week. This and all subsequent figures, however, are subject to inevitable price fluctuations.

Turning to specific cases, International Houseboats in the California Delta (Woodland Hills, Calif. 91364) rents pontoon boats that sleep six for $320 per seven-day week and ten-sleepers for $425. Holiday Flotels, Lake Shasta, California, offers Leisure Craft for $300 to $485 weekly. Off-season rates generally run 20 percent lower.

Moving eastward, Hutchinson's Boat

Works at Alexandria Bay, New York, handles River Queens at $450 to $650 a week. Seaway Marina, Peoria, Illinois, rents Chris-Crafts for $450 a week—$300 a weekend.

Rental periods vary from operator to operator, with possibilities including renting by the day, the weekend, Monday through Friday or the full week.

As a general rule, for a 40-foot boat sleeping six to eight you can count on spending from $100 to $200 for a weekend and $300 to $600 for a week, depending on the type of boat rented. Putting it another way, a Monday through Friday jaunt for four on a 32-foot houseboat comes to roughly $35 per person. When you get right down to it, a houseboat vacation will cost less than spending the same amount of time at a resort or motel.

Choosing Your Boat

Houseboat rental units range from comfortable pontoon boats that average a leisurely 6 miles an hour to sleek steel-hull or fiberglass cruisers that really get up and go.

Which is the best boat for you? That depends on the kind of vacation you have in mind. Different families have different ideas of fun. Some enjoy the thrill of skimming across the water at 20 to 30 miles an hour. Others

Operators overhaul their rental units during the off-season months: Here she comes out of the water.

prefer to meander along with time out for a sunbath on the top deck, an afternoon's fishing in a shallow cove or a chat with fellow houseboaters at anchor under a willow tree. Still others will look for a boat that caters to such special interests as skin diving, water-skiing and entertaining.

Keeping your vacation needs in mind will help you choose between a pontoon or a cruiser-hull model. Let's see what each has to offer.

Pontoon Hulls

Pontoon units generally consist of a platform and cabin constructed on two long pontoons—

This model is blocked up for complete going-over.

large floating compartments that are round, semicircular, square or rectangular in shape. Pontoon boats generally run from 18 to 50 feet in length, but there is no limit to their size.

These boats are extremely stable in the water and not overly sensitive to passenger movement. They have the added advantage of being able to carry tremendous weight without undue difficulty. They offer limited speed, however, and are generally powered by an outboard motor. Count on about 6 to 8 miles per hour. They also lack the maneuverability of cruiser hulls. On the plus side, this type of boat is generally easy to handle and operate, it can easily be pulled up to shore and it is ideal for quiet exploring in a variety of waters.

Among the popular pontoon rental units are Boatel, Leisure Craft and Kayot. Rental operators are partial to houseboats of this type because a novice can give them pretty rough treatment without doing any damage. Also you will find that since the operator does not have as large an initial investment, rates are comparatively low. You can count on pontoon houseboats to provide extremely enjoyable vacations at reasonable cost.

Cruiser Hulls

In spite of a number of variations, cruiser hulls are usually shaped in a deep or modified V and are constructed of either steel, aluminum or fiberglass. Their main appeal is directional stability and maneuverability. Most cruising houseboats boast modified V hulls (fairly flat in some boats) and 160- to 325-horsepower stern drive inboard/outboard power plants, either single- or twin-engine, which provide the added attraction of speed.

These are boats in the truest sense of the word. They can travel up to 30 miles an hour and navigate through the water with the ease of a cruiser. Some names to look for are Seagoing, River Queen, Nauta-Line, Drift R Cruz and Lazy Days.

This may be the type of boat for you if you are planning a long cruise in a limited amount of time. Keep in mind, however, that some of these units can be tricky for a beginner to handle, especially the twin-engined variety. There is also more speed and weight involved

here, with a more expensive boat at stake in case of a collision.

If you are planning a rough-water adventure, then a cruiser hull is a must. As we have seen, houseboats were originally designed for space and comfort, not heavy seas, and there is always some danger that water will come through the large front windows under the pressure of a big wave. But manufacturers are now coming up with cruiser-type models constructed to take the roughest seas. Further information on these and all other types of rental units can be attained by simply writing to a sampling of rental agencies (see Houseboat Rental Guide, Appendix pp. 189-193) and requesting their brochures.

A House Away from Home

Although you will find tremendous differences in handling between cruiser-hull and pontoon-hull units, their inner cabin accommodations are on the same high level. Both offer the space and modern conveniences that do so much toward making a water vacation a success. Units obviously vary in floor plans, plumbing, kitchen appliances, etc., but their basic aim is the same—to provide you with a cozy, practical home away from home.

Until you actually step aboard you can't imagine what a houseboat is really like. Perhaps the closest approximation is the interior of a luxurious mobile home. Among the amenities you are likely to encounter are carpeting, drapes, a shower, bunk beds, a toilet, a large dressing area, heat, hot and cold running water and air conditioning.

Let's take a stroll through some of the more popular units and see what they offer.

Leading off with one of the Rent-A-Cruise of America units, we enter through a spacious, uncluttered, carpeted wheelhouse, containing the center control console and a setee that folds out into a double bed. Two steps lead down to a starboard (right-hand) galley and a portside (left-side) dinette. The galley boasts a three-burner gas stove, a 4½-foot deluxe icebox, stainless steel sink with hot and cold water, and overhead galley cabinets. The dinette converts to a bed sleeping two.

Aft (rear) quarters include a full-length upper and lower berth to port with a private lavatory with full vanity, mirrored cabinet, hot and cold water, plus a completely separate shower on the starboard. There is life cushion and package storage in the locker under the pilothouse instrument panel. Suitcases and bulky items go under the pilothouse floor, bedding goes in the lockers under the dinette seats, suits, coats and other hanging items store in the hanging locker just behind the galley on the right-hand side. Drawer space is provided under the bunk in the aft stateroom.

A tour of one of the popular River Queens begins in the 23-foot-long cabin. This is broken down into a forward area measuring 9 by 9, a galley-dinette section 9 by 6, and a completely private aft stateroom 7 by 9. For maximum visibility the stateroom has an aft 4-foot sliding patio-type door that looks out over the water. In the daytime these sleeping quarters convert into a family lounge. Bathroom facilities include a marine toilet (standard boat toilet), a dressing table with a luxurious 30 by 38 inch mirror, and plenty of storage space. This light and airy model sleeps six and comes equipped with air conditioning, heat, avocado-colored carpeting, drapes and interior walnut paneling.

Houseboat manufacturers really outdo themselves when it comes to the galley area. You may well find that the kitchen facilities on your rental unit are superior to what you have at home. The River Queen, for example, boasts a 6 by 3 foot galley that is really designed with chow in mind. There is a three-burner range and oven directly adjacent to the sink, a large counter area opposite the stove, a built-in roller towel and a garbage slot. Three lights mounted directly over the 7 by 15 inch overhead storage cabinet provide excellent illumination for the work area, and two large picture windows offer a view. The counters are lipped to keep their contents from sliding off, and a 4-cubic-foot electric refrigerator adds a final practical touch. Best of all, to reach the dinette area all you have to do is turn around.

This spacious rental unit features an adjoining galley and dinette.

The Boatel, another popular make, also sports an attractively compact galley. A three-burner gas stove with a thermostat oven, a refrigerator and a stainless steel sink supplying hot and cold water help make mealtime easy and fun.

What Should You Bring?

When it comes to what is included in your rental houseboat, operators today furnish almost everything except the customer himself. Some throw in more extras than others, but you will always find the necessary basics for a good water vacation. Here is an idea of what you can expect:

Boating accessories. One rental operator furnishes propane gas, a compass, horn and bell, life jackets, pillows, deck chairs, a boating ladder, a charcoal broiler, a pike pole, fenders and other safety equipment. Another goes even further and equips his boats with spotlights, a dual horn, a ship's bell and an aluminum dinghy.

Livability accessories. Of course you will expect rental operators to provide the basic boating accessories such as anchor and line, etc., but most provide a lot more. For example, Holiday Flotels (at the California Delta, Lake

GOOD HOUSEKEEPING AND MAINTENANCE CHECK LIST

"our customers expect clean, properly equipped houseboats for comfort and safety"

HOUSEBOAT No. _____   DATE _____

OUT	IN		OUT	IN	
		hull			windows & screens
		engine			roman shades
		gas			110v dockside cord
		oil			deck chairs (4)
		battery # 1			propane gas
		battery # 2			gas range
		outdrive unit			fresh water
		propeller condition			water pressure
		steering			head functioning
		ventilating blower			shower
		instrument panel			ice box
		horn			galley equipment
		search light (portable)			solo cup holders (8)
		running lights			vacuumed wheelhouse
		anchor light			vacuumed galley & dinette
		catwalk lights			vacuumed stateroom
		interior lights (12v)			vacuumed deck carpets
		interior lights (110v)			stateroom beds, bed spreads
		bell			hide a bed
		anchor & line			blankets (4)
		tie lines (2)			pillows (6)
		fenders (4)			fire extinguishers (2)
		life buoys (2)			disposable galley kit
		life cushions (6)			clean linens & towels
		docking pole			tool kit
		bilge pump			captains chair
		air conditioner			

Most rental operators use a checklist like this to ensure that your boat will be ready to go.

Shasta and Clair Engle Lake locations) include a garbage can, broom, mop, dishes, silver and glassware plus a complete set of cooking utensils.

Some operators go even further than this. Rent-A-Cruise of America offers such niceties as bedspreads, blankets, pillows, a disposable galley kit, a coffeepot and cup holders. And Northernaire Floating Lodges, based in International Falls, Minnesota, goes all the way in their "Executive" houseboat rentals with a hi-fi, ice-cube maker, television, indoor barbecue pit, screened-in front porches and, believe it or not, a large aerated minnow tank.

As mentioned earlier, an important part of the operator's job, and one that is vital to the success of your trip, is a thorough checking out of all boats to ensure spic-and-span cleanliness and tip-top performance. Each has a standard procedure of his own, designed to guarantee customer satisfaction.

An idea of what may be involved can be obtained by glancing at one of the larger company's checklists, above, which includes fifty-two items ranging from strictly boating maintenance items such as steering, ventilating blower, outdrive unit, and battery through such livability equipment as water and water pressure, disposable linen, and deck chairs. The list also itemizes vacuuming and complete cleanup. When the checkout is completed, the list must be signed to certify that the boat is equipped, cleaned and provisioned in accordance with company standards.

The Checkout

Once your boat is ready for you, the operator has one last vital step to perform—readying you for your boat. Since at least 80 percent of today's houseboat vacationers have never been on the water before, the operator will insist on a careful checkout when the customer shows up at the dock to take possession of his rental unit.

Here is typical dockside procedure on departure day at one of California's leading rental operations:

The operator greets the family and shows them to their boat. Once it has been decided who is to be "skipper," he and the operator (followed by an inquisitive crew) start at the front of the boat and go through it thoroughly from stem to stern.

The operator shows the skipper how to tie up at night facing the wind, how to drop anchor 50 feet out, the fine art of tying up to a tree, how to check water depth with a pike pole. He points out the special nature of the area's bridges and alerts the skipper to other potential water hazards.

Moving sternward, the engine is next studied in detail—how to start it, how to shift gears, how to check the oil and gasoline, where to find spare shear pins and how to change them, how to raise and lower the motor.

Now it is time to familiarize the cook and bottlewashers with the appliances (the oven, the refrigerator, the water heater, etc.) and to make sure that the entire family knows how to relight the pilot light. The operator also explains what to do about the refrigerator if you ground on a sandbar and the tide goes out, how to cope with a water pressure pump and how to use the toilet. Special emphasis is given to the difference between water use at home and on board a houseboat. Since most units have a

The rental checkout. The skipper learns how to check the fuel level.

The operator explains how to run the engine and the care it will need en route.

The operator makes sure the family understands how the appliances work.

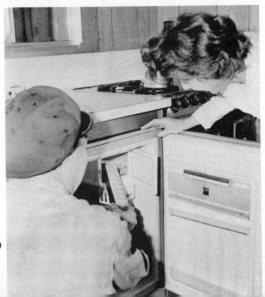

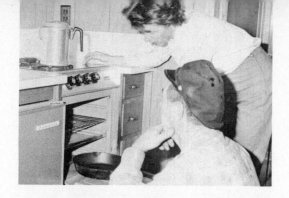

Every detail is checked to ensure a successful rental vacation.

The skipper learns how to check water depth with a pike pole.

The operator points out places of interest along the way.

limited carrying capacity of 40 to 100 gallons, water must be used with care and the tank must be refilled whenever possible to avoid running dry along isolated stretches. The hot-water tank should be secured to eliminate damage to coils or elements.

Now that the family members have a more nautical gleam in their eye, it is time to head out into the channel for a shakedown run.

While the skipper familiarizes himself with the handling of the boat, the operator stands alongside and explains such fine points as how to take a wave if a powerboat comes by, how to compensate (or overcompensate) for slow steering response, how to back up, ease in and dock. He then gives a quick rundown of the rules of the road (see pp. 104-106) and explains horn signals. The details of the water checkout vary with the type of boat you are renting.

Once back at the dock, the operator sits down with a detailed chart or large area map and shows the family some of the nearby places worth exploring. One operator sends his first-time renters on what he calls the "milk run"—a five-day trip through placid yet scenic waters, which allows them to go out one way and come back another. He then clues them in on the amount of time it takes to travel between various points of interest, indicates the best fishing spots along the route, and pinpoints the marinas and overnight stopping places on the map. He explains that they can stop and plug in at a marina for about ten cents a houseboat foot; or, if they prefer, simply pull up onto an open beach or tie their boat to a tree.

The rental operator also explains how to get help if something goes wrong. Sometimes a battery will run down or the engine will act up. In most areas you'll be close to civilization during the entire trip, and if there's any trouble you can simply pull into a marina or wave down a passing boat and have it call home base. Most operators have service men available and keep a service boat handy in case of such trouble. Or if the repairs are minor, the majority of boats carry a few small tools so that the renter can do it himself. (See pp. 173-176 for a listing of common motor troubles and suggested ways to correct them.)

A first-time family checks in. This is what it's really like.

One last important point is the matter of water safety. Rental operators tend to stress this most emphatically, showing the family where the cushions and life jackets are stowed and giving them an idea of how they work. One operator gets the whole family out on deck and goes through an emergency drill, including donning the jackets. This not only impresses the children but gets the rest of the family water-safety conscious as well. Water safety is covered in detail in Chapter 11. Read this chapter carefully before you embark.

Charts and Cruising Information

The further you can plan ahead, the more enjoyable your houseboat vacation will be. As mentioned earlier, begin by writing to as many names as possible on the Houseboat Rental list (Appendix pp. 189-193). Once you have settled on a probable area, write to the Chambers of Commerce of nearby towns for as much back-ground material as possible. Then check with the appropriate state travel office (see Appendix pp. 186-188) for overall material. Last but not least, write away for charts and maps covering the territory you intend to houseboat (see Appendix pp. 188-189).

Good charts or maps of an area will help you get a lot more out of your water vacation. Sit down with them for a few minutes before you leave the dock and take an overall look at your watery vacation route—pinpointing marinas, state parks and other possible points of interest. Check again with your operator to be sure there's nothing you've missed.

Once under way, take out your charts from time to time and give them another look. You'll be surprised at how much more they show you now that you're afloat.

Make it a habit to mark your chart as to the last fuel dock, pay telephone booth, food supplies, and so on. The possibility of sudden illness or observing an accident warrants this safety measure.

CHAPTER FOUR

Gear, Games and Grub

Once your major decisions are made—the kind of vacation you are looking for, the section or sections of the country you would like to visit and the type of houseboat that will best accommodate the kind of cruising you have in mind—you will be ready to make your reservation.

A word of caution here. Since houseboating is fast becoming one of our most popular outdoor activities, operators may be booked up months in advance. Although more and more units are being added to rental fleets around the country to accommodate the growing demand, you should still plan as far ahead as possible to avoid disappointment.

It is a temptation in preparing your trip to simply pick out the rental area nearest to you and give it a try. But with the whole wonderful world of houseboating crying out for exploration, why not follow the example of one family we know? Sit down with a list of rental operations in a number of areas that seem appealing, plot these out on a big map, discuss the attractions of each and then start writing for brochures. And when you write, ask about add-on charges such as sales tax, etc.

A number of operators include a reservation coupon along with their brochure. When you have made your choice, simply fill out the form and send it back with your deposit—usually from $50 to $150. Insist on a confirmed reservation. As a general rule, if you cancel far enough ahead so that your boat can be placed elsewhere, operators will refund your deposit. If you take possession of your boat as planned, this amount will often automatically become a security deposit (most operators carry from $50 to $100 deductible insurance on each boat). Your deposit will be refunded in full when you bring your rental unit back to port, assuming you return the boat clean and undamaged.

As departure day draws near, you will find yourself faced with the inevitable problem of packing. Once again, planning in advance will help ensure a fun-filled, relaxed cruise. Here are some tips on what to take along.

Clothing

As a general rule, the clothing you'll want will be similar to what you would wear to loaf around the house. It should be lightweight, comfortable, practical and easy to wash, featuring fabrics that show as little dirt as possible. Wash-and-wear, knits, and other no-iron fabrics are high on the desirability list. Be sure to pack enough of everything to allow for plenty of changes.

Men favor T-shirts and faded blue denims or wash-and-wear trousers and other sportswear as cruising garb. Women tend toward slacks or jeans. Shorts and bermudas are also popular. In line with this loose and comfortable look, pants torn off just above the knee are ideal for houseboat wear.

Children's clothing should be expendable (something they can tear or get wet). Don't

Reserve well ahead. Many companies are booked far in advance.

Clothing should be light, comfortable and easy to wash. Don't forget tennis or canvas-sole shoes.

forget swimsuits and perhaps lounging gear for the entire family.

Proper footgear is of extreme importance on any kind of boat. Since decks can be very slippery, each family member should have a tennis and/or canvas-soled shoes, and should *wear* them. Barefoot is very dangerous.

For rainy weather, take along slickers, ponchos or plastic raincoats. You can always take refuge in the "house" in case of a downpour, but it is a good idea to prepare yourself for showers on trips ashore.

Since some parts of the country get really cold at night, don't forget to pack a few sweaters plus a warm jacket. Sweat shirts are also welcome on a chilly day. You may be glad to have mittens or gloves as well. Conversely, include some sort of head covering for everyone in the family, to combat the combined effects of sun and water.

Household Effects

The number of domestic items that are included in your rental will vary greatly from

Keep headcovering handy to combat the sun afloat.

Don't forget to pack a warm sweater and jacket.

boat to boat. Some operators automatically provide a list of what they furnish plus suggestions for what you may want to bring along. If this is not the case, question them as closely as possible in advance to eliminate last-minute surprises.

As a general rule, you will probably want to bring along a few woolen blankets for each bed and in many cases bed linen as well. As an alternative, many renters simply stretch out sleeping bags on their bunks, eliminating the fuss of bedmaking. Also bring your own towels and wash cloths. Kitchen utensils are usually furnished, but check this out by consulting the brochure provided by your rental operator. You may have to supply your own.

Another way of cutting down on household chores is by utilizing the extensive range of paper products available on today's market. In addition to paper cups, plates and other disposable tablewear, manufacturers now put out tough, pleasantly textured, attractive sleeping bags, blankets, sheets and pillowcases. If you supplement these with paper ponchos, diapers and dresses, you can cut cruise upkeep to a bare minimum. Most of these products come in a variety of colors and can be reused or thrown out as you choose. A list of manufacturers of paper products with approximate prices is given on Appendix p. 193.

You will find that the more personal items you include in your luggage the more enjoyable your trip will be. For example, most boaters do not consider a hot-water bottle a necessity, but it is reassuring to have one aboard. And don't forget shaving equipment, toothbrushes and toothpaste, nail clippers, disposable tissues and medicine. Another welcome item is a few extra rolls of toilet paper. Operators furnish these, but an additional supply of your own will come in handy. (Only cheap single-ply paper will work in chemical toilets.) Other useful items include a fingernail brush, disinfectant, plenty of soap, scissors, poison oak and ivy lotion, mosquito repellent, a magnifying glass, a sewing kit and toothache remedy.

Although most boats come equipped with a first-aid kit, it is wise to make up one of your own. Be sure to include a snakebite kit as well. This last item may sound odd for a boating vacation, but in some areas you will find yourself in snake-infested country. A list of emergency first-aid procedures as well as detailed directions on what to include in your kit will be found on pp. 180-184.

Other extras brought from home that will add to the pleasure of your trip are a radio, a portable battery-powered TV (unless a 110-volt generator is on board), a cassette tape player, games, books, magazines and a portable ice chest for cold drinks.

If you are considering taking a pet along and plan to rent a houseboat, check first with the rental operator. Some allow pets, others do not.

No special preparations are needed for taking pets aboard. Some pet owners like to take along a familiar blanket or a box for the animal. A few pets become sick on the water. If yours has the tendency to get carsick or seasick, or to wander off, leave the animal at home if possible. Finally, all animals will need some time on shore each day to relieve themselves and to exercise.

Recreational Equipment

One of houseboating's main attractions is the base it provides for a number of fun-filled activities. You can profit from these most fully if you step on board armed with the proper equipment.

Most Americans are expert browsers, and the houseboat provides excellent opportunities for water exploration. Once again: Don't forget to do your homework ahead of time so that you are thoroughly familiar with the waters, history and attractions of the area to be traveled.

A camera will prove invaluable. Not only will you have the fun of cruising about in search of memorable shots, but you can compile a scrapbook of your trip once you get back home. This will allow you to relive your vacation all winter long and share it with your friends. Along with a camera, tuck a notebook into your suitcase so that you can jot down your impressions along the way. Bring along an additional guidebook or two to study and read aloud en route. This will further enrich the trip for the entire family.

Budding or confirmed birdwatchers will find their observations enriched by a good reference book: *A Guide to Familiar American Birds* (Golden Nature Guide), *Birds of North America* (Golden Field Guide), *Birds of America* (Gilbert Pearson Doubleday), *Birds of Prey* (Bantam), *Field Guide to the Birds* (Peterson Field Guide, Houghton Mifflin), *Field Guide to Western Birds* (Peterson Field Guide, Houghton Mifflin), among others. Binoculars (preferably 7 x 35) are helpful.

You and your family may decide to study other forms of life on or along the water. Even if you are not seasoned naturalists, you will enjoy seeing what you can come up with. These inexpensive books will help you with your identification: *Trees* (Golden Nature Guide), *Trees of North America* (Golden Field Guide), *Flowers* (Golden Nature Guide), *Field Guide to Wild Flowers of North Eastern and North Central North America* (Peterson Field Guide, Houghton Mifflin), *Pond Life—A Guide to Common Plants and Animals on North American Lakes and Ponds* (Golden Nature Guide), *Seashore Life of Southern California* (Joel Hedapeth, Naturegraph), *Seashells of North America* (Golden Field Guide), *Seashores—A Guide to Shells, Seashells, Sea Plants, Shore Birds and Other Natural Features of the American Coast* (Golden Nature Guide), *Seashells of the World* (Golden Nature Guide), *Fishes of the World* (Dutton).

To get the most out of any rock-bound country you may encounter, encourage the family to pick up anything they stumble across, and take along a good rock and mineral book such as *Gold, Rocks and Minerals* (Golden Nature Guide) for classification purposes, or *Rock Hunter's Field Manual* (D. K. Fritzen, Harper & Row). Other useful tools include a geologist's pick, a cold chisel and a magnifying glass. And don't forget a few gold pans. Once you've gotten hooked on this pastime, you will realize what made the '49ers tick.

The thrill of stargazing from your deck will be increased by a telescope and a good guidebook such as *Stars, a Guide to the Constellations, Sun, Moon, Planets and Other Features of the Heavens* (Golden Nature Guide) or *Stars and Outer Space Made Easy* (Carlos S. Mundt, Naturegraph).

Other items useful for making a houseboat trip enjoyable include sketching supplies, a jacknife for whittling, musical instruments, anything else you can think of that "the crew" would enjoy.

Skin and scuba diving enthusiasts will of course find their equipment a great addition to the enjoyment of a houseboat cruise. And you will find that you can get a lot of extra fun from a one-man life raft, a fishing boat, a water-skiing boat, or any other type of runabout or inflatable you might stow on board. Some rental operators provide a small separate boat or dinghy with every houseboat.

As far as fishing gear is concerned, if you don't already have equipment of your own you can outfit a family of four for less than $12 with a cane pole, a spool of line, a couple of hooks, a sinker, a bobber and a can of worms. You'll be surprised to see what fun it is when everyone throws out their lines together on deck.

It is wise to take along a few supplies specifically designed for children. A portable typewriter will enable them to put out a daily newspaper describing in headlines and news stories what they see and do during their cruise. Carbon copies can be passed out to family members. If you do not want to lug along a machine, the paper can be printed by hand.

Kites are fun to fly from the deck, and a wastebasket will make for deckside fun with family members seeing who can sink the most of their fifteen playing cards at six paces. Beanbags can provide hours of simple fun.

Another activity that youngsters enjoy is print making, using the different leaves they pick up along the way. For this you will need fresh leaves, a soft rubber roller, a sponge or washcloth, newsprint, small tubes or jars of watercolor paints (two or three harmonious colors will do), an 18 by 24 or an 18 by 36 inch

You will be surprised what fun it is to throw out your line on deck. It is not at all unusual to run into luck like this.

Prepare games for the children in advance for that inevitable rainy day.

piece of heavy oil cloth and paper (a small art sketch pad, for example). For the "press" you will need a flat, hard surface such as a boat deck, two big towels and another hard surface (a breadboard or an 18-inch-square piece of ¾ plywood will do nicely). When you are ready to print, pour a bit of paint onto one corner of the oil cloth and roll the roller back and forth over the paint until the roller is well coated. Then roll it firmly across the leaf. Next, spread out one of the towels on deck and top it with a sheet of paper. Place the leaf on the paper, paint side down. Cover with a sheet of newsprint, the second towel and the top board. Have the youngsters step on the press with both feet and move around the surface. Every time you change colors, swab off the oilcloth thoroughly with the sponge or washcloth.

Kids also love making prints with blueprint paper. Buy fresh blueprint paper from a drafting supply house before you leave, cut it into typewriter paper-size pieces and keep it well wrapped. When you are ready to begin, lay a sheet of paper flat on the houseboat deck and fasten it down by placing a small rock at each corner. Keep it shaded under an umbrella or another protective covering. Arrange leaves, stones or shells on the paper, then expose it to direct sunlight. When the paper fades from deep blue to neutral gray, carry it into the shade, remove the objects and immerse it in water, printed side down. Soak for several minutes, then spread out flat to dry.

Another game you can prepare for in advance is one children enjoy because it's related to the very trip they are taking. Divide several large cards (one for each player) into nine, fifteen or twenty-five squares. In each square jot down things you are likely to see during your cruise—a young boy fishing, a maple tree, a jet vapor trail, a water-skier, a ferryboat, a bait shop, a tugboat, etc. Players fill in each square with time and place as they find the called-for items. The first one to complete his card wins.

While we are on the subject of games, here are a few more to keep up your sleeve for that inevitable rainy day. They are designed not only to keep the youngsters occupied but at the same time to heighten their sense of observation and help them remember what they've seen and done on their vacation.

Place ten different objects in a paper bag. Take them out one at a time, giving the youngsters a brief glimpse of each, then return them to the bag. Now have the youngsters try to list the objects in order. Include leaves, flowers, twigs, berries, pine needles, rocks, sand, bark and other items you have picked up along the way.

A variation of this is to put a number of objects that you have all observed together into a bag, blindfold the players and make them guess what each object is by touch alone. Seed pods, soil, sinkers, fish line, lichens, moss, ferns, sticks, mushrooms, berries, lava rock, pine cones, nuts, rotting wood and shale can be utilized.

In the same vein, try a nature's travelers game. Have each family participant collect in advance as many of nature's travelers (seeds or seed pods) as he can find; they can be picked up on hikes, from the water and even on the houseboat deck. Then try to identify them. Here are some representative shapes:

(1) Winged—box elder, ash, maple

(2) Parachutes—dandelion, milkweed, cattails

(3) Seeds with hooks—burs

(4) Seeds that shake out—poppies, columbine

(5) Seeds that pop out—jewelweed, violet

Many nature books and reference works including the *World Book Encyclopedia* list seed types with examples. Check one of these for more specific details.

And for the smallest of the small, simply have them look about them. What do they see? Nothing but water or another boat? Then help them to look more closely. What about the colors of the water and the sky? The shapes and sizes of the clouds overhead (a warm day creates all sorts of configurations in the sky—marching men, a witch's face, animals and mountains)? The texture of the water surface

On any vacation chow time is a large part of the fun.

(the ripples made by stones, etc.)? How about the tiny insects in the air? How do they look? How do they sound?

And let's not forget what is probably the greatest and most enriching game of all—handling and tending the boat itself. The more the entire family participates in this the more fun your trip will be. Plan to assign chores the moment you step on deck, with everyone trying their hand at swabbing, polishing, cleaning, KP—and everyone making their own beds. All but the tiniest should get their turn at the wheel (under the strict supervision of the skipper, of course). And make the pleasures of map reading, course plotting and deciding on the day's activities a shared, family affair.

Food and Menus

This is another area in which foresight really pays off. In fact, seasoned houseboaters say that when it comes to meals, careful advance planning is absolutely essential.

In the galley (or kitchen) a houseboat really shines. Notice the stainless steel sink, three-burner stove and vinyl top. Food preparation aboard should be simple, quick and casual.

You can always pull in for some fill-in food shopping en route.

On any vacation chow time is a large part of the fun. But you can make the necessary cooking a pleasure or a chore, depending on how you approach it. Veteran cruisers agree on certain basic rules: Food preparation should be simple, quick and casual.

Some family cooks prepare a number of foods at home, including spaghetti dishes, lasagna and chili. Then they freeze them and pop them into the houseboat's icebox or refrigerator on arrival. Others take no pre-cooked dishes and a minimum of standard food items, and simply buy everything in prepared form. At dinnertime all that is needed is to add water and heat.

Savvy houseboaters usually buy the bulk of their food at home since they know where to go for the best buys and widest selection. Some, however, wait to stock up until they reach the last large town along the way, and even the most efficient shoppers occasionally pull up for some fill-in shopping at marinas en route.

When it comes to planning houseboating menus, a good rule to follow is this: Keep them as uncomplicated as possible. After all, the cook is on vacation too. With this in mind you may want to rely heavily on the ever-growing list of convenience foods available on the market.

Convenience foods divide into two basic categories: dehydrated and freeze-dried foods. They range from dehydrated potatoes and freeze-dried steak to the dry, lightweight sports-man foods prepared by such specialized com-panies as Bernard and Richmoor.

In planning vacation menus, variety is another important factor. Instead of the same breakfast every morning, for instance, try serv-ing three hot and three cold ones during a six-day cruise.

Breakfast menus should be planned around these basic foods:

(1) fruit juice or fruit

(2) cold cereal

(3) eggs and bacon, ham or sausage, steak, etc.

(4) pancakes

(5) hot beverage such as coffee or cocoa

Dehydrated milk, individually packaged dry breakfast cereals and packaged instant "toaster type" foods are definite timesavers here. And the specially prepared sportsman foods (the prices are higher than for conventional foods) allow you to stock up on orange drink, instant tomato juice, oatmeal with sugar and milk, scrambled egg and bacon, Western omelet, pancake mix, maple syrup mix and a French toast mix. In addition, sportsman foods come in complete breakfast packages. Here is a sampling from one company's brochure (all breakfasts include a butter substitute):

Breakfast #1
Instant applesauce, pancake mix, maple syrup mix, sweet milk cocoa

Breakfast #2
Orange juice drink, eggs and bacon, hash brown potatoes, sweet milk cocoa

Breakfast #3
Peach slices with sugar, brown and serve sausages, corn cake mix, maple syrup mix, sweet milk cocoa

Breakfast #4
Instant applesauce, scrambled eggs with freeze-dried ham, hash brown potatoes, sweet milk cocoa

Breakfast #5
Fruit cocktail with sugar, "Mel-Betts" melba toast, French toast mix, maple syrup mix, sweet milk cocoa

At lunchtime, only a really committed cook will want to go to any extra work. Most put up sack lunches at breakfast or simply lay out all the fixings and let each family member fend for himself. Plan lunches around these items:

(1) Sandwiches—canned or package lunch meats, peanut butter, cheese

(2) Fresh or dried fruits

(3) Milk, tea, coffee, fruit drinks

(4) Cookies

Here again, the sportsman line of dried prepared foods will come in handy, offering a variety of tasty instant spreads, drinks and desserts.

At dinnertime the rule is again simplicity. This does not mean, however, that meals must lack imagination or variety. There are endless variations on the theme of meat, starch and vegetable. Casseroles are especially popular on board as they involve a minimum of dishwashing. Accompany them with a refreshing green salad made of easy-to-conserve ingredients and round off with soup and a dessert.

Here are six sample timesaving menus:

First Dinner
Tomato soup, fresh steak, fried onions, mashed potatoes, lettuce-tomato salad, canned pears

Second Dinner
Tomato soup, beef stew, mashed potatoes, cabbage, Jello

Third Dinner:
Onion soup, hamburgers with all the trimmings, apple dumplings

Fourth Dinner
Tuna or salmon casserole, carrots, instant butterscotch pudding

Fifth Dinner
Vegetable soup, ham and pineapple, pears, instant chocolate pudding

Sixth Dinner
Chicken noodle soup, macaroni, hot dogs, carrots, instant pudding

Preparation time can be minimized if you lay in a supply of instant soups and bouillon cubes, instant potatoes in a variety of types, instant rice dinners and instant puddings. Canned tuna and salmon are quick and handy additions to casserole dishes, and the wide range of available prepared foods includes everything from Western hash to no-bake brownie mix.

Many families make lunch a do-it-yourself meal.

Like breakfasts, sportsman dinners can be purchased in complete menu packages. These include:

Dinner #1
Chicken rice soup, Chili Mack with beef, chocolate pudding, fruit punch beverage

Dinner #2
Freeze-dried corn, chicken à la king, instant mashed potatoes, vanilla pudding, orange beverage

Dinner #3
Tomato noodle soup, vegetable beef stew with dumplings, butterscotch pudding, pineapple-orange beverage

Dinner #4
Vegetable beef soup, quick chicken rice dinner, French apple compote, lemon beverage

Dinner #5
French onion soup, beef stroganoff with noodles, banana cream pudding, grape beverage

In spite of all the above mentioned shortcuts available to the modern cook, some vacationers enjoy spending their leisure time fooling around in a galley. If you are in the mood to experiment one evening, here are a few streamlined casserole recipes designed to delight a hungry captain and crew.

TACO BEEF CASSEROLE

(serves 6 to 8)

1 medium-size onion, finely chopped
1 tablespoon salad oil or olive oil
2 pounds ground beef chuck
1 package (about 1¼ oz.) taco seasoning
1 cup water
1 small can corn (whole-kernel 8¾ oz.)
1 can (6 oz.) pitted ripe olives
6 corn tortillas
1 can (10 oz.) enchilada sauce
2 cups shredded sharp Cheddar cheese
1 avocado

In large frying pan sauté onion in oil until golden brown; push to sides of pan. Add ground chuck and sauté until browned, stirring. Add taco seasoning and water, cover and simmer 10 minutes. Remove from heat and add corn. Reserve ⅓ cup of olives for topping; coarsely chop remainder and add to meat.

Cut tortillas into quarters, dip each piece into enchilada sauce and arrange half of them in the bottom of a greased 9- to 10-inch round baking dish (about 2 inches deep). Cover with meat mixture. Sprinkle with 1 cup of cheese. Repeat layers, ending with cheese. Bake uncovered in a 350° oven for 20 minutes, or until hot. Before serving, garnish top with avocado slices and remaining olives.

CHICKEN AND VEGETABLES

(serves 6)

2 broiler-fryer chickens (about 2 to 2½ lbs. each), cut up
½ cup flour
1 teaspoon salt
1½ teaspoons pepper
⅓ cup salad oil
1 large onion, sliced
3 stalks celery, sliced
½ green pepper (seeded, membrane removed, sliced)
1 large can (28 oz.) tomatoes
½ cup water
1 teaspoon chicken stock base, or 1 chicken bouillon cube
1 bay leaf
Cooked rice

Wash the chicken pieces and pat dry with paper towels. Place a few at a time in a plastic bag with the flour, salt and pepper. Shake until all the pieces are coated with flour. Reserve excess flour. Using a large frying pan, heat the oil, put in about half the chicken pieces and fry until nicely browned on all sides. As the pieces are browned, set aside; continue frying until all the chicken is browned. To the drippings that remain in the pan, add the sliced onion, celery and pepper. Cook until soft, then add remaining ingredients. Simmer for 15 minutes. Serve with the chicken over hot cooked rice.

MEATBALL STROGANOFF

(serves 6 to 8)

2 pounds ground beef
½ pound mushrooms
4 tablespoons margarine
1 medium-size onion, finely chopped
1 teaspoon salt
¼ teaspoon pepper
¼ teaspoon sweet basil
1 tablespoon flour
½ cup canned tomato paste
1 can (10 oz.) condensed beef consommé
2 teaspoons Worcestershire sauce
1 tablespoon vinegar
1 cup sour cream
Buttered French bread

Shape meat into bite-size balls. Slice mushrooms and sauté in a large frying pan in 2 tablespoons of margarine; turn out of pan and set aside. Add remaining 2 tablespoons margarine to pan and sauté onion until golden; push to sides of pan. Add meatballs and sauté, shaking pan to turn meatballs until browned. Sprinkle with salt, pepper, basil and flour. Add tomato paste, consommé, Worcestershire, and vinegar. Cover and simmer 10 minutes. Add mushrooms to meat and remove from heat. Stir in sour cream. Serve with hot buttered French bread.

CAPTAIN'S MEATBALL STEW

(serves 6)

1½ pounds ground beef
1 egg, slightly beaten
1 cup small bread cubes
¼ cup finely chopped onion
1 teaspoon salt
2 tablespoons shortening
1 can (16 oz.) sliced carrots, drained
1 can (15 oz.) whole white potatoes, drained
1 can (8 oz.) small white onions, drained

Combine beef, egg, bread cubes, onion and salt. Shape into balls. Brown in shortening in skillet, pour off fat and add remaining ingredients. Cook over low heat 20 minutes, stirring occasionally.

The houseboat provides an ideal base for a number of fun-filled activities.

SALMON AND CHEESE PIE

(serves 6)

Generous 9-inch pastry shell
1 cup shredded American or Cheddar cheese
1 can (16 oz.) salmon, drained; or 2 cups cooked salmon (leftover barbecue or baked salmon can be used)
1 tablespoon flour
2 tablespoons butter or margarine
1 bunch green onions, with about 2 inches green tops, sliced
1 can cream of mushroom soup
¾ cup sour cream
1 teaspoon dill weed
⅛ teaspoon pepper
2 eggs, slightly beaten

Using your own recipe, or a pie crust mix, prepare 1½ times the amount of pastry required for a 9-inch pie shell. Roll out as directed and transfer to a 9-inch pie pan, building a firm standing edge. Bake and cool.

Sprinkle half the cheese into the cooled pastry shell. Remove any bones and skin from salmon, break into chunks, mix lightly with flour and place in shell. In a pan, heat butter or margarine and sauté onions until soft. Add undiluted soup, sour cream, dill weed and pepper. Heat and stir until the mixture boils. Remove from heat, mix in eggs and pour over salmon. Sprinkle top with remaining cheese. Bake in a 325° oven for 30 minutes, or until set. Let stand 5 to 10 minutes before serving.

CREWMAN'S DELIGHT

(serves 6)

½ pound sliced frankfurters
1 can (15 oz.) whole white potatoes, drained and diced
½ small onion, sliced
2 tablespoons margarine
1 can cream of mushroom soup
¼ cup water
1 can (16 oz.) cut green beans, drained

Cook frankfurters, potatoes and onions in margarine until onions are tender. Add soup, water and green beans. Simmer 10 minutes, stirring occasionally.

One of the greatest joys of houseboating is the handling and tending of the boat.

GROUND BEEF AND CHEESE PIE

(serves 6)

Serve wedges of this main-dish pie for brunch or a light supper, accompanied with fresh asparagus or a green salad. Quick pastry recipe follows for a 9-inch pie plate.

½ teaspoon salt
1½ pounds lean ground beef
1 medium-size onion, chopped
¼ teaspoon pepper
1 whole egg
1 egg white
1 pint large-curd cottage cheese
⅓ cup shredded Parmesan cheese
Chopped parsley (optional)

Quick pastry: In a bowl combine 1 cup biscuit mix, 1 egg yolk and 2½ tablespoons milk. Mix with a fork until blended, then press into a ball. Roll out the pastry on a lightly floured board, then line a 9-inch pie pan, making a fluted edge.

Sprinkle salt in a frying pan, add beef and cook over medium heat, stirring until juices begin to form. Add onion and pepper. Cook, stirring until meat loses all pinkness and liquid has evaporated. Turn into the prepared crust. In a bowl, mix together the egg, egg white and cottage cheese. Spoon mixture over the meat in the pie. Sprinkle top with Parmesan cheese. Bake in a 375° oven for about 25 minutes, or until top is set. Serve hot, sprinkled with parsley if desired.

THE ADMIRAL'S SUPER SUPPER

(serves 6)

½ cup uncooked rice
1 pound ground beef
2 chopped onions
2 tablespoons butter
1 can (16 oz.) tomatoes
½ teaspoon chili powder
½ teaspoon mustard
1 teaspoon salt
Dash of pepper
1 can (16 oz.) green beans

Cook the rice while you fry the ground beef and chopped onions in butter. Add the prepared rice. Stir in remaining ingredients. Cover skillet and simmer for 15 minutes.

CREW'S CASSEROLE

(serves 4 with leftovers)

1   tablespoon cooking fat
1   pound ground round
1   onion, chopped
1   quart water
1   pound medium noodles
1   teaspoon salt
½   teaspoon monosodium glutamate (m.s.g.)
½   teaspoon pepper
1   can cream of celery soup
1½ cups milk
2   eggs
¼   pound sliced Cheddar cheese

Melt fat in frying pan or dutch oven. Add meat and chopped onion, and cook until meat loses its color. While cooking the meat, pour 1 quart of water into a three-quart pot. Bring to a boil and add noodles. Cook until tender. Arrange meat and onions in a casserole. Add seasonings. Drain noodles and place ½ of them on the meat mixture. Mix celery soup with ½ cup of milk. Pour half of the soup into casserole, then add another layer of meat and noodles, then the remaining soup mixture. Lightly beat two eggs with the remaining cup of milk and pour over the casserole. Top with cheese slices. Bake at 325° for 35 minutes.

ZANE VEST'S PORK CHOP CREOLE

(serves 6)

6   pork chops
1   tablespoon margarine
Dash of pepper
6   onion slices
6   green pepper rings
1   can tomato soup with rice
½   soup can water
1   tablespoon Worcestershire sauce

Brown chops on both sides in margarine. Pour off drippings. Sprinkle each chop with pepper and top with an onion slice and a green pepper ring. Combine soup and water. Pour soup over chops, add Worcestershire sauce. Cover. Cook 45 minutes over low heat, stirring occasionally.

The following are several inexpensive cookbooks featuring easy recipes suitable for houseboat cooking: *Easy Can-Opener Cookbook* (Pyramid), *Ground Beef Cookbook* (Sunset Books), *Better Homes and Gardens Casserole Cookbook* (Bantam), *Jiffy Cooking* (Better Homes and Gardens).

CHAPTER FIVE

Navigation for the Novice

When you first step aboard your houseboat, you are going to have to unlearn most of what you have been taught about driving an automobile.

Houseboats, like any other boat, have both steering and power located at the rear. To navigate, you simply change the direction of the stream of water shot out behind the propeller. If your boat is equipped with an outboard motor or a stern drive, you will alter your course by turning the entire drive unit to one side. In most cases you will find action and reaction relatively positive.

However, with other types of boats, especially single-engine inboards, changes of direction are made by throwing the wheel over hard. You must learn to allow for a brief lapse of time between the moment the maneuver is made and the boat responds.

When you embark on your maiden voyage, what are some of the basic navigational problems you will be faced with, and how can they be most effectively solved?

Let's begin, as you will, with leaving the dock. To accomplish this maneuver smoothly, the main factor to keep in mind is wind direction. Figs. 1-5 illustrate how to cast off under all possible wind conditions.

Leaving the Dock

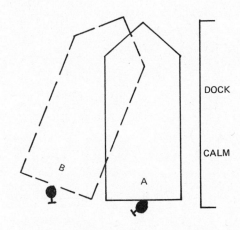

Fig. 1: No wind—cast off stern, then bow lines. Turn engine away from dock and run in reverse (A). Turn engine back and swing boat parallel to the dock.

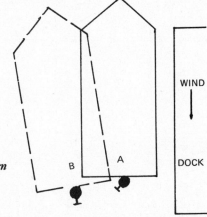

Fig. 2: Wind ahead—push boat clear (A). Turn engine away from dock and reverse.

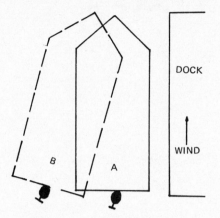

Fig. 3: Wind at rear (astern)—push boat clear (A). Turn engine away from dock and reverse.

The other side of the coin is bringing your boat into the dock. There are two general rules to remember here: First, try to draw up against the wind or tide, for they will act to slow you down. Second, if the dock looks crowded, sit back and wait until it clears. Figs.

Approaching the Dock

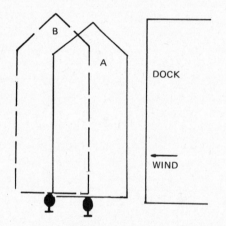

Fig. 4: Wind off dock—let wind blow boat clear after casting off both lines, then move forward.

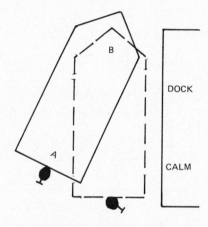

Fig. 6: Approaching dock with wind calm, ahead, or off dock—come in slowly at angle, turn engine toward the dock and run in reverse to bring stern in.

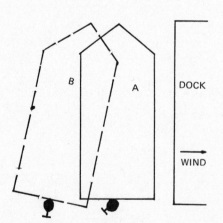

Fig. 5: Wind toward dock—after casting off lines, push boat clear. Turn engine away from dock and run in reverse.

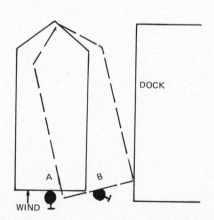

Fig. 7: Wind at rear (astern)—bring boat in parallel to dock (A). Halt, turn engine toward dock and run in reverse to bring stern in (B).

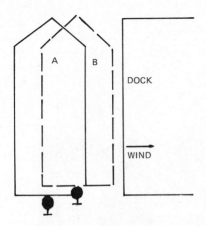

Fig. 8: Wind toward dock—stop boat parallel to dock (A). Wind will blow boat in.

6-8 illustrate proper docking procedures in a variety of winds.

Once you are safely in harbor, you will be faced with the problem of tying up to the dock. This may seem tricky to the novice boater, but it is easy once you get the knack. If you want to secure your boat to a post, throw your rope around the post and lay it over its own starting point. Then bring the rope around the pole once more, pass the end under the rope and tighten. To make sure your line doesn't slip, simply throw in another hitch.

Securing to a Post: Throw the rope around the pole and lay it over its own starting part (A), bring the rope around the pole once more (B), carry the end under the rope and tighten (C), throw in one more hitch (D).

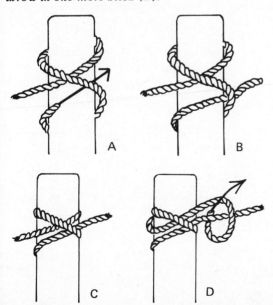

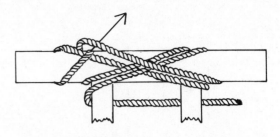

When tying to a cleat, turn the line over the horns a number of times. Then tuck the end under one of the loops to make a hitch.

To tie to a cleat, turn your line over the horns six or eight times, then tuck the end under one of the loops to make a hitch.

Next on the list is turning and stopping. For an ordinary turn, just twist the wheel. But if you want to turn tightly, remember to throw the wheel over hard and gun the motor briefly.

Stopping is accomplished by shifting the boat into neutral, then reversing the engine. Keep in mind, however, that you are dealing with several thousand pounds of boat and tremendous momentum, so this may require more time and space than you think. Begin by practicing in open water. This will help you gain the experience and assurance necessary to react properly in more complex situations.

Before beginning your cruise, take time out to perfect the basic maneuvers.

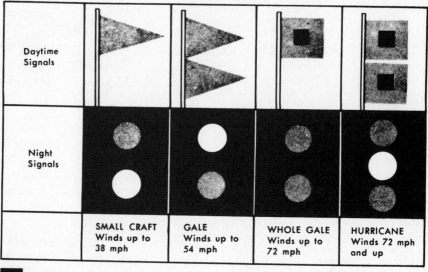

Daytime Signals				
Night Signals				
	SMALL CRAFT Winds up to 38 mph	GALE Winds up to 54 mph	WHOLE GALE Winds up to 72 mph	HURRICANE Winds 72 mph and up

■ BLACK   ▪ RED

In fact, before heading out on your cruise, take the time to perfect all the basic maneuvers. This is sure to save you headaches later on. And remember that one of the main ways to avoid having to navigate your way out of a tight spot is by keeping a sharp eye on the weather. This can be done in a number of ways. The Coast Guard posts daytime and nighttime storm warnings (a chart of storm signals and how to read them will be found above) at Guard Stations, yacht marinas, municipal piers and other points. The National Weather Service also broadcasts routine weather and marine information. These reports can be picked up on 162.55 MHz for most stations or on 162.40 MHz. These radio weather transmissions repeat taped messages every four to six minutes. Tapes are updated periodically every two to three hours. In addition local AM or FM commercial radio stations provide frequent updated weather reports. If your houseboat has a radio, keep yourself posted at all times.

You can often predict the weather, of course, by simply watching the sky. Keep in mind that any sudden weather change can spell trouble, and that on large bodies of water high winds inevitably mean high waves and rough handling. A recent industry forum concluded that the successful handling of a houseboat in a storm depends on the skipper's experience. Also, as we have seen, not all houseboats are built for open waters and high waves. So unless you have a boat specially designed for all conditions, sit out the heavy storms ashore and as a novice and/or renter, *never* try to tackle really bad weather.

A wise precaution before you leave port is to equip yourself with a coastal warning facilities chart, available from the Superintendent of Documents, U.S. Government Printing Office, Washington D.C. 20402. Information provided includes a list of places from which small craft and other warnings are flown, telephone numbers of various weather bureaus and a broadcast schedule of weather reports from local stations.

The Art of Cruising

Now that you are feeling more secure behind the wheel, you will be impatient to get under way. A word of advice here. Houseboats can travel from 50 to 100 miles daily, and you will be eager to cover as much ground as possible. But try to limit yourself to 10 to 15 miles of cruising per day (less in slower boats).

Try to limit yourself to 10 or 15 miles of cruising per day.

There's no better vehicle for exploring back-country shallows than a houseboat.

Learn to scan the water before you for an indication of what lies beneath.

To get the most from your vacation, concentrate on your boat's unique ability to water explore rather than speed. Most houseboats draw less water than a very small cabin cruiser and allow you the fun of creeping in under large trees, grounding on islands, penetrating shallow lagoons and inlets and visiting spots you would never see otherwise. Here are a few tips designed to help you navigate your boat with maximum efficiency through the picturesque lakes, rivers and bayous of houseboating country:

Coastal rivers have 2- to 6-foot tidal action. The shallower the water you want to explore, the farther forward you should shift your load Although you obviously cannot move the fuel or water tanks, you can displace your anchors, portable ice chests, picnic equipment and other bulky items. This reduces speed, and as the front of the houseboat goes down, the rear rises up, lifting the propeller several inches. If your propeller begins turning in sand or mud, shut off the engine immediately. When forward motion ceases, tilt the motor out of the water. If you have a stern drive or outboard, lock it up until you are clear

of existing hazards. Then check your propeller for possible damage.

Keep a weather eye out for rocks, sunken logs and reefs. Some pontoon and metal-hull cruising houseboats are built specifically for grounding on a beach, and most houseboat hulls are wider and flatter with more hull surface per pound of houseboat weight than a conventional cruiser. But running aground or striking a submerged object can still mean trouble. If you have any doubts about what is underneath you, *proceed slowly.*

Obviously, the shallower the water the greater the danger of collision with an underwater obstruction. Learn to scan the waters ahead of you for indications of what may lie beneath. Moving water will ripple slightly when passing over sandbars, sunken posts or logs. Water color provides additional clues. Dark blue or green indicates deep water. Brown and yellow mixed with mud or silt spells shallows. (Some deep rivers, of course, have a constant muddy look, but these are exceptions to the rule.)

Even the most experienced navigator will graze against a submerged object or scrape the

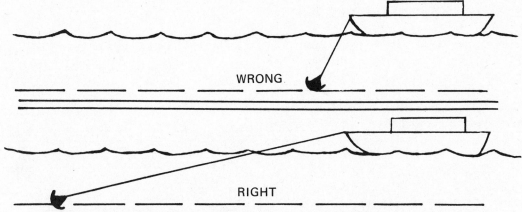

For proper mooring, anchor line should be five or six times longer than water depth.

bottom from time to time. In the event that this occurs, stop the boat at once. There is always the risk of injury to the hull, propeller, shaft or struts.

Immediately examine the bilge for signs of damage. Rising water means a leak. If you don't have an automatic bilge pump, get out the manual pump and have someone start pumping while you try to locate the trouble spot.

Once you have found the leak, cover any large or medium-size holes with a flat surface such as a section of a mattress, a cushion, a piece of waterproof clothing or a length of canvas. Patch small holes with bits of canvas or strips of waterproof clothing. You can also plug them with tapered wooden plugs.

Now check the propeller. Is it dented or bent? If the boat vibrates excessively when you run the engine, or if there is a drop in full-throttle speed, you have probably damaged the propeller or the shaft. Continued running at cruising speed can strip the bearings. Push the throttle all the way in and proceed slowly to the nearest marina equipped with the proper repair facilities. If the vibration is really bad, shut off the engine and ask for another boat to tow you in, or notify the boat's owner of your location and condition.

Running aground is likely to be a less serious matter, given the special construction of houseboat hulls. You may find, however, that you have grounded so hard that it takes more than your own engine to get you going again.

In most cases you can simply push the boat off the obstruction. If this fails, try shifting your passenger weight to the point in the back of the boat that is farthest from the obstruction and see if you can float yourself off. Next, toss or row the anchor out into deep water and try to haul the boat free by "pushing against" the anchor line aboard the boat.

If your boat still won't budge, call for help on your radio phone or hail a passing boat and ask for a tow.

To work your way landward for closer exploration of off-shore water, reduce your speed a short distance out and glide in slowly. If you plan to pull all the way up to shore, kill the motor and coast in on your momentum.

Be sure you have someone on deck continually measuring the water depth (on most boats, about 2 feet) as you near land. If you plan to land, come in straight and tie the boat's stern to shore on both sides at enough of an angle to prevent the stern from coming into shore. Keep the boat at a 90° angle with the shore until it is securely moored by running the motor with a slight amount of throttle.

If you are a first-time renter you will probably want to anchor for the night. You may choose to simply stay where you are if you have discovered a tempting exploration point, rather than heading for a regular marina. If so, keep in mind that mooring overnight in shallow water is an art, particularly in an area of sudden winds. On a sandy bottom, anchor with the bow facing open water and the stern tied to anything handy. Make sure you tilt the motor out of the water to keep the prop from burrowing its way into the mud.

In deeper water, bring the boat to a complete stop, heading into the wind or current. Then throw the anchor out. Reverse the boat and allow the line to play out. After you have five or six times the water depth, stop and jerk the line to make sure it is firmly hooked (see illustration p. 103).

Or you may feel in the mood to try some night cruising. To do this in safety, remember that ordinary landmarks disappear from sight as darkness falls. In order to navigate properly, pick out your position on the chart at dusk, then note the location of onshore and off-shore lights. Some houseboat rental operators insist that novices not operate their boats after dark, since buoys marking channels are hard to find. In other areas unless you are completely familiar with the channels it's both difficult and dangerous to travel at night.

In many houseboating areas today you will have the thrill of passing through one or many locks. Lock handling may seem intimidating at first but it can be quickly mastered. It is important, however, to follow the directions of the lockkeeper and navigate locks with caution.

As you approach a lock from either direction, you will see a traffic light ahead. Green means the standard come-ahead; red indicates that the lock is not ready. Remember that commercial traffic receives preference at locks. If the light is red, stop at a safe distance from the lock gates (usually 150 feet) and wait. When it is time to advance, proceed slowly and with care. Do not approach the lock walls at an angle; instead, nuzzle up (see diagram above). Because many lock walls are rough, you will usually want to place fenders between them and your boat. Never tie on to the snubbing posts, bullhooks, ropes or other facilities you may find on a lock wall. Make sure your line can easily slip through or around them as the water level rises or lowers. Be sure to have a boathook and an adequate supply of lines handy if you intend to navigate a lock.

Caution must also be exercised when

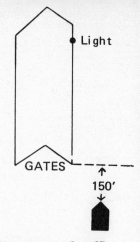

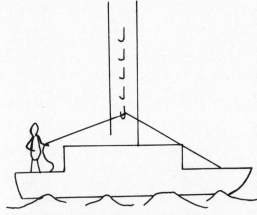

How to enter a lock:

(A) **Stop here away from gates and traffic. When coming downstream with current, stay at least 600 feet above lock gates.**

(B) **Do not tie to bullhooks or anything else you may find on the lock wall. Let ropes slide through them.**

cruising on or near dams. Make a point of avoiding all areas outside the navigation channel immediately above or below dammed areas. Waters around the spillway discharge will be dangerously turbulent, while those above the dam are sure to be treacherous.

Rules of the Road

Safe boating, like safe driving, is largely a matter of following the rules. These rules are extremely simple, and veteran boaters obey them meticulously. It is the novice cruisers who tend to hog the road, either through ignorance or sloppiness, thus creating potentially dangerous situations.

Lock handling may seem intimidating at first, but can be quickly mastered.

Caution must be exercised while cruising on or near dams.

Here is a basic list of what you should know in order to act and react properly afloat:

(1) When you meet a boat head-on or nearly so, pass to the right. Show you intend to do this by swinging your bow in that direction. The signal is one blast of the whistle from either boat, answered by a return blast from the other.

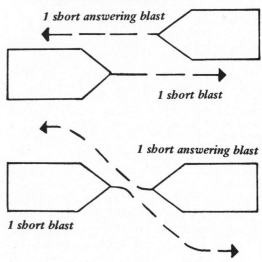

1 short answering blast

1 short blast

1 short answering blast

1 short blast

(2) When you meet a boat coming toward you, but a safe distance to your right, either boat should signal two short and distinct blasts, which means it is going to stay on course. The other boat should then answer with two blasts.

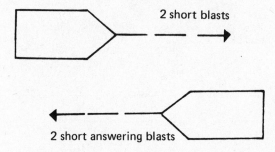

2 short blasts

2 short answering blasts

(3) When you meet another boat at an approximate right angle, any boat on your starboard (right) has the right-of-way $112\frac{1}{2}°$ right of bow center. He should sound one blast. You should reply with a single blast, slow down and pass behind him. Enter his wake on a 20 percent angle to eliminate rolling motion of your boat.

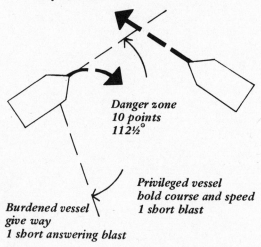

Danger zone
10 points
$112\frac{1}{2}°$

Privileged vessel
hold course and speed
1 short blast

Burdened vessel
give way
1 short answering blast

(4) When you prepare to overtake, remember the other boat has the right-of-way. If you intend to pass on his right (starboard), signal one blast, then wait for the answer before passing. The same

procedure is followed for passing to left (port), except that you use two blasts. If the maneuver appears unsafe, the other boat will signal back. Do not pass until he answers and idles slowly so that you can pass at fast idle, whereby no one suffers wake damage.

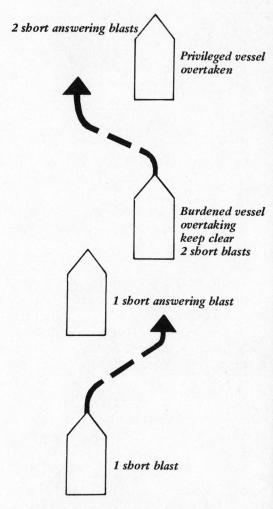

2 short answering blasts

Privileged vessel
overtaken

Burdened vessel
overtaking
keep clear
2 short blasts

1 short answering blast

1 short blast

(5) If danger of collision exists, the following signals must be given on your whistle or horn:

ONE BLAST: I will leave you to my port.

TWO BLASTS: I will leave you to my starboard.

THREE BLASTS: My engines are in reverse.

FOUR BLASTS: D A N G E R—stop boat.

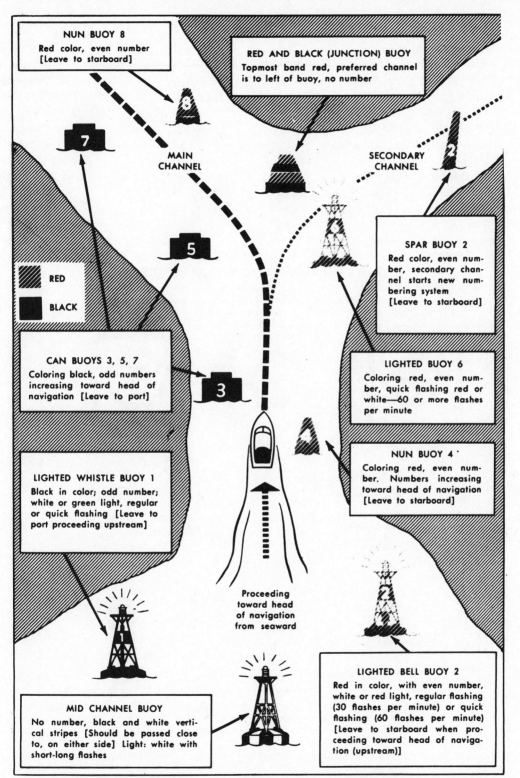

NUN BUOY 8
Red color, even number
[Leave to starboard]

RED AND BLACK (JUNCTION) BUOY
Topmost band red, preferred channel
is to left of buoy, no number

MAIN
CHANNEL

SECONDARY
CHANNEL

RED

BLACK

SPAR BUOY 2
Red color, even num-
ber, secondary chan-
nel starts new num-
bering system
[Leave to starboard]

CAN BUOYS 3, 5, 7
Coloring black, odd numbers
increasing toward head of
navigation [Leave to port]

LIGHTED BUOY 6
Coloring red, even num-
ber, quick flashing red or
white—60 or more flashes
per minute

NUN BUOY 4
Coloring red, even num-
ber. Numbers increasing
toward head of navigation
[Leave to starboard]

LIGHTED WHISTLE BUOY 1
Black in color; odd number;
white or green light, regular
or quick flashing [Leave to
port proceeding upstream]

Proceeding
toward head
of navigation
from seaward

MID CHANNEL BUOY
No number, black and white vertical stripes [Should be passed close
to, on either side] Light: white with
short-long flashes

LIGHTED BELL BUOY 2
Red in color, with even number,
white or red light, regular flashing
(30 flashes per minute) or quick
flashing (60 flashes per minute)
[Leave to starboard when proceeding toward head of navigation (upstream)]

"Red Right Returning"—an illustration of the kinds of buoys you might see heading for
port, and how to interpret them.

The Meaning of Markers

In addition to the preceding rules of the road, you will be guided by a variety of markers. These are the waterway equivalent of highway signs. Knowing how to interpret them correctly is essential to proper navigation.

The most common of these signposts is the buoy. These floating markers are strung out along the United States waterways in a lateral system and come in a variety of shapes, sizes and colors. Some bear numbers; others are outfitted with lights and whistles.

The catch phrase "red right returning" has long been popular among seafaring men to remind them that when proceeding from open sea into port (upstream), all red buoys must be on the right and all black ones on the left. The red buoys bear even numbers and the black ones are odd-numbered. Conversely, when proceeding toward the sea or leaving port, red buoys are left to port and black buoys are right to starboard.

Since all channels do not lead from seaward, boaters apply arbitrary rules for the sake of consistency. On the Atlantic Coast,

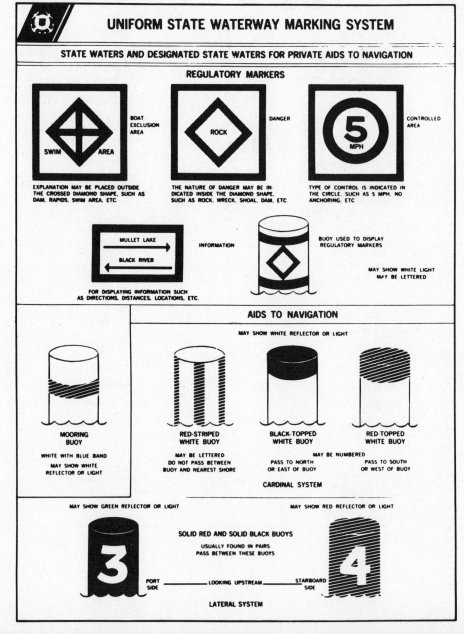

proceeding from seaward is considered to be in a southerly direction. On the Gulf Coast, westerly and northerly. On the Pacific Coast, northerly. In the Great Lakes (except for Lake Michigan, where it is southerly) it is interpreted as proceeding westerly and northerly. On the Intercoastal Waterway, proceeding southerly along the Atlantic Coast and westerly along the gulf is considered proceeding from seaward. On the Mississippi and Ohio rivers you will find red buoys on the right side, black on the left when going from the sea upriver.

On many inland waterways, under the uniform state waterway marker system, there are two categories of waterway markers: regulatory markers and aids to navigation.

Regulatory signs are white with black letters and a wide orange border. These mark speed zones, restricted areas, danger areas and direction.

Red and black buoys are aids to navigation and mark channel limits (see pp. 107-108).

Pass between a red buoy and its companion black buoy. Buoys that are not paired indicate dangerous water. The color points out the direction of the dangerous water from the buoy. Pass white buoys with black tops to the north or east; danger lies to the south or west. White buoys with red tops should be passed to the south or west; danger lies to the north or east. Do not pass between a vertical red and white striped buoy and the nearest shore; danger lies inshore of the buoy.

Instruction Courses You Can Take

If you feel you would like professional instruction in navigation before embarking on your cruise, this is available through the Coast Guard Auxiliary, which offers free public instruction courses in small-boat handling and seamanship by qualified Auxiliary members.

The United States Power Squadrons, a nationwide association of boatmen, also conducts an extensive program of boating instruction. The local squadrons throughout the country present a basic course of twelve lectures, known as the USPS Piloting Course. This is open to all boating enthusiasts. For starting dates and locations of classes in your community, contact the Squadron Commander in your area, or write to USPS Headquarters, 50 Craig Road, Montvale, N.J. 07645.

For courses in your area, ask your boating dealer or contact the nearest Coast Guard Office. For further information, write to the Director of Auxiliary at the following address closest to you:

*1st Coast Guard District
J. F. Kennedy Federal Building
Government Center
Boston, Mass. 02203

*2nd Coast Guard District (WR)
1520 Market St.
St. Louis, Mo. 63103

2nd Coast Guard District (SR)
1600 Hayes St., Suite 304
Nashville, Tenn. 37203

2nd Coast Guard District (ER)
550 Main St., Room 4020A
Cincinnati, Oh. 45202

2nd Coast Guard District (NR)
PO Box 693
Dubuque, Ia. 52001

*3rd Coast Guard District (NA)
Building 104, Room 101
Governors Island
New York, N.Y. 10004

3rd Coast Guard District (SA)
c/o USCG Base Gloucester
King & Cumberland Streets
Gloucester, N.J. 08030

*5th Coast Guard District
431 Crawford St., Federal Building
Portsmouth, Va. 23705

*7th Coast Guard District
51 SW First Ave.
Miami, Fla. 33130

*An asterisk denotes district offices which are Boating Safety Branches.

*8th Coast Guard District
Custom House, Room 333
New Orleans, La. 70130

*9th Coast Guard District (ER)
New Federal Building
1240 East 9th St., Room 2021
Cleveland, Oh. 44199

9th Coast Guard District (CR)
U. S. Post Office Building, Room 207
Federal & Jefferson Streets
Saginaw, Mich. 48605

9th Coast Guard District (WR)
2420 S. Lincoln Memorial Dr.
Milwaukee, Wis. 53207

*11th Coast Guard District
19 Pine Ave., Heartwell Building
Long Beach, Calif. 90802

*12th Coast Guard District
630 Sansome St.
San Francisco, Calif. 94126

*13th Coast Guard District
618 Second Ave.
Seattle, Wash. 98104

*14th Coast Guard District
677 A la Moana Blvd.
Honolulu, Hi. 96813

17th Coast Guard District
FPO Seattle, Wash. 98771

CHAPTER SIX

Buying Your Own Houseboat

Once you have experienced the joys of a rental vacation, you may be tempted to invest in a houseboat of your own. One thing you can be sure of as you set out to explore the market: There's no lack of choice.

Current available models range in price from $1000 to over $50,000, and in size from 18 feet to more than 59 feet. You will be shown houseboats with pontoons, others with conventional cruiser hulls and even some you can trailer. You will learn about kits that allow. you to build your own unit at home. You will discover that some models come pretty well stripped inside, while others are fitted out with a number of luxury compartments. You will be presented with boats equipped to navigate intriguing shallows and others ready to tackle the open seas.

Which to choose?

Here are some guidelines to keep in mind in making your selection.

In buying a houseboat, as in renting one, your primary consideration should be *how you intend to use it*. If you want a getaway family boat for leisurely weekend cruising, stick to the pontoon models. Several manufacturers produce this kind of craft, with prices ranging from $4500 to $13,000, and lengths from 18 to 50 feet. All models are powered by outboard motors and can do from 6 to 12 miles per hour. Interiors are pleasantly comfortable.

Should you prefer something that can handle long cruises with ease, really moves and looks more like a conventional boat, consider the cruiser hulls. Conventional hull types come in steel, aluminum and fiberglass. They are powered by single- or twin-engine inboards and reach speeds of over 30 mph. Prices range from $6995 to over $50,000, and sizes from 30 to 59 feet. Numerous livability features and a wide variety of interior designs are available, with a trend toward sleeker exteriors.

Or perhaps you like to lake hop or cruise unconnected rivers. Then you will find it worth your while to investigate the versatile, ultracontemporary trailer-type models. You can pull these amphibious recreational vehicles from place to place behind your car, enjoying them both as trailers in the campground and as seaworthy crafts ready to take to the water for a day, a weekend or a month of cruising.

There are a variety of available models. Some houseboat manufacturers simply construct flat houseboat hulls designed to buoy up conventional campers or travel trailers. Other units resemble tent trailers with sides that fold up or down. Several float on pontoons. But the majority look much like conventional cruiser-hull houseboats, complete with typical houseboat-style living quarters.

Most trailerable houseboats incorporate forward-looking design elements within and without. These include fiberglass hulls, molded fiberglass, plastic or fiberglass over plywood cabins, and foam flotation between the walls and in the bulkhead areas.

Some of the cruiser types sport the latest refinements in hull construction as well, fea-

The pontoon: ideal for family weekend cruising.

Cruisers offer speed and maneuverability.

Trailerables are equally at home on land or afloat.

Trailerables are ideal for lake-hopping or cruising unconnected waters.

turing seaworthiness and including such sophisticated innovations as tri-planing and quick-planing hulls with as little as seven inches of draft.

Manufacturers power the smaller, lighter trailerable houseboats with outboard motors with 10 to 90 horsepower. The heavier, more luxurious models operate on 90- to 210- horsepower inboard-outboard engines. The smaller trailerables cruise lazily up to 10 miles an hour, while the larger units have real get-up-and-go and can plane like a regular high-speed boat, pulling along water-skiers at up to 37 miles an hour. But think twice about the fuel costs involved in propelling this much weight at the necessary speeds before you invest in skis. And think about the weight you will be regularly loading and unloading in the case of the larger trailerables.

The new amphibs sell anywhere from $2500 to $13,000, weigh from 1500 to 8000 pounds and range in length from 18 to 30 feet. Most come equipped with horn, running lights, compass, fire extinguisher and other safety equipment. The majority tow on their own boat trailer, but a few feature retractable wheels.

Although some trailerable houseboats offer relatively basic interior combinations, a typical cruiser model boasts a completely equipped galley with formica cabinet tops, lots of storage, a self-defrosting gas/electric refrigerator, a four-burner gas range and oven and twin sinks with hot and cold running water. The head comes complete with a self-contained toilet and shower and a large vanity.

There is plenty of carpeting and wardrobe space. In addition, the typical cruiser model sleeps seven with a variety of accommodations. You also have the option of purchasing such additional refinements as air conditioning and a large generator.

As with travel trailers, the self-containment feature of this type of unit is an added plus. It permits you to be independent and nonpolluting for days at a time of water or land travel. When the holding tank fills, simply dump it at the nearest campground sanitation station.

And when it comes to land travel, these versatile amphibs compare favorably to camping with any other recreational vehicle.

There are other considerations. Do you plan to do a lot of entertaining aboard? Then you will want to keep an eye out for space, carpets and drapes, a bar and a well-designed galley.

Are you planning to join the growing number of full-time houseboaters? If so, you will want to consider such year-round living needs as separate living areas, beds that do not

Most trailerables incorporate slick, modern design elements.

Some trailerable houseboats simply consist of a boat hull and a conventional travel trailer. These are powered by an outboard.

One of the more unusual trailer-houseboats.

Launching a trailerable. A roller system guides this model along the trailer runners.

interfere with other functions when unfolded, a completely equipped galley and adequate electric power.

And remember, whether or not you live on board full-time, livability is an extremely important factor afloat. Some families like to rough it, in which case a simple interior design will suit their tastes well. Others prefer a more finished, upholstered decor. But in all cases, check for adequate storage area, efficient galley space with the necessary appliances (many meals are cooked and consumed during a lengthy trip, and you will want the conveniences of home), a time-saving floor plan (how close, for example, is the kitchen sink to the dinette area?) and a comfortable head with a good mirror and adequate primping space.

The second major factor to keep in mind when making your choice is *size*. Many boaters make the mistake of buying a boat that is too small, only to find that they have to trade it in

within a year. Consider carefully whether the cabin space is sufficient to give the children enough elbowroom, and if the boat will comfortably handle the number of people you expect on board for the type of cruising you want to do. For instance, a family of four can get by fine for an afternoon's cruise on an 18-footer, but will be pretty uncomfortable on a week-long vacation. In addition, several families together might enjoy a day cruise, but the minute you take them out overnight, space becomes critical. Boat size is so important that several experts agree you should forget what you think you are going to need and *buy the biggest boat you can afford*.

This leads to the all-important element of *price*. Here is a rundown of what is available in the various brackets:

$1000 to $3000: This pretty well limits you to do-it-yourself kits. There are several on the market that make up into good, serviceable

If you like luxury, you can get it with today's houseboat designs.

If you like to rough it, this kind of houseboat may be all you need.

A rule of thumb in buying: Choose the biggest boat you can afford. Arrangements vary considerably with individual floor plans. You can get almost any combination you want today.

houseboats. Hull materials include steel pontoons, wood and Ferro-cement.

$3000 to $8000: This price range includes the pontoon types to about 35 feet, some of the smaller cruiser hulls to 28 feet and just about half of the trailerables.

$8000 to $19,000: For this sum you can buy a larger, more luxurious pontoon boat to

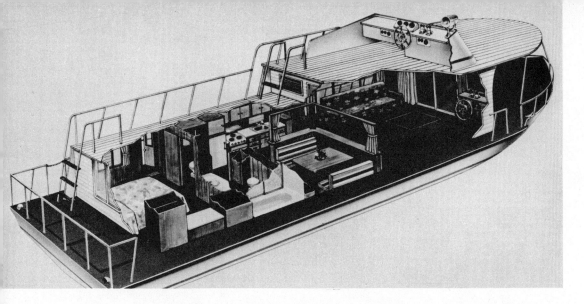

Notice the spacious living area in this unit.

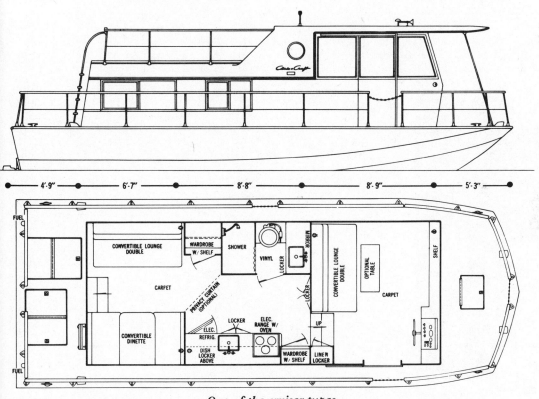

One of the cruiser types.

about 42 feet, a basic cruiser-hull boat to about 35 feet and the larger trailerables to about 28 feet. Power here is primarily by a single engine. ***$19,000 to $30,000:*** Now you are beginning to purchase real luxury. All boats here are the cruiser type (37 to 50 feet) and include the latest in interior appointment and twin engines. ***Above $30,000:*** You get the best in cruiser-hull houseboats 50 feet and over. Most models come with a large lounge and many extras.

This model has three cabins.

This model has a stateroom below.

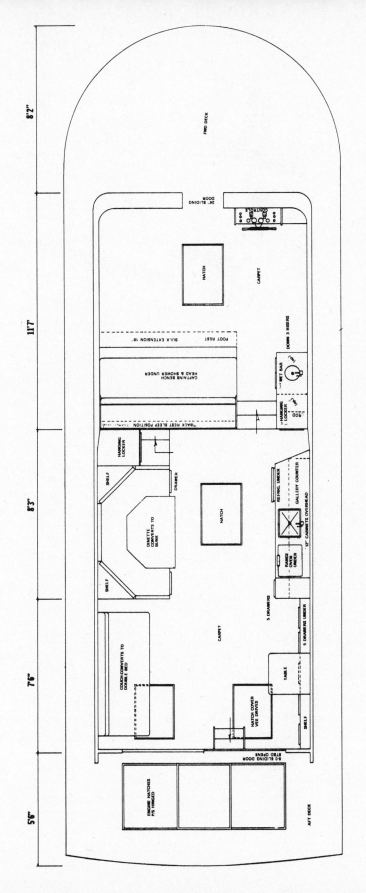

Note the dinette and kitchen arrangement in this unit.

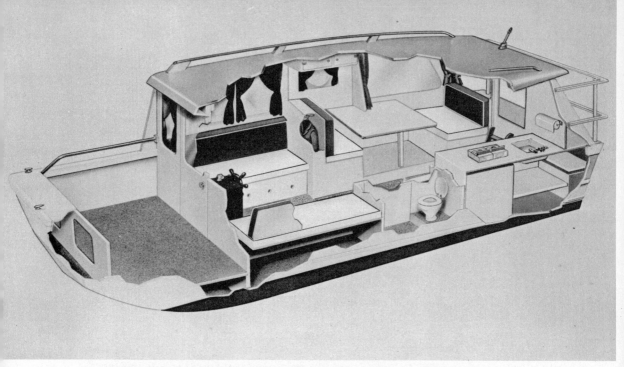

Trailerable houseboats offer good, compact interior arrangements. Some even come equipped with self-defrosting gas/electric refrigerators and more.

All the preceding prices are basic. The next thing to consider is how you want your boat equipped. The boat that sells for $18,000 with a single engine and the basic necessities might cost $10,000 more when equipped with twin engines, a ship-to-shore radio, a flying bridge, draperies, air conditioning, an automatic bilge pump, a monomatic toilet and extra fuel tanks. The price would be further increased with the addition of dual air horns, a spotlight, stereo speakers, a microwave oven, a generator pack and an electric "gas sniffer."

To avoid unpleasant surprises, check to be sure you have the price on the model you want *equipped the way you'd like it.*

Another factor leading to discrepancy in the price that you are quoted initially and what you end up paying can be traced to transportation costs. These can either be calculated FOB the dealer's address or FOB the factory. If the price quoted is to the factory, find out ahead of time what the additional charges will be.

Next consider *operating costs.* These are directly related to fuel consumption.

The heavier the boat and the greater the speed, the more fuel you will use. Twin engines on a heavy boat might use a great deal of fuel, for example, while a fairly powerful engine on a lightweight boat might consume only three to six gallons an hour. In many cases your dealer can show you fuel consumption curves at various speeds. Look at these figures carefully, keeping in mind that hull shape and material play a determining role here. Chapter 7 explains why this is so, with suggestions on how to choose the best hull depending on your pocketbook and cruising needs.

An additional factor to take into account is *real carrying capacity.* How much of your footage can actually be utilized for passenger needs? A 28-foot houseboat, for instance, might comfortably handle as many vacationers as some 40-footers, since passenger capacity depends on the design space of the bunks and the dining, lounge, cooking and other primary areas. Such things as sundecks, catwalks and fore and aft decks can also be attractive features.

If you have a used boat, give careful consideration to the possibility of a trade-in. You can make a deal on your boat subject to a physical inspection or on "as is" condition at

In choosing a design, be sure the galley area is adequate, with plenty of storage space.

Can your family spread out comfortably? Can you entertain without feeling crowded?

an agreed-upon price. Keep in mind, however, that the heart of the matter is not what you are offered but the cash *difference* between your trade-in and the new model. This is what really counts. If the dealer cannot afford to take your trade-in, he won't be there when you need warranty service.

Also, take a good hard look at the warranty. What does it cover? Parts and material, or labor too? Does it give complete protection? Does the dealer have the facilities to perform the warranty work? These questions are important since the answers can mean many extra dollars to you if your new boat has problems that need correcting.

Consult pp. 194-201 for a list of major houseboat manufacturers throughout North America, complete with a rundown of available models, specifications and prices in the cruising houseboat, trailerable, floating home and do-it-yourself lines.

Finally, larger houseboats, up to 18,000 to 20,000 lbs. or more, must be launched with special equipment such as a crane or a Travelift which picks up houseboats like a baby in a cradle. Ordinarily you will buy a houseboat already in the water at a dealer's place of business or he will have it launched for you at the location of your choice. Anytime the larger boats are removed from the water you will have to go to a marina with special facilities. Transporting houseboats today is a special problem. Vessels up to 12 feet wide can be moved in most states with a permit. A number of states are now considering the possibility of allowing loads up to 14 feet wide on the Interstate Highway System.

The Kenosha Auto Transport Corp., 202 Greenfield Road, Lancaster, Pa., and Morgan Drive Away Inc., Elkhart, Ind., will move certain kinds of houseboats for you. Larger vessels can also be moved by rail.

Trailerable houseboats can be hauled along the highways on boat trailers just like the smaller boats and launched in 3 to 4 feet of water. Ordinarily the larger trailer wheels used with these boats make it necessary to get the trailer some distance out in the water to float the boat. In addition, at these weights the boat won't slide when tilted. However, launching is usually simple and the boat will float off the trailer easily.

Trailerables can usually be taken out of the water without difficulty.

Judging a Used Boat

When you set out to buy, consider the possibility of a second-hand model. By purchasing a used boat, you eliminate the "new commission" and can usually bargain over the price more easily than with a new unit.

It may take a while, however, to come up with exactly the houseboat you want, so be prepared to bide your time. Visit as many marinas as you can. You might also run an ad in your local newspaper and see what happens.

A word of warning. Once you have found your dream boat, be sure it's really the good buy it's cracked up to be. The best way to establish this is to call in a marine surveyor. (You will find a listing in the yellow pages in many cities.) For a flat fee he will look over your boat and rate its value.

The surveyor will not only tell you if your boat is worth the money, but on the basis of an extensive examination he will present you

Buying a used boat: Check the gears for clashing or growling. Are there any unusual vibrations when running?

Check out the hull carefully. On fiberglass, look for bubbly or cracked surfaces. On steel, check for widening seams where the welds converge.

with a list of problem spots. He may even estimate the repair costs. Armed with this report, you can then either ask the seller to adjust the price accordingly or put the boat in better condition.

If you prefer to judge the boat on your own, be sure to check it out carefully. Start with the cabin. Keep an eye open for unpleasant odors, rot, water marks, peeling paint, damaged or worn carpet and cushions. These are usually signs of general abuse. Be sure that all equipment is in good operating order, including the refrigerator, the heater and the air conditioning. Check the water system to be sure it pumps water readily and that the water is clear. Since it is illegal to flush toilets in the waterways of many states, toilets should be connected to a holding tank or other approved systems (see Chapter 9). Look over sinks, wash basins and showers and make a careful note of anything that does not work.

Next, check the hull for possible damage:
Steel hulls: Keep an eye out for splits or widening seams where the welds come together. Inspect inside for rust or other signs of leakage.
Fiberglass hulls: Look for bubbly or cracked surfaces and warp next to the keel. Check the bilges. If they are wet and foul-smelling, you probably have a problem. Take a knife point and check the inside supports lightly—if the blade goes in the wood without effort, there may be dry rot. Finally, does it feel solid?
Aluminum hulls: Inspect for loose or missing rivits plus signs of corrosion.

After that, no matter how qualified you feel you are, have an experienced marine mechanic inspect the engine. Let it run several hours, then get his expert opinion. Always get a compression check.

Now shift the gears and check them out for grinding or unusual noises. If there is excessive vibration, it could indicate a bent propeller, a damaged crank shaft or a twisted drive shaft.

Last of all, take the houseboat out and open up the throttle for a brief period. Does it slice cleanly through the waves? Does it seem stable? Are the high-speed turns sloppy or clean? Does it come to plane easily? How well does it respond? Does it handle well in tight quarters?

Consider all of the preceding factors in making your choice. When you buy, starting off on the right foot can save you a lot of money later on!

How to Estimate Additional Costs

In making any houseboat purchase, you must remember that the cost of your unit doesn't stop when you sign the dotted line. Supplementary expenses are reasonable on the whole, but you will want to keep them in mind. Here is the general idea of what to expect.

Financing cost: The first thing you will run into is the cost of financing. This will be discussed in detail later on in the chapter, but generally speaking you will be required to put down about a quarter to a third of the total price, and pay 7 percent or more a year on the balance. For instance, if you have a $6000 balance, your handling charges will run around $420-plus for the year.

Insurance cost: Houseboat insurance is one of the best purchases you can make. Both hull insurance and liability coverage come within one policy. Typical rates for one company run in the neighborhood of $112 for a $5000 houseboat, $175 for a $10,000 model, $248 for a $15,000 unit and $310 for a $20,000 boat. Liability rates are relatively modest, with one company charging only $37 annually for $300,000 coverage (on a houseboat of less than 30 feet). The mechanics of insuring your boat are covered on pp. 128-129 of this chapter. Request a three-year rate, and next year your rate cannot go up.

Taxes: Taxes can mount up to a considerable total. They vary from state to state and even from county to county. Sales taxes, for example, range from nothing to 7 percent. Hence in California, which charges 5 percent sales tax per boat, you will pay $400 on an $8000 unit; in Maryland, which has a 3 percent title tax in lieu of a state sales tax, it will cost you $240 for the same boat.

Most states also insist that you register and get an operator's number. Again, charges vary from state to state. Alabama, for example, charges a $6 registration fee per year for houseboats 26 to 40 feet, and $12 a year for 40 feet up; California assesses a $5 registration fee for one year, $3 for renewal; Maryland charges $8 per boat from 18 to 26 feet, $10 for anything over this; Vermont's fees are $10 for a houseboat 26 to 40 feet, and $25 for 40 feet and over.

Finally, you will find a personal property tax in many counties and school districts. One California county charges 11.78 percent on the assessed evaluation of the houseboat (which is 27 percent of the total cost). This means if you purchase an $8000 houseboat, your personal property tax in this county will be $254.45 a year. Your boat dealer can tell you what the taxes are for your state and area.

Berthing and upkeep: Unless you own a trailerable houseboat you will need to keep your houseboat at a marina. Some marinas offer slips only (a place where you can secure your boat alongside a pier or wharf), others offer a choice between a slip or a mooring. At a mooring the boat is left in the water at anchor off-shore in the marina area. This anchor is usually marked by a small buoy which keeps the anchor line on the surface. Slips run from about $3 to $4 per foot length of your boat to $16 to $18 a foot for a 5 to 7 month season. Moorings cost from about $35 to $250 for the season.

Then, if your houseboat has a steel or aluminum hull, it will have to be hauled out of the water and repainted every twelve or fifteen months. However, by using the new Colortox tin base paint (in the range of $48 a gallon) you may be able to keep repainting intervals to three years or more.

Typical charges for hoisting up your boat run between $60 and $160. Dry-docking costs, including painting, average $2.65 per foot.

Operating costs: As we have seen, operating costs, based mainly on fuel consumption, vary with the size and weight of your boat, its hull design, the kind of power plant you use and how often you go cruising.

One owner, with a popular steel-hull model equipped with two 210-horsepower Chrysler engines, estimates his total operating expenses at about $300 per year. This includes four gallons of fuel per hour per engine, for a yearly average of 110 hours; an oil change every 50 hours; plus having the valves ground every 500 to 600 hours and going in for a major overhaul every 1000 hours.

Operating costs for a houseboat powered by an outboard vary. Two twin 110-horsepower Mercury engines use approximately fourteen gallons an hour. On the other hand, cost for a week's cruising with a 55-horsepower Homelite outboard averages out to $15 to $17. You can make a guess at what your own boat might cost you by judging it in relationship to these figures.

These are the essential expenses to keep in mind when you estimate your yearly costs. With a little time and thought you can cut some of them significantly, however. For instance, a fiberglass houseboat will probably cost a little more initially but will entail less yearly upkeep. Insurance, however, will be slightly higher than for a steel hull. You can also lower costs by shopping around to find the most advantageous financing and insurance packages. Minimizing your power plant to what you really need and keeping your houseboat in states and counties that charge less for registration and have little or no property tax will result in further savings.

Financing Your Houseboat

Financing a houseboat today is a relatively simple matter. This was not always the case, however. Until recent years many banks and financial institutions would not touch boats, due to the fear of losses and the conviction that this type of financing was too risky.

But this proved untrue, and now many banks welcome such business and will finance a used houseboat just as readily as a new one. Some financial institutions may shy away from innovations and unconventional boats, but in general if you are considering buying a standard houseboat with a conventional hull, built by a reputable manufacturer, you will have little trouble obtaining the financing you need at reasonable rates.

What a bank will look for can be divided into two categories: the condition of the boat itself and the financial condition of the owner.

In the first instance, many banks require a survey by a competent boat surveyor for any model five years old or older. Some require a similar survey for *any* used boat, regardless of age.

On a used boat, the surveyor looks basically to see how clean it is and if there is evidence of dry rot. He checks for thin spots, looks at the underwater fittings and checks for such additional signs of depreciation as peeling paint. Actual value is then determined by the use of a blue book (similar to the price book for used cars) which lists the approximate value plus the surveyor's report.

In addition to this, the banks look at you. This means drawing up a credit report, examining your general financial picture and investigating how you pay your bills.

Most concerns also want to establish your ability to pay for your boat over a period of time. "We realize," explains one banker, "that there are a lot of hidden expenses here that the first-time buyer doesn't take into account." Here is an example of what he means.

In a typical case for a small houseboat payments will run to $117 a month, *with* additional costs of $300 a year insurance fees, $300 worth of annual taxes, a per annum docking rental charge totaling $480 and an annual upkeep outlay in the neighborhood of $100. What the bank wants is not only a record of good pay, but assurance that you will also be able to take care of these "included" extras.

The amount you will be able to borrow and the terms involved vary with the area and the lending institution. Banks usually require one-fourth to one-third down; lengths of terms vary. There was a time when banks would not lend over an extended period, but today practically all banks make marine loans for five years;

YACHT INSURANCE APPLICATION

NAME _____

ADDRESS _____

LOSS PAYABLE _____

ADDRESS _____

OCCUPATION _____ INSURANCE EFFECTIVE _____

YEAR BUILT _____ YACHT LENGTH _____ BUILDER _____

TYPE OR CLASS _____ NAME OR NUMBER _____

HULL INSURANCE AMT. _____ COST NEW _____

PROTECTION AND INDEMNITY INSURANCE—(INDICATE ONE)
(Bodily injury and property damage liability,
 including $1,000.00 medical payment insurance.)

☐ 10,000/20,000   ☐ 25,000/50,000
☐ 50,000/100,000   ☐ 100,000/300,000

ADDITIONAL MEDICAL PAYMENTS
☐ 2,000
☐ 3,000
☐ 4,000
☐ 5,000

WATERS TO BE NAVIGATED _____

HOME PORT _____ MAKE & H.P. OF ENGINE _____

DOES YACHT HAVE THE FOLLOWING: ☐ GASOLINE   ☐ DIESEL
☐ AUTOMATIC CO-2 SYSTEM   ☐ DEPTH INDICATOR   ☐ SHIP TO SHORE RADIO
☐ RADAR   ☐ FUME DETECTOR   ☐ RADIO DIRECTOR FINDER   ☐ COMPASS

DINGHY (INCLUDING O/B MOTOR SERIAL NO.) AND VALUE _____

PRESENT INSURANCE COMPANY _____

YACHTING EXPERIENCE IN YEARS _____

LOSSES SUSTAINED DURING PAST 3 YEARS _____

INDICATE DATE & AMOUNT _____

NAVIGATIONAL COURSES COMPLETED _____

DATE _____ PHONE _____ SIGNATURE _____

Current houseboat or yacht insurance applications reflect the credits possible. A marine insurance specialist can tailor your insurance to meet your needs.

institutions that specialize in this type of business allow from seven to ten years to pay.

If you are looking for low-rate financing, it pays to survey the market. Almost any established dealer can arrange your financing for you, but before committing yourself, check a bank that knows you. Many buyers have found that they can arrange loans through their regular banking channels at rates several percentage points under what they would pay elsewhere. "Also," one expert advises, "if you're after the best going rate, check on a couple of other institutions as well, explaining what you want and asking the banker what kind of a loan he will make, on what terms, for how long and with what kind of interest." This kind of careful comparative shopping has been

known to save buyers anywhere from 2 to 4 percent.

Marine Insurance

When it comes to insuring your houseboat, the first thing you will probably want to know is what kind of coverage is available.

One of the possibilities you might want to consider is simply calling up your regular insurance broker and asking him to add liability for the boat to your regular insurance policy. There is a problem here, however. Your day-to-day coverage does not adequately provide for the special problems you may have afloat. Suppose, for example, you run into someone else's boat and sink it. Your standard coverage will pay to have his boat repaired, but what about the cost of bringing it up from the bottom?

A second possible solution is to take out a marine perils policy. This type of insurance is actually the oldest form of insurance in existence, dating back over 400 years. The marine perils policy does exactly what it says, protecting you against a number of perils at sea. All risks covered are specifically listed on the policy. The company is not liable for anything not noted.

It is amusing to observe this type of insurance, so heavily steeped in tradition, still includes coverage for piracy, a very real hazard in the old sailing days.

A third option, and one that marks the present trend for boats today, is the Protection and Indemnity Policy (P&I). (See p. 128 for a typical P&I application form.) Unlike the marine perils policy, it protects against all losses *except* those named on the policy. Excluded items are few and far between, including marine borers, war, wear and tear, etc.

Protection and liability coverage (the protection part of the P&I policy) is actually a combination of three things: (1) hull insurance; (2) bodily injury and property damage liability; (3) medical payments insurance.

Hull insurance simply insures the houseboat itself, including all the fittings, furniture and other equipment. The amount you are insured for depends on the value of your boat, which as we have seen is determined by a system similar to the automobile price book rating for used cars.

Unlike automobile insurance, however, the hull policy does not dock you for depreciation. Known in the industry as new for old, it simply means that if you buy a new boat and it is completely destroyed in a collision, you will be able to replace it with a brand new houseboat without regard to depreciation.

As with a car, your bodily injury and property damage liability is listed as the maximum amount payable to any one person and the maximum amount payable in any one accident.

Basically, you purchase insurance in amounts of $10,000/$20,000, $25,000/

$52,000, $50,000/$100,000, $100,000/$300,000.

The policy automatically includes $1000 medical payment insurance, but you can also specify additional amounts up to $5000.

The rates for full insurance and protection and liability are ordinarily figured separately, then added together for a total premium. Rates for a houseboat (all coverages) are extremely reasonable.

Besides the basic hull rate, it is also possible to get percentages off in cases where the company feels that there has been a reduction in the risk. For example, the rate is adjusted downward by one firm 10 percent for any skipper having three or more years of experience, for boats with diesel rather than gas engines and for models with steel rather than fiberglass hulls. And up to 10 percent allowance is also made for limiting the geographical area in which the houseboat operates.

It is also possible to get up to 5 percent credit for having on board an automatic CO_2 system and certain navigational aides (including a depth indicator, ship-to-shore radio, radar, radio director and finder and a compass). There is a 2½ percent consideration made if the skipper has taken a navigational course. Most companies have similar reductions.

One word of warning, however. Houseboat insurance is an extremely variable item. Unlike other forms of insurance, rates on marine policies are not controlled and can differ for identical boats depending on the company involved. Here too, shopping around can pay off in significant savings, but as this is an extremely complex field, it is unlikely that you will be able to arrive at the best solution on your own. Your best bet when it comes to marine insurance is to put yourself in the hands of a marine insurance specialist. Any broker can insure your boat for you, but it is the specialist, with his inside knowledge of which companies offer the best rates for the coverage, who will come up with the standard package most advantageous for you. When you buy your houseboat, your dealer will probably recommend such a specialist. If not, look for listings in the yellow pages.

CHAPTER SEVEN

Which Hull Is Best?

If you inspect a variety of houseboats, you will observe that no two manufacturers seem to come up with the same type of hull. In fact, the differences far outweigh the similarities. This is due to the tremendous influence a boat's shape underwater has on its general performance.

Hull shape, for example, is responsible for a craft's stability, is a controlling factor in the water speed a given engine can attain, and determines how well a unit will handle in rough seas. It directly affects a boat's ability to come up to plane and influences its maneuverability at planing speeds. In addition, it determines the minimum water depth a boat can safely explore.

Kinds of Hull Design

Hull design falls into two broad categories: displacement hulls and planing models.

A displacement hull is based on the principle that a certain amount of weight displaces so much water. The boat simply settles down until it displaces water equal to its weight. When in motion, it therefore plows through the water rather than riding along the surface.

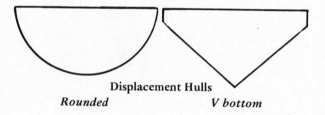

Displacement Hulls
Rounded　　　　　　*V bottom*

Examples of crafts with displacement hulls include tugboats, battleships, sailing vessels and *the majority of pontoon houseboats*.

In contrast to this, a planing hull is one that rides or "surfs" over the water under full power. On a small boat as much as 50 to 85 percent of the hull rides out as the boat skims along. For larger planing hulls this figure is substantially lower. When a boat planes, it pits its surfing potential (based on buoyancy) against the pull of gravity. At planing speeds the hull functions like the wing of an airplane, acting to support the craft's weight. Hence its design is a major factor in the boat's surfing performance.

Most houseboats today are a variation of some kind of planing hull. To understand more clearly how hull design influences a boat's planing potential, let's take the familiar example of the surfboard, which operates on the same principle.

Like a surfboard, a hull's efficiency depends on the way it cuts through the water at the point where its sides join its bottom (the chine) and its back. If you've ever tried to skim a board across the water, you've observed that the square edges along the side and back act to trap water beneath the board. This water quickly accumulates into a wave that lifts the board out of the water and on which it then rides.

As you begin to round off these edges slightly (rounded chines), you allow some of the water beneath to escape. The more you

A boat's shape under water has tremendous influence on its performance.

Most modern pontoon houseboats use some shape other than round. Today you will find square, diamond shape, deep V—and much in between.

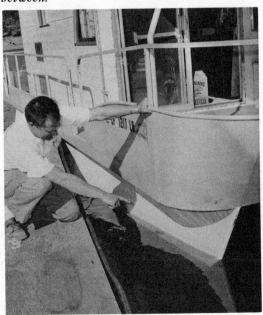

round them off, the more water is freed and the lower the board or boat will sink.

Since it takes substantial power to bring any boat to a plane, look for a boat designed to come up easily. Poor design not only results in higher operating costs, but often even with substantial increases in horsepower you will get only a slight increase in speed.

A boat's planing ability is, of course, only one factor in its general performance, and the boat designer must balance this characteristic against other important needs. The craft must be stable as well; handling without rolling, wallowing in the trough, or pitching and yawing. It must also be able to travel over rough water without excessive pounding. You may have observed how some boats cut through the waves smoothly with the rise and fall, whereas others literally slam down on the water. Hull designers aim to give the smoothest possible ride, not only for passenger comfort but to keep split seams and ruptured bulkheads at a minimum.

Planing Hulls

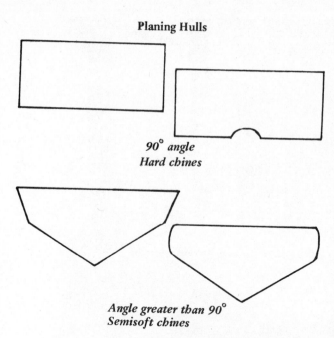

90° angle
Hard chines

Angle greater than 90°
Semisoft chines

Hulls showing the angle of the chines. These are good planing hulls.

Choosing Your Hull Type

There are three main types of hulls on the market today: pontoon, cruiser and catamaran. Let's examine them one by one.

As we have seen, the majority of early cruising houseboats were of the pontoon variety. These simple crafts consisted of two long, enclosed tubes, supporting a platform and a house. Some of the early pontoon manufacturers simply bought large steel pipes and sealed over the ends to make floating compartments. Today, however, pontoon design is highly sophisticated, and models can be square, round, triangular, a deep V shape or anything in between.

Pontoon boats are extremely stable and can carry large amounts of weight. Although the pontoon itself offers quite a bit of water resistance, today's forward-looking designs

The pontoon: a larger houseboat for less money. Although a pontoon offers quite a bit of water resistance, today's sophisticated designs allow greater speed.

allow for greater speeds and sometimes even planing. But without a doubt, the main advantage of the pontoon boat is the fact that it offers a larger houseboat for the money.

The pontoon's main disadvantages, on the other hand, are a relative lack of speed and maneuverability.

In choosing among the various pontoon models, remember that completely round pontoons have the disadvantage of allowing the boat to be blown sidewise fairly easily. Diamond and other shaped models that penetrate more deeply into the water avoid this problem by actually acting as a stabilizing keel that makes drifting difficult.

Modern cruiser hulls are basically compromises between a rounded bottom and a deep V shape. They are designed with an eye to providing some of the advantages of both.

A modern houseboat hull is a compromise between the rounded bottom and the deep V—the flatter the bottom, the more easily it will plane.

133

The cruiser hull: narrowing the performance gap between houseboats and the conventional cruiser.

The catamaran: a smooth ride and directional stability.

For instance, the flatter a boat's bottom, the more easily it will plane and the less water depth it requires for navigation. On the other hand, a deep V handles more efficiently, has good directional stability and maneuvers well. The V also offers a more comfortable ride in rough water and is less affected by wave action than a flatter model.

The third type of hull on today's market is the picturesque catamaran. This, in reality, is a set of twin deep V hulls that operate by trapping an air bubble between them, producing a lifting effect.

Catamaran hulls offer excellent directional stability and rise and fall on the waves with a smooth motion.

Hull Materials

In addition to the hull's shape and type, you will also want to consider what it is made of. Hulls today are generally fashioned from aluminum, fiberglass or steel. Less common materials include wood and Ferro-cement. Whereas wooden commercial models seem to be a thing of the past, a number of very progressive companies are now experimenting with Ferro-cement, and it may well see greater use in the near future.

What do each of these materials have to offer?

Aluminum: This is the lightest of the hull materials and is widely used today. Aluminum boats offer low fuel consumption per boat size (due to their light weight) and require less power to produce high speed.

There was a time when aluminum hulls were afflicted with corrosion and pitting problems, but protected with the proper coating they now require little maintenance. In addition, it offers complete immunity to marine borers. And from the manufacturer's standpoint, aluminum is easier to manipulate and form than steel.

On the minus side, you will find it difficult to do your own repair work on an aluminum hull since it requires special tools, special techniques and special know-how.

Fiberglass: Durable, popular fiberglass is primarily a plastic reinforced glass fiber material. When molded into a hull shape it is then braced with reinforced fiberglass-wood cross members.

Fiberglass hulls are completely seamless, yet resilient enough to take considerable pounding without injury. They require no upkeep except an occasional touch of fresh paint.

Fiberglass is also extremely strong and can be easily patched—in fact, you can "do it yourself." Keep in mind, however, that a fiberglass hull costs slightly more than the same size hull made of another material. It is also heavier.

Steel: This extremely tough material can be formed into an almost seamless hull. It will take a lot of punishment without puncturing and does not require any internal support. But if you do manage to damage a steel hull, you can't repair it yourself the way you can a fiberglass model. It is off to the boatyard for a welding job!

Wood: Although there are a number of homemade plywood hulls afloat, wood is not used today in commercial houseboat construction. This material does, however, offer strength and good resilience. It is also the least expensive of the materials and does not easily transmit vibrations. Your main problem here will be the yearly painting necessary to keep your hull in shape. Wood also is more fire-prone than the other materials.

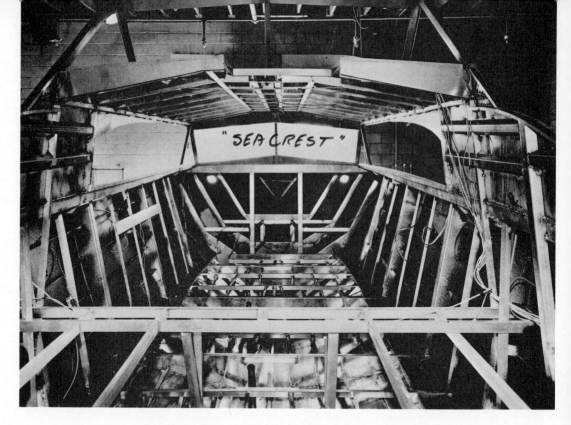

An aluminum hull. This is all-welded aluminum construction.

Working on a large fiberglass hull. These hulls require very little upkeep.

Putting a fiberglass hull together at the plant. Note the supporting cross members.

Fiberglass hulls are completely seamless and will take considerable pounding.

Steel hull construction in the early stages. Note the minimum of internal support. Steel can be formed into an almost seamless hull that will take a lot of punishment.

Ferro-cement: This newcomer to the field is actually a highly reinforced type of concrete developed by the Italian Professor Pier Luigi Nervi. It consists of a dense mortar, composed of Portland cement, fine sand and pozzolana (a powdered volcanic rock used in making hydraulic cement). This is troweled onto a framework of pipe, rod and chicken wire. The result is maintenance-free, fireproof, rot-proof and strong. This, however, is the heaviest of all hull materials, averaging ten pounds per square foot for a ¾-inch hull.

Equipped with the preceding guidelines (aluminum for speed, steel for strength and durability, and fiberglass for low maintenance), you should find it easier to make a selection based on which factor is most important to you. Before making your choice, however, here are a few final items to take into account:

(1) When buying, keep in mind the relationship between fuel consumption and speed. The fastest boats often require tremendous amounts of fuel and tend not to be the best handlers in rough water or the most stable at slow speeds.

(2) Try to work out a compromise between the "house" and the hull. If you want a boat that will achieve reasonable speed without undue fuel consumption, keep the total weight down.

(3) Consider where you will be cruising. If you plan to take to the open sea or navigate rough waters, you will need a hull that can take a rough chop and come down gently without breaking open. It must also be tough enough to withstand the sudden shock of yawing, pitching or jolting, as well as the impact of hitting a dock or bumping up on a beach.

Even if you intend to begin by limiting yourself to exploring the stillest waters, you will probably be tempted to try some more adventurous cruising later on, so insist on a hull that can plane reasonably well and has good strength and upkeep factors.

And above all—don't choose a hull for its flashy appearance. Styling is important, of course, but it's far from the main consideration.

CHAPTER EIGHT

Power Plants

Now let's take a look at the heart of the matter—selecting the engine that will best propel your boat along the byways of houseboating country.

When it comes to power plants, today's houseboat skipper has a number of options. He can choose among inboard or stern-drive models, 4-cylinder, 6-cylinder or 8-cylinder engines and a wide range of horsepowers. A boat can adapt itself to any of these solutions. It's really a question of deciding which best answers the individual owner's needs.

Here is a basic rundown of what is available on the market, plus some general guidelines aimed at helping you make the right choice.

Engine Types

There are three basic categories of power plants in use today: outboard, inboard and stern drive.

Modern outboards are extremely sophisticated mechanisms. Many have an ignition key starting, single lever remote control generators, alternators and very stylish covers (shrouds). Most are 2-cycle, but at least two manufacturers now produce a very efficient and economical 4-cycle engine. At cruising speed the large outboard consumes about six to eight gallons of gas per hour. This type of motor is used extensively on pontoon houseboats.

The inboard operates on the same principle as the automobile engine, but it is designed to do a basically different job. The engine

proper is installed inside the hull with an under hull drive shaft and propeller. Horsepower here ranges from under 20 to over 600 but today's houseboats generally stick to inboards within the 160 to 325 horsepower range.

When it comes to popularity, it is the stern drive that is currently ahead. These models were originally called "inboard/outboard" because the engine was installed inside the hull while the lower unit was geared by a coupling through the transom (the back of the boat) to an outboard-type drive unit.

Outboards are used extensively on the pontoon-type houseboats and some of the lighter cruiser hulls. New models have high horsepower.

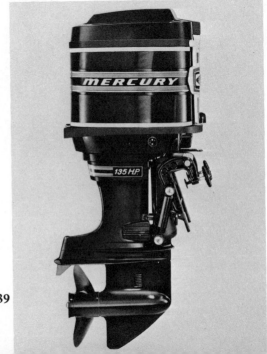

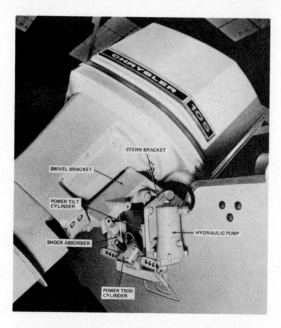

Some outboards are tilted out hydraulically.

The stern drive combines the advantages of both the inboard and the outboard engines and has been instrumental in making the houseboat the versatile cruiser-explorer it is. You can tilt up the motor to allow beaching or poking around in shallows. You can also crank it free of the water to clear a fouled propeller. Another plus for the stern drive is that it has a lower fuel consumption than the outboard.

In addition to these three engine types, some houseboat manufacturers now offer a fourth option: the diesel. These models have no spark plugs, wires, coils, condensers or other ignition parts, but simply ignite by air compression to an exceedingly high temperature inside the cylinders. Diesels use a cheaper, lower grade fuel and are almost twice as efficient as the gas models. They also offer the advantages of a greater speed range and longer service life, and it is easier to pinpoint a problem because they lack an ignition system.

Keep in mind, however, that the diesels are considerably heavier than gasoline engines

Inboards like this are found in many of today's larger houseboats. Some models use either a single engine or twins. The inboard operates on the same principle as the automobile engine.

The popular stern drives are a relatively new development. The stern drive power package combines the advantages of both the inboard and outboard engines, and has a relatively low fuel consumption.

Cutaway view of the power drive unit of a stern-drive engine. This unit provides smooth, easy shifting.

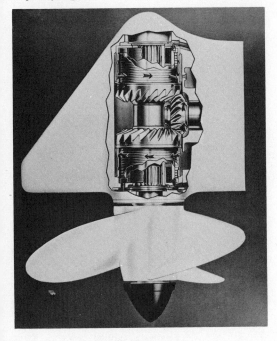

and more expensive to overhaul and maintain. They also cost two to three times as much as a comparable gasoline-powered model.

This power package is recommended if you intend to use your houseboat every day or extensively and expect to keep the boat at least 5 years. Lower fuel bills and a greater time interval between overhauls will eventually off-set the higher engine cost.

Twins Versus Singles

Twin engines provide ease of handling and offer decided safety advantages. With two propellers located some distance apart, you can swing around sharply by simply throwing one into forward and the other into reverse. In addition, you will have added speed in case of emergencies, and a second engine to fall back on if the first one fails.

Your initial investment, however, will be twice as high, and you will have greater fuel consumption. Actual operating figures show that although twin engines do not double fuel consumption as might be expected, they do increase it from 35 to 60 percent.

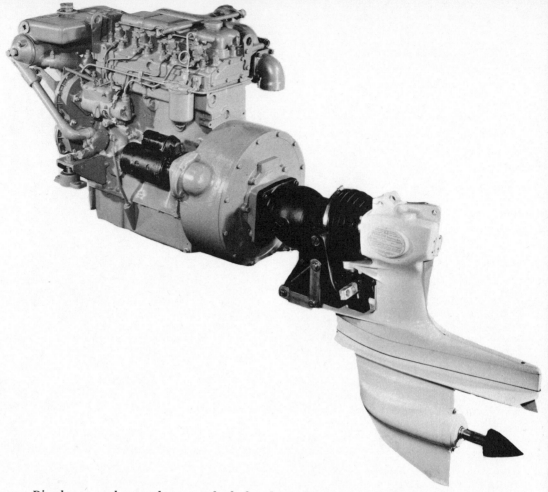

Diesels use a cheaper, lower grade fuel and are almost twice as efficient as gas models. They are extremely heavy, however. Normally they have a longer service life than a gasoline engine.

Twin outboard engines provide ease of handling and offer decided safety advantage.

Twins are generally recommended if you intend to take extended trips, if you plan to use your houseboat off the coast or in potentially dangerous water, or if you really crave the added speed and maneuverability they provide.

On the other hand, any single engine recommended by the manufacturer is perfectly adequate for cruising on protected waters. In fact, this power package is better suited to a relaxed vacation than the speedier twin. Should you want to do some water-skiing, you will do better buying an additional ski boat than investing in twins. The cost of pulling skiers at the necessary speed with a 12,000-pound boat is pretty prohibitive.

Suiting Your Engine to Your Boat

A typical manufacturer today will present you with a bewildering number of power possibilities. Here, for example, is what one firm offers for a given model: a single 225-horsepower Chrysler engine, a single 270-horsepower Mercury engine, a single 160-horsepower Perkins diesel, 215-horsepower Mercury twins, 225-horsepower Chrysler twins, and 170-horsepower Glastron twins.

In making a selection, keep the following points in mind:

(1) You can get only so much performance out of a hull (see Chapter 7). Additional horsepower can increase speed and efficiency up to a certain point, but beyond that you are just wasting fuel.

(2) It takes four times the power to double boat speed. This is because the boat hull has an enormous contact surface with tremendous friction drag. Therefore, if your boat is powered with a 160-horsepower engine, and you step it up to 320-horsepower, you will increase your speed roughly by half (depending on the hull design).

(3) The proper engine and hull combinations that produce reasonable speed and good fuel consumption in a houseboat must be worked out individually for each boat type. Your dealer or manufacturer can help you do this.

(4) In buying an engine, keep in mind the load-weight ratio. This can vary tremendously. To give you a graphic example, here are six optional engine packages compared on a pounds per horsepower basis:

Price	Package	Pounds of Houseboat Weight Pushed by Each Engine Horsepower
$1829.00	225 Chrysler	53 lbs. per horsepower
1565.00	270 Mercury	44 lbs. per horsepower
5839.00	160 Perkins diesel	75 lbs. per horsepower
3837.00	215 Mercury twins	28 lbs. per horsepower
3569.50	225 Chrysler twins	27 lbs. per horsepower
2536.00	170 Glastron twins	35 lbs. per horsepower

Boat weight . . . . 12,000 pounds

Each of the above options is well adapted to the particular boat in question, but you will notice a significant discrepancy in individual load-weight ratios. Although all of these power plants meet acceptable performance and economy standards, look to the engine with the *lowest* load-weight ratio to do the most effective job. Remember, however, that the efficiency factor must be balanced against the engine's initial cost and the higher fuel outlay required to produce a lower pound-per-horsepower ratio.

(5) In making a final power decision, weigh performance against dollars and cents. The smallest engine offered by the manufacturer will do a satisfactory job. It will not,

however, give you top speed or performance. As you step up in horsepower, you will obviously increase your cruising speed as well. You will also see a rise in operating costs, but less than you might think since operating time per mile is less.

A list of selected power plant manufacturers follows. For further information, send for any brochures they may have available.

Selected List of Manufacturers

Outboard Motors

Chrysler Corp.
PO Box 2641
Detroit, Mich. 48231

Evinrude Motors
4143 N. 27th St.
Milwaukee, Wis. 53216

Fisher Pierce Bearcat Inc.
1149 Hingham St.
Rockland, Mass. 02370

Johnson Motors
Waukegan, Ill. 60085

Kiekhaefer Mercury
Fond du Lac, Wis. 54935

Stern Drives

Chrysler Corp.
PO Box 2641
Detroit, Mich. 48231

Eaton Yale & Towne
Eaton Marine Division
24275 Northwestern Highway
Southfield, Mich. 48075

Graymarine Corp.
498 E. Chicago St.
Coldwater, Mich. 49036

Kiekhaefer Mercury
Fond du Lac, Wis. 54935

Outboard Marine Corp.
Galesburg, Ill. 61401

Inboard Engines

Chris-Craft Corp.
Pompano Beach, Fla. 33061

Chrysler Corp.
PO Box 2641
Detroit, Mich. 48231

Graymarine Corp.
498 E. Chicago St.
Coldwater, Mich. 49036

Holman & Moody Inc.
PO Box 27065
Municipal Airport Station
Charlotte, N.C. 28208

Diesel

Barr Marine Products Co.
Philadelphia, Pa. 19134

Caterpillar Tractor
Industrial Division
Peoria, Ill. 61602

Chrysler-Nissan
Marine Division, Chrysler Corp.
PO Box 1
Marysville, Mich. 48040

Crusader Marine
25140 East St.
Warren, Mich. 48089

Cummins Engine Co., Inc.
Columbus, Ind. 47201

Daytona Marine Engine Corp.
701 S. Beach St.
Daytona Beach, Fla. 32015

Detroit Diesel Engine Division
General Motors Corp.
13400 W. Outer Dr.
Detroit, Mich. 48233

Graymarine Corp.
498 E. Chicago St.
Coldwater, Mich. 49036

Lehman Manufacturing Co.
800 E. Elizabeth St.
Linden, N.J. 07036

Perkins Engines Inc.
24175 Research Dr.
Farmington, Mich. 48024

Starrett Corp.
Diesel Division
Tampa, Fla. 33602

CHAPTER NINE

Furnishing Your Floating Home

As we have seen, one of the main areas in which the houseboat really excels is livability afloat. In buying a boat, you can generally count on the shipboard equivalent of the following basic floor plan: a large draped and carpeted living room, a well-appointed kitchen and a covered patio. Most models also come with full-length sliding doors at the rear. These provide light, a view, a feeling of spaciousness and an outdoor-indoor living area that is hard to beat.

How to install and furnish the interior of your boat will depend on your tastes and your pocketbook. Let's take a look at some of the household equipment you will be considering and see just what's available, starting with the galley.

Appliances

The modern houseboat galley is a far cry from models of only a few years back and differs vastly from the cramped cooking space available on cruisers. Taking a lesson from trailer design, manufacturers started early to equip their houseboats with three-burner LP (liquified petroleum) stoves, ovens and LP gas or electric refrigerators. But this was only the beginning in a trend toward greater and greater modernization.

Today, for instance, one popular make boasts a spacious, well-designed galley featuring teak cabinets, a rotisserie oven, a teak spice rack, a seven-cubic-foot electric refrigerator, a seven-cubic-foot freezer with an automatic ice-maker, and a double stainless steel sink equipped with a single-lever mixing faucet.

There are numerous supplementary options available in the oven and stove line, including a removable double rotisserie unit, a microwave oven and ranges that are made in a variety of colors. Sea rails are available to safely anchor utensils.

Refrigerators have also evolved tremendously over the years. At first, most houseboats came equipped with iceboxes. These were followed by small LP gas* refrigerators, electric refrigerators and combination gas/electric refrigerators. Now you can buy apartment-size refrigerators and freezers, table-top or wall-mounted models and icemakers that spew out up to 400 cubes a day.

Galley counter tops and wall surfaces are usually of washable, durable plastic laminates. And when it comes to your dinette table, you can request a number of shapes and materials up to and including a teak pedestal table that can be lowered to cocktail level or raised and extended to a family-size dining table!

Moving on to a related area, some houseboats still get their water by hand pump from a tank. Others use a high tank fed by gravity. A number of modern boats, however, utilize as standard equipment compact units that create pressure in the tank or simply pump water when needed. A number of boats also come equipped with 40- to 100-gallon water tanks. And if you wish, you can add water-carrying

*LP gas units of all types should be operated with due caution (following the manufacturer's instructions) as LP gas can be dangerous in high concentrations.

The modern houseboat galley is a far cry from the cramped spaces of yesteryear. Note the double stainless steel sink and three-burner LP stove and oven.

This modern unit features a built-in rotisserie.

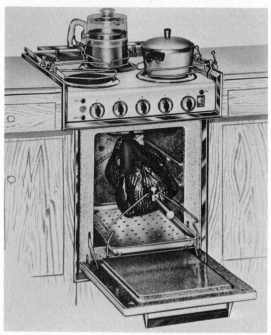

LP units can be extremely compact. This one has all the conveniences of home yet occupies a minimum of space. Note overhead oven.

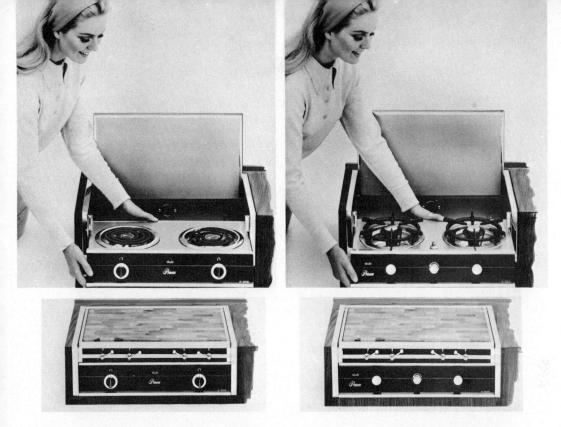

This convenient electric cooktop operates on 110 volts at dockside or on alcohol afloat. Note removable, reversible cutting board.

capacity up to several hundred gallons. You may also want to consider a purifier that will provide you with safe water anywhere.

Hot water heaters range from about four to twelve gallons and operate on either electricity or LP gas. Units are also available that attach to the cold water faucet and provide an instant and continuous flow of hot water. You will also find an eight-gallon, glass-lined tank that operates on AC at dockside or uses a heat exchanger to draw heat from the engine cooling water while under way.

Another area that has seen tremendous modernization over the past years is heating units. Once again, the credit for the revolution goes to the trailer manufacturers. Today you can choose among such models as a trailer type heater, 9 by 21 inches, vented to the outside; a flameless, compact, ventless, flush-mounted heater that operates for less than one cent an hour; a forced-air ducted heater with electrical blowers; and a 16,000 BTU forced-air gas furnace with a wall thermostat.

You can also buy portable radiant propane heaters, floor electric heaters and an open fireplace that fits into a space 12 by 12 by 10 inches deep.

Looking at the other side of the coin, you will find a number of air conditioning units on the market, including a 10 by 24 inch unit that both cools and heats. (A list of selected appliance manufacturers will be found on pp. 155-156.)

This brings us to another of the convenient features of houseboating—the fact that you can carry your own power with you. As a rule, houseboats have two electrical systems: 110 volts (just like at home) and a 12-volt system that works off batteries.

Many houseboats also have their own 110-volt generator. But you will find that your 12-volt system will be quite adequate to operate such items as the bilge pump, sump pump, cabin lights, running lights, compass light, marine radio, searchlight, windshield wiper, depth sounder and anchor lights.

Sea rails are available to safely anchor utensils. These are extremely useful.

And as we have seen, you can usually pull into any marina at night and plug into their power for about ten cents a foot (length of boat). This will permit you to run a regular television set and some of your larger electrical units.

Beds Aboard

A houseboat's sleeping arrangements depend largely on its general floor plan. Many forward lounges provide hide-a-bed sleeping units plus couches that make into beds in the aft stateroom or lounge. Some also have separate staterooms with molded fiberglass beds.

Ingenuity is the key word here. Houseboat designers have outdone themselves in devising a variety of sleeping combinations aimed at achieving maximum space plus comfort aboard, depending on individual family needs.

If you intend to entertain a number of guests, for example, you will want to keep in mind solutions that achieve maximum privacy. These include models with separate staterooms, as well as boats with lounge areas that convert into staterooms that can be sealed off with sliding partitions.

You will also find a convertible combination for children with a conventional-style bedroom for the owners, V-bed arrangements with specially designed mattresses, and upholstered foam convertible couches that fit into the pattern of the room. Double-bed arrangements are available as well. And for super space saving you might investigate bunks that double

Small portable refrigerators are useful for entertaining.

as couches when the upper section is tilted against the wall to form an upholstered back for the lower bunk; convertible dinette tables; and bunks that serve as combination beds, desks, chests and cabinets!

Sanitary Facilities

Considering the tremendous advances in general houseboat design in recent years as far as the basic "house" and galley are concerned, it is surprising how the installation of the head or bathroom area has lagged behind. Until only a few years ago, you were likely to find luxurious houseboats equipped with only the skimpiest vanity facilities. But fortunately, all of this has changed today.

Now, for example, one houseboat manu-

facturer provides a large, carpeted head with a marine toilet tucked underneath a folding vanity shelf, a built-in vanity and a large mirror with theatrical lighting. In addition, there are numerous decorative touches designed to brighten the bathroom area.

As to the toilet itself, current emphasis on water pollution and new state laws are forcing most houseboat owners to use something other than the standard marine toilet that simply pumps the untreated boat sewage overboard. Currently, there is a choice of four types on the market: flush with holding tanks, recirculating, incinerator and treatment (macerator-chlorinator). (See chart on p. 151.)

The flush-type toilet works just like a home toilet, simply flushing water through the bowl. This is the principle behind the conven-

Wall-type heaters make houseboat heating extremely convenient. These have thermostats with manual or automatic controls.

tional marine toilet. But the discharging of waste directly overboard is now forbidden in many areas, and waste matter must be trapped inside a holding tank attached to the unit. It is later discharged into dockside facilities.

A recirculating toilet, unlike the ordinary flush toilet, uses the same water over and over again. When you flush the toilet the waste drops into a reservoir, to which chemicals are added. On the next flushing the waste is filtered and the solids are deposited in a holding tank. The newest types of recirculating toilet systems claim up to eighty or more flushes of an initial charge of about four gallons of water. When coupled to a large water tank and a 40-gallon holding tank, it is possible to get up to 600 flushes without filling the holding tank to capacity.

Look like home? This is the guest stateroom aboard one of the larger houseboats.

Marine Sanitation Systems

System	Method	Advantages	Disadvantages
Marine toilet	Raw sewage is pumped manually overboard	Low cost	Prohibited in most areas
Flush—with holding tank	Waste is dumped into a holding tank for later removal	No treatment required; can go a considerable time without emptying	Tank must be emptied
Recirculating	Filters remove the solids while the water is used a number of times	Reuses the water; solids are trapped	Must be emptied
Incinerator	Waste is burned	Raw sewage is burned, leaving a dry residue	Takes about fourteen minutes to recycle
Macerator-chlorinator	"Treated waste" is dumped overboard after being broken down mechanically and treated with chlorine	Treated sewage can be dumped— tank does not have to be emptied dockside	Prohibited in some areas

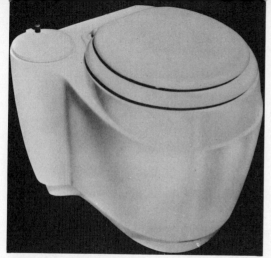

This Mono-matic toilet is a self-contained, electrically operating, recirculating flush unit. It can be converted to discharge waste at dockside or empty treated waste overboard where permitted by law.

With one popular make, the Monomatic, you simply pour in four gallons of fresh water and add one charge of the chemical sanitizer. To operate, you need only press a button, which activates a timer controlling the flushing cycle.

If overboard discharge is permitted, the Monomatic discharges waste through a second fitting by means of a discharge pump.

Two companies also manufacture a toilet with a built-in grinder and discharge pump that permits discharge into dockside tanks, even when a marina does not have a system of sewage suction pumps.

The incinerator model operates on a completely different system. Functioning on both LP gas and 12-volt battery power, it simply burns the waste matter into ash and collects it in a chamber. With one brand the user activates the blower and burner cycles when he lifts the lid off the bowl. After use, there is a fourteen-minute burn cycle, followed by several minutes of cooling.

In the macerator-chlorinator system, a marine toilet is connected to a tank with a grinder, which chews up the solid matter. Then chlorine is added to bring the bacteria count down to acceptable levels, and the whole thing is discharged overboard.

In one model, using dry chlorine tablets, you simply push a button on the bulkhead, which sets the macerator in action for a measured length of time. In a more advanced unit, the chamber breaks down the waste at 10,000 rpm; the chlorine container, resting on a spring-loaded switch, breaks the circuit when the bottle is empty.

The problem with these systems, however, is that even though the discharged waste is of a higher quality than most treated sewage, it is still waste discharge and may be prohibited in some areas.

The following list of manufacturers of sanitation equipment and toilet systems can provide you with further information on available models. Before investing in sanitation equipment, familiarize yourself with your state's current laws regarding such facilities—*as well as the expected trend of legislation in the future.*

Ball-Hed Marine Products Co., Inc.
5219 Sangamore Rd.
Washington, D.C. 20016

Carlson Division (Koehler-Dayton, Inc.)
401 Leo St.
Dayton, Oh. 45404

Corlon Manufacturing Co.
1910 N. Cogswell Rd.
South El Monte, Calif. 91733

Craft Division of Craftor, Inc.
193 Genesee St.
Auburn, N.Y. 13021

Gross Mechanical Laboratories
1530 Russell St.
Baltimore, Md. 21230

Jensen Sanitation Systems
1946 E. 46th St.
Los Angeles, Calif. 90058

LaMere Industries, Inc.
277 N. Main St.
Walworth, Wis. 53184

Mansfield Sanitary, Inc.
132 First St.
Perrysville, Oh. 44864

Monogram Industries, Inc.
10131 National Blvd.
Los Angeles, Calif. 90034

Raritan Engineering Co.
1025 N. High St.
Millville, N.J. 08332

Saniware Division, Mission West Mfg. Co.
3238 W. 131st St.
Hawthorne, Calif. 90250

Thetford Corporation
PO Box 1285
Ann Arbor, Mich. 48103

Townsend Products Corp.
182 Avenue D
Rochester, N.Y. 14621

Zurn Industries, Inc.
Recreational Products Division
Erie, Pa. 16512

Agencies Concerned With Houseboat Waste Disposal

State	*State Agency Involved*
ALABAMA	State Board of Health and Director of Conservation, Montgomery, Ala.
ALASKA	
ARIZONA	
ARKANSAS	Bureau of Environmental Engineering, State Board of Health, Little Rock, Ark.
CALIFORNIA	
COLORADO	
CONNECTICUT	
DELAWARE	
FLORIDA	
GEORGIA	State Water Quality Control Board, 47 Trinity Ave., S. W., Atlanta, Ga.
HAWAII	State Dept. of Health, Honolulu, Hi.
IDAHO	
ILLINOIS	
INDIANA	State Stream Pollution Control Board, Indianapolis, Ind.
IOWA	

State	State Agency Involved
KANSAS	
KENTUCKY	State Water Pollution Control Commission, Frankfort, Ky.
LOUISIANA	
MAINE	
MARYLAND	
MASSACHUSETTS	
MICHIGAN	
MINNESOTA	Water Pollution Control Commission State Board of Health, St. Paul, Minn.
MISSISSIPPI	
MISSOURI	Water Pollution Board, State Dept. of Public Health, Jefferson City, Mo.
MONTANA	
NEBRASKA	
NEVADA	
NEW HAMPSHIRE	
NEW JERSEY	
NEW MEXICO	
NEW YORK	Division of Motorboats, State Conservation Dept., Albany, N.Y.
NORTH CAROLINA	Sanitary Engineering Div., State Board of Health, Raleigh, N. C.
NORTH DAKOTA	State Water Pollution Control Board, Bismarck, N. D.
OHIO	

State	State Agency Involved
OKLAHOMA	State Dept. of Health, 3400 N. Eastern, Oklahoma City, Okla.
OREGON	State Sanitary Authority, State Board of Health, Salem, Ore.
PENNSYLVANIA	
RHODE ISLAND	
SOUTH CAROLINA	
SOUTH DAKOTA	State Health Dept., Pierre, S.D.
TENNESSEE	Stream Pollution Board, Department of Public Health, Nashville, Tenn.
TEXAS	
UTAH	State Dept. of Health, Salt Lake City, Utah
VERMONT	
VIRGINIA	
WASHINGTON	
WEST VIRGINIA	
WISCONSIN	
WYOMING	

Laws governing waste disposal vary with the states—many no longer permit standard marine toilets without holding tanks. Many require on-board inspection to make sure toilet complies. Check with the state agencies involved as listed above.

Selected Appliance Manufacturers

Heating

Duo-Therm Division
Motor Wheel Corp.
LaGrange, Ind. 46761

Koldwave Marine Division
Heat Exchangers Inc.
8100 N. Monticello
Skokie, Ill. 60076

Mobil Temp Inc.
11871 E. Grand River Rd.
Brighton, Mich. 48116

Suburban Manufacturing Co.
PO Box 399
Dayton, Tenn. 37321

Therm'x Corporation
1280 Columbus
San Francisco, Calif. 94113

Wagon-Master Inc.
3308 Harbor Ave. SW
Seattle, Wash. 98126

Air Conditioning

Duo-Therm Division
Motor Wheel Corp.
LaGrange, Ind. 46761

Frigiking Division
Cummins Engine Co., Inc.
10858 Harry Hines Blvd.
Dallas, Texas 75220

Marinaire Corp.
3233 SW 2nd Ave.
Fort Lauderdale, Fla. 33315

Way Wolff Associates
45-10 Vernon Blvd.
Long Island City, N.Y. 11101

Stoves

Homestrand Inc.
37 Plain Ave.
New Rochelle, N.Y. 10801

Magic Chef
City of Industry, Calif. 91744

Princess Mfg. Corp.
741 Fremont Ave.
Alhambra, Calif. 91803

Sattler Mfg. Corp.
9313 Sorenson Ave.
Santa Fe Springs, Calif. 90670

Ward & Son Inc.
Elkhart, Ind. 46514

Refrigerators

Dometic Sales Corp.
2900 W. Mishawaka Rd.
Elkhart, Ind. 46514

General Thermetics Inc.
Brookdale Pl.
Mt. Vernon, N.Y. 10550

Morphy-Richards, Inc.
128 Ludlow Ave.
Northvale, N.J. 07647

Ward & Son Inc.
City of Industry, Calif. 91744

CHAPTER TEN

Boating Accessories and Safety Equipment

Boating accessories fall into two basic categories: those required by law and those that are optional. Choosing among the latter will partly depend on how elaborate an installation you desire and what you want to spend. Let's begin with legal requirements:

According to Federal regulations*, all motorboats today must be equipped with fire extinguishers, lifesaving devices, backfire flame arresters, ventilation devices, bells, horns (called whistles) and proper lights.

As you begin shopping around, you will find a variety of available merchandise within each of these categories. Take fire extinguishers, for example. Some models use dry chemicals (2 to 3 pounds, $7 to $30); others rely on foam (2½ gallons, $25 to $50); still others utilize carbon dioxide (5-pound size, $40 to $60).

Each type is classified by letter (indicating the type of fire it is meant to combat) and number (designating the unit's size). "A" stands for ordinary combustible materials, "B" for gasoline, oil and grease fires, and "C" for fires in electrical equipment. To meet with legal requirements, portable fire extinguishers must be Coast Guard approved (see pp. 158 and 160).

*A pamphlet listing all requirements, "Pleasure Craft, Federal Requirements for Motorboats"—CG 290, is available from the Superintendent of Documents, Washington, D.C. 20402 or from the nearest Coast Guard Office (see pp. 109-110).

The Coast Guard sometimes boards small craft for inspection of the equipment. Be sure your gear fulfills government requirements.

Required Equipment

	Class 1 16' to less than 26' in length	Motorboats Class 2 26' to less than 40' in length	Class 3 40' to 65' in length
PERSONAL FLOTATION DEVICES All must be marked "Approved by U.S. Coast Guard" and be in good, serviceable condition	One life preserver, buoyant vest, ring buoy, special purpose water buoyant safety device, or buoyant cushion for each person on board	Same as Class 1	One life preserver or ring buoy for each person on board
BELL	Not required	One which when struck produces a clear, bell-like tone	Same as Class 2
SOUND-PRODUCING DEVICES (Hand, mouth or electric sirens are not approved)	One device—hand-, mouth- or power-operated—producing a blast of two seconds audible half a mile (not required under 26')	One hand- or power-operated device, producing a blast of two seconds audible one mile	One power-operated device producing a blast of two seconds audible one mile
FIRE EXTINGUISHERS PORTABLE (When no fixed fire extinguishing system is installed in machinery space)	At least one B-1 type approved hand-portable fire extinguisher	At least two B-1 type approved hand-portable fire extinguishers; or at least one B-II type approved hand-portable fire extinguisher	At least three B-1 type approved hand-portable fire extinguishers; or at least one B-1 type plus one B-II type approved hand-portable fire extinguishers
(When fixed fire extinguisher system is installed in machinery space)	None	At least one B-1 type approved hand-portable fire extinguisher	At least two B-1 type approved hand-portable fire extinguishers; or at least one B-II type approved hand-portable fire extinguisher

VENTILATORS	At least two ventilators fitted with cowls or the equivalent for ventilating each machinery and fuel tank compartment	Same as Class 1	Same as Class 1
BACKFIRE FLAME ARRESTER	An approved backfire flame arrester on carburetors of gasoline engines installed after April 25, 1940, except outboard engines	Same as Class 1	Same as Class 1

Coast Guard Approved Equipment (Personal Flotation Devices and Fire Extinguishers)

"Coast Guard Approved Equipment" is equipment that has been approved by the Commandant after it has been determined to be in compliance with the various Coast Guard specifications and regulations relating to the materials, construction and performance of such equipment.

Personal Flotation Devices

Prior to 1972, only motorboats were required to carry personal flotation devices. Now all boats (with a few exceptions) must carry these devices.

Life Preservers. Kapok, fibrous glass or unicellular plastic foam is used as flotation material in life preservers. They are either of the jacket or bib design and are acceptable for use on all types of motorboats and vessels. Adult sizes for persons 90 pounds and over, and child sizes for those less than 90 pounds are available. Coast Guard approved life preservers bear markings showing flotation material used, size and U.S. Coast Guard approval number. All Coast Guard approved life preservers manufactured after 1949 are Indian orange.

Buoyant Vests. Coast Guard approved buoyant vests use the same flotation materials as life preservers but may be any color. Approved buoyant vests come in three sizes: adult, child medium and child small. Weight ranges of the child sizes are included in the Coast Guard approval markings. It should be noted that buoyant vests provide less buoyancy than life preservers do. They are not acceptable on motorboats 40 feet in length and over, or on vessels carrying passengers for hire.

Buoyant Cushions. Buoyant cushions approved by the Coast Guard contain kapok, fibrous glass or unicellular plastic foam. They come in a variety of sizes and shapes and may be any color.

Cushions are not acceptable on motorboats 40 feet in length and over, or on vessels carrying passengers for hire.

Approved buoyant cushions are marked on the side (gusset) showing the Coast Guard approval number, and other information concerning the cushion and its use. Buoyant cushions are intended for grasping and should never be worn on the back.

Ring Buoy. Ring life buoys can be made of cork, balsa wood or unicellular plastic foam, and are available in 30-, 24-, and 20-inch sizes. Their covering is either canvas or specially surfaced plastic foam. All buoys are fitted with a grab line and may be colored either white or orange.

Cork and balsa wood ring buoys must bear two markings, the manufacturer's stamp and the Coast Guard inspector's stamp. Plastic foam ring buoys bear only a nameplate marking.

Special Purpose Water Safety Buoyant Devices. Approved special purpose water safety buoyant devices are manufactured in many designs depending on the intended special purpose, such as water-skiing, hunting, racing, etc. Additional strength is added where needed for the intended purpose of the device.

Special purpose devices include those to be worn and those to be grasped. They are acceptable on Classes A, 1 and 2 motorboats not carrying passengers for hire. Devices to be worn are available in adult and child sizes. All special purpose devices show U.S. Coast Guard approval number E25/160.064 . . ., include instructions on use and care, and other necessary information. The devices intended for grasping also are marked with the wording: "Warning—Do not wear on Back."

Fire Extinguishers

Approved types of fire extinguishers are identified by any of the following:

(a) Make and model number of extinguishers manufactured before 1962. Check markings on nameplate with the Coast Guard.

(b) "Marine Type" marking. Check nameplate marking on Underwriters' Laboratories, Inc., listing manifest showing the words, "Marine Type USCG" followed by the Coast Guard classification such as "B-I, B-II."

(c) Coast Guard approval number. Check for marking of Coast Guard approval number on nameplate.

Stored pressure dry chemical extinguishers manufactured after June 1, 1965, that have the propellent gases and extinguishing agent in the same bottle, must have a visual pressure indicator—a pressure gauge or similar device that shows the state of internal pressure charge.

Dry chemical extinguishers manufactured prior to June 1, 1965, without pressure indicating device are still acceptable if: (1) inspection record shows weight check within the past six months, (2) weight is within one fourth ounce of weight stamped on container, (3) external seals or disk in neck are intact and (4) there is no evidence of damage, use or leaking.

Required Fire Extinguishers

Each fire extinguisher is classified, by letter and number, according to the type of fire it may be expected to extinguish, and the size of the extinguisher. The letter indicates the type of fire: "A" for fires in ordinary combustible materials; "B" for gasoline, oil and grease fires; "C" for fires in electrical equipment. Extinguishers approved for motorboats are hand-portable, of either B-I or B-II classification.

NOTE: Carbon tetrachloride extinguishers and others of the toxic vaporizing-liquid type such as chlorobromomethane are not approved and are not accepted as required fire extinguishers.

Fire Extinguishers

CLASSIFICATION (type-size)	FOAM (minimum gallons)	CARBON DIOXIDE (minimum pounds)	DRY CHEMICAL (minimum pounds)	FREON (minimum pounds)
B-I	1¼	4	2	2½
B-II	2½	15	10	—

Most models can be purchased with a handy bulkhead mounting bracket. You will probably want to install your units in such a way that there will be one handy on deck (preferably near the engine) and one in the "house" close to the galley. Directions on how to operate portable models are given in Chapter 11.

Current laws also require that there be one Coast Guard approved lifesaving device on board per person (see pp. 158 and 159-160).

Children twelve years old and younger, *in or about* a boat, must securely wear a life vest. If aboard a Class 3 vessel, they must wear life jackets. Again there is a variety of choice. Life preservers come in kapok, buoyant fibrous glass and unicellular plastic, with prices ranging from $7 to $15 per unit. Cork and balsa wood, previously common flotation materials, are being phased out. Jackets are probably the most satisfactory should you end up in the water, but they can be uncomfortably bulky on board. Lightweight buoyant vests ($3 to $7) are more agreeable for boat wear and come in a variety of materials, patterns and sizes designed to outfit the entire family.

Cushions are also popular devices. They are low-priced ($3 to $7) and easy to stow, with the added plus of serving as extra seats on board. Unfortunately, however, they are the most difficult of the lifesaving devices to hang onto in the water, and they lose their buoyancy after they've been sat on awhile. Cushions serve best as additional or optional safety measures.

Ring buoys are another model much in demand, largely because they can be thrown to sea quickly and accurately in case of emergency. Models made of cellular plastic are priced from $17 to $25, while cork rings retail at $7 to $25.

A third requirement under current boating laws is a Coast Guard approved back flame arrester (see p. 159). Again there are several types: one model attaches to the engine air intake through a flame-tight connection, another operates through an attachment to the engine air intake system that discharges back-fire flames to an area where they can't do any harm, a third type utilizes a gasoline engine specifically approved by the Coast Guard and equipped with an engine air and fuel induction system that prevents backfire flames in the atmosphere.

Fourth on the list of regulation gear is a system of ventilators (see p. 159). These serve to keep volatile fumes out of the lower portion of the boat and are required on all but pontoon-type houseboats. Both intake and exhaust mechanisms are required. The intake duct must extend below the carburetor intake, and the exhaust duct must service the lowest portion of the bilge. Each ventilator must be fitted with vents (cowls) at the openings (see illustration above).

Legal requirements can be met by simply installing an intake vent on one side of the

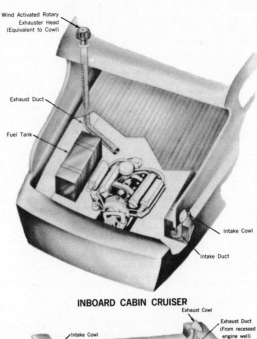

INBOARD CABIN CRUISER

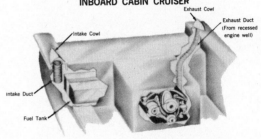

INBOARD-OUTBOARD STERN DRIVE
Combined Fuel Tank and Engine Compartments

Ventilator exhaust systems are required on all but pontoon-type houseboats.

engine compartment and an exhaust vent on the other. But to ensure maximum safety, you would do well to have a marine-type electrically driven blower inserted in the line of one bilge exhaust vent. As the blower draws stale air out, fresh air rushes in. It is best to let the blower run for at least five minutes and preferably ten before turning on the engine. Some ignition switches are equipped with a blower position through which the switch lever must pass before you can turn the ignition on.

Horns (referred to afloat as whistles) are also obligatory on board. Hand- or power-operated models fulfill regulations on houseboats under 40 feet. A power-operated horn (whistle) is required for all larger boats.

Models range from a hand-operated trumpet model, functioning on a compressed Freon can ($18), to permanently installed twin air horns with their own compressor ($260), with numerous possibilities in between.

If your houseboat measures over 26 feet, the law calls for a fog bell (which is sounded during foggy weather) as well. These range in price from $7 to $30. There are a number of medium-size brass bells on the market that do a good job.

Lights

Specific laws govern what lights your houseboat must display while under way or at anchor (except in "special anchorage areas"). These fall into two categories: the Motorboat Act and International Rules. On inland waters you can conform to either set of regulations; on the high seas (waters outside of national jurisdiction) you must abide by the International Rules.

Both sets of rules require lights to be visible from certain directions, expressed in terms of points. Each point equals 11¼ degrees.

Sidelights and forward combination lights show red on the left, facing forward (port); green on the right, facing forward (starboard). By law, these lights cast a 10-point arc (112.5 degrees) measured from dead ahead. Other lights—anchor, single bow and stern—are white.

Under both sets of rules, when anchored you must have a 32-point (360°) white anchor light visible for two miles. On the Great Lakes the anchor light must be under 20 feet above the hull and visible for a mile minimum.

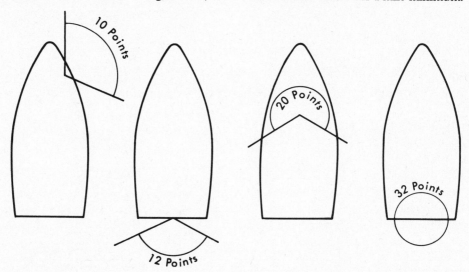

Standard light apertures of 10, 12, 20 and 32 points. These apertures are usually, but not exclusively, associated with the positions shown.

With a little experience you will be able to judge what a boat is doing and how big it is by the lights you see.

Renting or Hiring Out Your Houseboat

Houseboat owners sometimes rent their houseboats when they themselves are not using them. Others infrequently carry passengers for a fee. Houseboats meeting general regulations can be rented without difficulty. "Boats for hire," however, have additional requirements. Every motorboat carrying passengers for hire must have an approved life preserver (buoyant vests, ring buoys or buoyant cushions will not do) for each person carried, with an additional number of approved life preservers suitable for children, equal to at least 10 percent of the total number of passengers carried, unless children are never carried. In addition, boats for hire cannot use liquified petroleum gases or certain flammable liquids for cooking, heating or lighting. A motorboat for hire, while car-

LIGHTS REQUIRED ON BOATS UNDERWAY
BETWEEN SUNSET AND SUNRISE

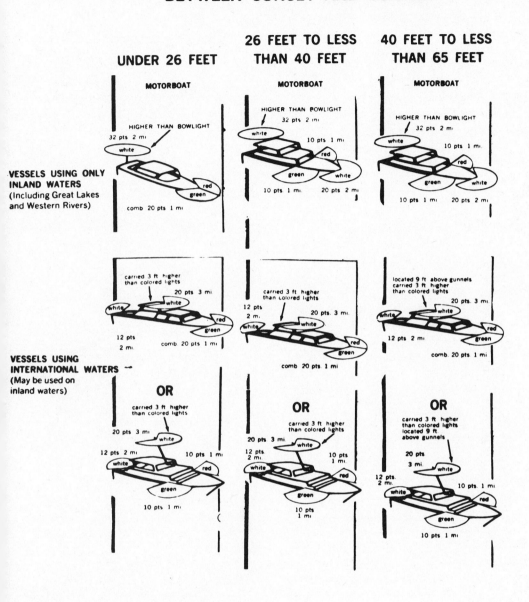

	UNDER 26 FEET	26 FEET TO LESS THAN 40 FEET	40 FEET TO LESS THAN 65 FEET

VESSELS USING ONLY INLAND WATERS (Including Great Lakes and Western Rivers)

VESSELS USING INTERNATIONAL WATERS → (May be used on inland waters)

IMPORTANT: LIGHTS MUST BE PLACED HIGH ENOUGH THAT THEIR LIGHT WILL NOT BE BLOCKED BY PERSONS OR PARTS OF THE BOAT OR IT'S EQUIPMENT.

LIGHTS FOR USE WHEN ANCHORED

POWER BOATS under 65 feet and all Sailing Vessels at anchor must display anchor lights except those under 65 feet in "special anchorage areas." An anchor light is a white light visible to a boat approaching from any direction, and is displayed in the fore part of the vessel.

rying passengers for hire, must be operated by someone licensed by the Coast Guard. Motorboats for hire must be inspected and certified by the Coast Guard.

Optional Items

You're obviously not going to leave shore without an anchor. But choosing among the many types on the market can be complicated. When you select yours, keep in mind what kind of bottom you will be cruising over.

Generally speaking, an anchor's holding power depends on its ability to dig in. This is particularly true over a soft bottom. Properly designed, it will be buried deeper and deeper by the pull of the anchor line until it reaches terrain solid enough to give it a firm grip.

Standard anchor types today are the kedge, grapnel, plow, Danforth, Northill utility and mushroom. For houseboating, your best bet is to get a Danforth 40-pounder for a 40-foot boat, and a 22-pounder for a 30-footer. You should also carry a secondary anchor—a plow if you are cruising over weedy areas, or a traditional yachtman's kedge for boating over rocks.

When it comes to line (anchor rope), nylon is unbeatable. Manila rope was once used extensively for this purpose, but nylon offers over twice the strength for the size. You will probably want to avoid chain. It's too cumbersome for most houseboats.

Other accessories you will want aboard are a boathook, fenders and some sort of spotlight. Boathooks (4- to 6-foot-long metal or plastic poles tipped with a small hook) have a variety of uses, from docking to helping bring another boat alongside. Fenders, protective units designed to cushion your boat against whatever you are coming against, prevent unnecessary damage and are available in plastic, air-filled rubber and other materials. Spotlights are practical, fun for exploring and serve as helpful signal devices in times of distress; models range from relatively simple units to deluxe chrome-plated searchlights that sell in the neighborhood of $300.

Deck Seamanship

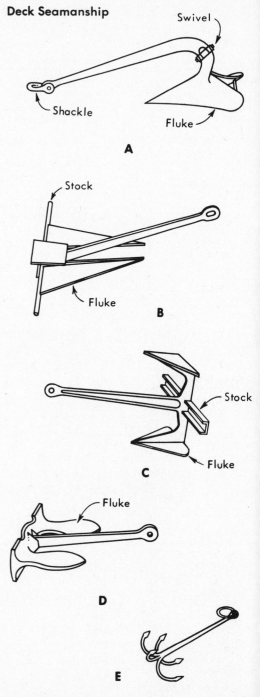

Commonly used types of anchors: (a) plow; (b) Danforth; (c) Northill; (d) Navy stockless; (e) grapnel. The latter is used only for anchoring skiffs or for dragging for articles lost overboard.

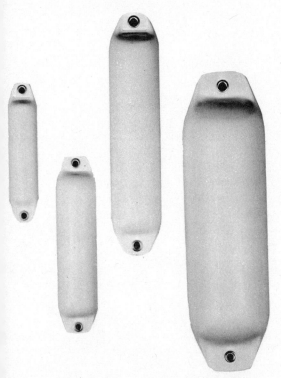

Boat fenders protect your houseboat from damage. They come in a variety of materials.

Some radiotelephones will mount almost anywhere. This is a six-channel VHF/FM unit.

HEATHKIT 6 Channel VHF/FM Radiophone, Model MWW-18

Electronic Devices

There are several electronic devices on the market that can take a lot of the work out of boating. Let's begin with communication aids:

You can pilot a houseboat without a radiotelephone, but more and more skippers are finding that having one aboard can come in very handy. If you are disabled and need assistance, it enables you to alert the Coast Guard or shore. Should you be delayed afloat, it serves to keep others· from worrying and prevents a needless search. Units range in price from about $165 up.

Currently the Very High Frequency— Frequency Modulation (VHF/FM) equipment (operating in the band 156-162 MHz) is enjoying increasing popularity. Boats equipped with transmitters and receivers using the frequencies reserved for boatmen can communicate within a limited range and will experience little interference from distant stations and atmospheric noise.

If you are planning to cruise on inland waterways, you will probably want a Citizen's Band radio instead of a marine radiotelephone. This is a short-range communication service over designated frequencies for business, personal and other uses.

Count on about $150 for a good unit. Some models operate on only one channel. Others offer a selection of two or three that can be chosen by a switch, and many can be tuned in manually to all twenty-three channels.

When you are out on the water with a group of boats, radio communication is an excellent way for everyone to keep in touch. It is also a valuable safety device, especially during night cruising. You can use your Citizen's Band on shore as well—in the car, at the office and at home. As a general rule, these units have a range of up to fifteen miles.

A license application blank comes with each Citizen's Band radio you purchase. If you buy a used set, write to the nearest Federal Communications Commission (FCC) Field Office (see list Appendix p. 202) and ask for the proper forms.

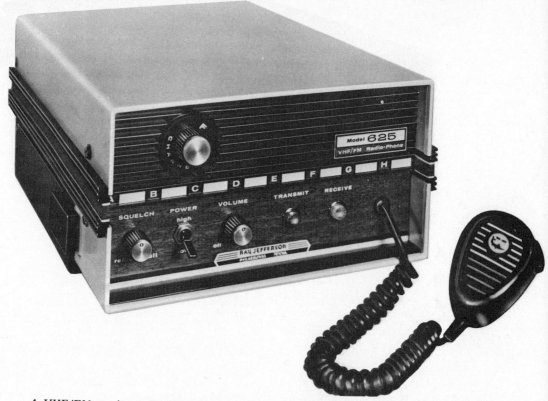

A VHF/FM marine radio. These units are becoming increasingly popular among boatmen.

Many houseboats are now being equipped with Citizen's Band radios. This unit operates on any of the twenty-three FCC-designated channels.

Depth finders are extremely helpful. They let you know how much water is under your keel at all times.

Radio equipment other than Citizen's Band requires a license for both the equipment and the operator. Contact the nearest FCC office, or write to the FCC, Washington, D.C. 20554 for information and forms.

You may also want to consider purchasing a radio direction finder. If you do much off-shore cruising, you will find this a welcome addition aboard. It enables you to find your position electronically by picking up signals from RDF-sending stations shown on the charts. By determining the positions of two such beacons with your radio direction finder, you can pinpoint your whereabouts. You can also follow one of the signals right to the transmitter if you choose. Most units are battery powered and have weather and marine bands as well as broadcast bands, thus serving a dual purpose. Prices range around $200 and up.

A depth finder is another item that is extremely useful for cruising. It is a good feeling to know just how much water is under your keel at all times, and this device not only serves as a good safeguard against running aground but helps you feel your way along in a fog as well.

These mechanisms operate basically by bouncing sound waves off the bottom and are equipped to indicate the bottom's nature as well as the water depth. A rocky bottom gives off multiple echoes, for example, while a mud bottom emits a broad signal that spreads further out across the dial. These units can be used to double check your depth soundings. Models in the $80 to $190 range are quite adequate for ordinary piloting needs.

A gas detector is another piece of electronic equipment that you will be happy to own. It serves as a constant watchdog, alert for signs of explosive gas in the bilge. The unit functions by sampling the air in the bilge and translating its gas content into current flow. When the indicator needle reaches the red sector, there is an explosive mixture present and the engine should be shut off immediately. Some detectors even flash a red warning light and ring a bell.

You can turn on your detector when first coming aboard to check out the condition of the bilge before starting the engines. It is wise to leave it running throughout your cruise. Models range from an elaborate unit that draws a sample of bilge air by pumping it through a plastic tube, to a do-it-yourself kit that you can assemble and wire at home.

Unfortunately there are more and more boat thefts in today's world, hence a growing need for boat alarms. There are two basic systems on the market—closed and open circuit ($30 to $200). In the closed-circuit units an alarm sounds when any circuit is open—a window or door is lifted or a wire is cut. In the open system the alarm sounds when the circuit is closed by opening a window to a certain point, stepping on or touching a small switch or something similar. With both systems you can install magnetic switches on all doors.

A list of selected manufacturers of electronic accessories follows:

Depth Finders

Columbian Hydrosonics
Freeport, L.I., N.Y. 11560

Electronic Laboratories Ltd.
Leigh Rd.
Haine Industrial Estate
Ramsgate, Kent, England

ERA Dynamics Corp.
67 Sand Park Rd.
Cedar Grove, N.J. 07009

Konel Corp.
271 Harbor Way
South San Francisço, Calif. 94080

Pearce-Simpson Inc.
Box 800
Biscayne Annex
Miami, Fla. 33152

Ray Jefferson
Main and Cotton Streets
Philadelphia, Pa. 19127

Raytheon
213 E. Grand Ave.
South San Francisco, Calif. 94080

Ross Laboratories
3138 Fairview Ave. East
Seattle, Wash. 98102

Sonar Radio Corp.
73 Wortman Ave.
Brooklyn, N.Y. 11207

Direction Finders

Kett Avionics
920 Santa Monica Blvd.
Santa Monica, Calif. 90406

Layton Industries Inc.
542 E. Squantum St. N.
Quincy, Mass. 02171

Simpson Electronics
2295 NW 14th St.
Miami, Fla. 33125

Sonar Radio Corp.
73 Wortman Ave.
Brooklyn, N.Y. 11207

Zenith
1900 N. Austin Ave.
Chicago, Ill. 60639

Radiophones—Citizen's Band

American Nucleonics Corp.
Team Products Division
1007 Airway
Glendale, Calif. 91209

Apelco Co.
213 E. Grand Ave.
South San Francisco, Calif. 94080

Aquadynamics Inc.
6940 Farmdale Ave.
North Hollywood, Calif. 91605

Arvin Industries
3209 N. Meridian St.
Indianapolis, Ind. 46208

Courier Communications
439 Frelinghuysen Ave.
Newark, N.J. 07102

Fisher Research Laboratories
1890 Embaracadero Rd.
Palo Alto, Calif. 94303

Lafayette Radio Electronics Corp.
111 Jericho Turnpike
Syosset, L.I., N.Y. 11791

Linear Systems Inc.
220 Airport Blvd.
Watsonville, Calif. 95076

Motorola
4501 W. Augusta Blvd.
Chicago, Ill. 60651

Pearce-Simpson Inc.
Box 800
Biscayne Annex
Miami, Fla. 33152

Simpson Electronics
2295 NW 14th St.
Miami, Fla. 33125

Walco Electronic Co.
9404 Ventnor Ave.
Margate City, N.J. 08402

Zenith
1900 N. Austin Ave.
Chicago, Ill. 60639

CHAPTER ELEVEN

Safety Afloat

Hundreds of thousands of vacationers go houseboating every year without running into trouble. But houseboating, like any type of boating, has its share of headaches. Houseboaters must therefore be prepared to handle engine trouble, fire, shipwreck, collisions, personal injuries and other water mishaps.

Water safety has been drummed into all of us with such intensity over the past several years that one might almost expect boating accidents to be a thing of the past. However, a recent Coast Guard report stated that among the 36 million enthusiasts afloat that year in 4½ million boats, there were 4113 accidents, 1312 fatalities and a total dollar damage in excess of $6 million.

Boating safety, the experts tell us, is primarily a matter of being aware of existing hazards, knowing how to cope with them and possessing a knowledge of correct boating procedures. This chapter is devoted to providing you with that information. (Consult as well the list of fundamental "rules of the road" given in Chapter 5.)

Prelaunching Precautions

Water safety begins on land. Before leaving shore, set aside the time to go over your houseboat from stem to stern, asking yourself these questions:

(1) Does my boat meet all Coast Guard requirements for bells, whistles, fire extinguishers and other lifesaving devices? (See chart pp. 158-159.) Are they in good condition and easily accessible?

(2) Do I have the required lights? (See p. 162.)

(3) Are the charts I need on board? Are they up to date?

(4) Am I equipped with such emergency items as a first-aid kit, flashlight and tool kit?

Before you cast off, make sure that there is adequate fuel on board, the lights and horn are in operating condition, the first-aid kit is fully stocked (see p. 184) and the life preservers are in place. Have an adequate anchor and sufficient line to assure good holding in bad weather. In addition, check the weather, familiarize yourself with your course and inform someone ashore of your itinerary. For any trip involving several days or more, it is good to file a "Float Plan" with the marina you leave from, or with a relative. A Float Plan will list such things as boat type and description, persons aboard, expected stopovers, anticipated return date, etc. See Sample Float Plan p. 170.

Many things can go wrong on the water, as anyone knows who has had to cope with unexpectedly heavy traffic, snarled lines or a guest or child overboard. To eliminate such crises—or reduce them to the minimum—it is essential to establish a set of shipboard rules ahead of time which are to be followed throughout your cruise. Here is a basic list, to which you will probably wish to add some rules of your own:

The Float Plan

1. Name (Person Reporting): _____

2. Telephone Number (Person Reporting): _____

3. Description Of Boat: Type: _____ Color of Hull: ____
   Trim Color: _____ Weight: ____ Registration Number: ____
   Length: ____ Name: _____ Make: _____
   Other: _____

4. No. Persons Aboard: _____

NAME	AGE	ADDRESS	TELEPHONE No.

5. Engine Type: _____ Horsepower: ____ Normal Fuel: ____ Gallons

6. Survival Equipment Aboard (CHECK AS APPROPRIATE):
   Life Jackets: ____ Cushions: ____ Flares: ____ Smoke Signals: ____
   Mirror: ____ Flash Light: ____ Paddles: ____ Food: ____ Water: ____

7. Radio? Yes ____ No ____ Frequencies: _____

8. Trip: Departure Time: _____ From: _____
   Going To: _____ Or: _____
   Will Return By (time): ____ In no event later than: ____

9. Miscellaneous Information: _____
   _____
   _____

10. Auto License No.: _____ Trailer License No.: _____
    Type: _____ Color: _____ Make: _____

11. If not returned by (time): _____ call the Coast Guard, or
    _____, Rescue Center: _____ (telephone,
    number), or _____ at _____

One example of a Float Plan.

170

Be sure you have all required safety equipment aboard.

(1) Print up a list of rules in advance for your guests (including what clothes and shoes to wear) so that they will know how to dress and behave on board.

(2) Check to be sure you have your boat keys before leaving home.

(3) Make sure all aboard understand how to use the life preservers. Preferably all children and nonswimmers should wear some type of flotation device at all times.

(4) See that at least one other person (preferably everyone aboard, including children under supervision) is acquainted with how to operate the boat.

(5) Do not overload or improperly load your boat.

(6) While under way, maintain a constant alert for obstructions, water traffic and other hazards. A special vigilance should be exercised for swimmers, who can be difficult to see, and skin divers (identified by a red flag with white diagonal aloft).

(7) Be sure your boathook is handy at all times to fend off obstacles.

(8) Check the mooring lines to make certain their inboard ends are secured to the appropriate boat cleats and the remaining line is neatly coiled.

(9) Recheck and triple check all mooring lines.

(10) Make sure you approach your slip by heading into the wind or current, whichever is stronger.

(11) Make sure your fenders are in place before you dock.

In addition to these rules, proper fueling procedures should be included in your pre-launching safety measures. If you have an outboard motor, fill the separate fuel tanks on the dock. If your motor is the inboard variety, run the engine-room ventilators before starting to fuel, and be certain the engine room is well ventilated.

The Coast Guard recommends the additional following procedures:

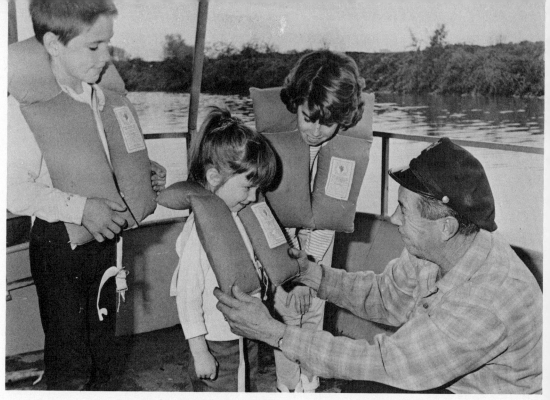

Be certain all children aboard know how to use their life jacket.

(1) Fuel before dark, except in emergencies.

(2) Do not smoke or strike matches while fueling; turn off all engines, motors, fans and other machinery; put out all pilot lights and galley fires.

(3) Make sure your boat is moored securely before starting to fuel; close all portholes, windows, doors and hatches; check condition of fuel tanks, vents and connections. Be sure you know how much fuel the tank will hold.

(4) Keep the nozzle in contact with fill opening during fueling to guard against sparks; make sure spilled fuel does not get belowdecks.

(5) Close fill opening after fueling; wipe up spilled fuel, open all portholes, windows, doors and hatches, and permit the boat to ventilate for five minutes.

(6) Make sure there is no gasoline odor in the bilges or belowdeck spaces before starting machinery or lighting fires.

(7) If necessary to carry additional gasoline, do so only in proper containers.

And take special precautions to prevent accumulation of vapor in confined places.

Engine Problems

Even the most experienced boater runs into engine trouble at one time or another. The following list will help you diagnose the more common motor troubles, and suggest ways to correct them.

Outboard troubles can often be fixed easily. Consult the repair information in the text.

Outboard Engines

Symptom	Possible Causes	Corrective Action
MOTOR WILL NOT START		
May start but then quits	Tank empty, fuel valve or vent closed	Fill fuel tank, open valve
Fuel drips from carburetor	Float valve stuck	Tap lightly to free float
Spark plugs damp	Crankcase flooded	Wipe clean, crank motor several times with plugs out, put plugs back in
	Fouled or defective spark plugs	Take plugs out. If fouled, clean and replace; if defective plugs suspected, put in spare set
Fuel will not drip from carburetor when float pin is depressed	Clogged fuel line	Disconnect fuel line or fuel pipe and strainer, remove obstruction
	Magneto points are fouled or out of adjustment, or ignition system is defective	Remove one spark plug, hold by its rubber boot and ground against the engine block where you can watch for a spark while the engine turns over. If spark is good and plug is in good condition, clean and adjust, replace breaker points
Motor will not turn over or turns over weakly	Battery weak or dead, or terminals loose	Check terminals for tightness, clean off any corrosion. If motor still will not turn over, battery will need recharging or replacing
MOTOR STOPS AND STARTS		
	Fuel tank air vent closed or clogged	Open and make sure vent is clean
	Tank empty or pressure system not feeding	Fill tank, check feeding
Runs a while, then stops	Fuel passage obstructed	Clean fuel pipes and filter; if carburetor is clogged, take motor to an outboard service station

Symptom	Possible Causes	Corrective Action
Runs a while, then stops	Loose or defective wiring. Inspect all wires for cracked or chafed insulation	Wipe clean and expose to sun until dry. Tape over breaks and make all connections tight
MOTOR MISSES	Spark plugs fouled or have wrong gap or heat range	Remove, replace or clean. Replace with proper spark plugs gapped as specified in your outboard maintenance book
	Carburetor out of adjustment	Readjust
	Dirt or water in fuel	Drain small quantity of fuel into container and check for dirt and water. If these are present, drain, flush tank, refill with clean fuel
	Loose or defective wiring	Check for faulty insulation, loose connections; wrap or tighten
	Magneto trouble	Check for spark (see p. 173)
	Manifold air intake leak	Listen for leakage while cranking motor. Tighten bolts or screws. When possible, have mechanic check
MOTOR KNOCKS	Fuel mixture too rich	Try with fresh, properly mixed fuels
	Carburetor not adjusted properly	Adjust carburetor
	Loose fly wheel	Tighten fly wheel nut
	Excessive carbon in cylinders	Motor needs overhauling and cleaning
MOTOR SUDDENLY RACES	Shear pin broken	Stop motor immediately, remove propeller and propeller nut, replace shear pin. Replace propeller and tighten nut

Symptom	Possible Causes	Corrective Action
MOTOR OVERHEATS		
	Wrong fuel mix	Check booklet to make sure you are using correct portions of oil. Mix thoroughly
	Not enough cooling water	Check intake for obstruction, then check the water passages
	Motor not deep enough in water	Lower slightly

Inboard Engines

Symptom	Possible Causes	Corrective Action
ENGINE STOPS		
Stops suddenly	Probably a defective primary electrical system	Check spark plugs
Slows down gradually	High voltage system problems	Check condenser and distributor
Coughs and sputters	Probably faulty fuel system	Check fuel line for clogging— check the carburetor needle valve, fuel pump and filters
Stops with a clanking noise	Needs major repairs	Do not restart—contact a boat mechanic
ENGINE WILL NOT START		
Does not turn over	Worn battery cables; disconnected or defective ignition wires, ignition switch, starter button	If battery cables are worn, replace. Reconnect disconnected ignition wires. Wrap chafed or frayed wires with electrical tape. For emergency, use a wire across the ignition switch or starter button
Turns over slowly	Probably weak battery or cables, or defective starter motor	Recharge or replace battery. If cable is loose, tighten; if worn, replace
ENGINE OVERHEATS		
	Incorrect gasoline octane rating	Check the manual for correct rating and replace. Check crankcase level—add oil
	Vacuum spark advances not working	Check vacuum line connection. Check slipping water pump belt, defective impeller— carry a spare impeller and replace or tape belt

Symptom	Possible Causes	Corrective Action
	Collapsed or obstructed water inlet hose	Check clogged water inlet scoop. Unclog, unobstruct inlet hose, check for faulty cooling system thermostat, replace
ENGINE MISSES		
Regular missing	Loose or broken spark plug wire, fouled spark plugs	Replace or repair broken wire. Tighten connections, clean spark plugs
	Broken or cracked distributor	Replace distributor
	Burned or improperly gapped points	Replace points or regap
	Broken valve spring; blown head gasket	Major repair
Irregular	Burned or improperly gapped distributor points	Replace points or regap
	Flooding carburetor; defective fuel pump	Replace
	Air leaks in fuel line	Check and replace line
ENGINE VIBRATES		
	Loose or bent propeller; bent drive shaft	Tighten propeller, replace if bent. Take boat to trained mechanic to straighten shaft

Spare Parts and Essential Tools

For repair and maintenance of your engine, be sure you have the following material aboard (if it applies to your particular power plant): extra fuel, an ignition coil, a condenser, breaker points, spark plugs, a fuel pump, propeller nuts, cotter keys and fuses.

Also equip yourself with a leaf-type feeler gauge for adjusting points and gapping spark plugs, a spark plug wrench, a regular and Phillips-head screwdriver, an adjustable end wrench, very fine sandpaper, paper for burnishing and cleaning breaker points, a set of ignition wrenches and wrenches for replacing the fuel pump and related uses.

Also carry a quart of proper weight marine oil (for inboard-stern drives). And make certain you follow the instructions for routine care and lubrication in the manufacturer's instruction pamphlet.

Fire and Shipwreck

Before beginning your cruise, carefully review procedures to be taken in case of fire or shipwreck. First, commit to memory the measures essential to fire *prevention*: proper fuel tank installation, proper ventilation, a proper electrical system and no smoking while fueling.

How to Use Your Portable Fire Extinguisher

Approved types

CARBON DIOXIDE

Carry to fire

Pull pin

Point at base of fire and pull trigger

DRY CHEMICAL (stored pressure) and **FREON**

Pull pin and free nozzle

Point at base of fire and pull trigger

DRY CHEMICAL (cartridge operated)

Pull pin and free nozzle

Point at base of fire and pull trigger

FOAM

Invert at scene of fire and "bank" discharge off sidewalls or arch stream onto surface

Then recheck to see that you have the proper firefighting equipment aboard and that it is in *working order*. One good fire extinguisher and a bailer or bucket can prevent a total disaster. Do not test fire extinguishers by squirting small amounts of the agent—the extinguisher might not work when you need it. (See above for instructions on how to operate an extinguisher correctly.)

Should a fire break out in spite of all precautions, proceed as follows:

For an oil or grease fire, use one of the smothering agents, such as dry chemicals, carbon dioxide or foam (do not use carbon tetrachloride in a confined space since it is toxic).

For burning wood, rags and mattresses, use water (fire extinguishers are also effective).

If the fire is burning in a confined space, close the hatches, doors and vents. This keeps fresh air from fanning the flames. If the fire is near the engine, shut off the gas supply.

If the fire breaks out when under way, stop, or reduce the speed to avoid fanning the flames. In addition, if the fire is in one end of the boat or the other, you can confine it by turning the boat so that the wind blows the flames away from the boat itself. If you can't put out the fire immediately, put on life preservers and signal for help.

In case of capsize or shipwreck by running aground, stay with the boat if it is afloat, even if it is filled. Distances at sea are deceiving, and you may find out too late that you can't swim to shore. You can also be more quickly located by rescuers if you remain with your disabled craft.

If you do decide to abandon ship, put on your life preserver and give distress signals. Wait to give signals until they are likely to be seen.

Distress Signals

If you find yourself in real trouble, signal for help by means of one or more of the following distress signals:

(1) If your radiotelephone works, broadcast for help on 2182 (KHz), the *calling and distress frequency*. Coast Guard ships and many other vessels keep tuned to this wavelength, and an increasing number of vessels listen in on 156.8 MHz as well. Simply call "Mayday" on either of the frequencies, and then in a slow, clear voice give your boat's name, position in latitude and longitude and your trouble. (See Coast Guard Information Sheet for details on correct calling practices.)

(2) Slowly and repeatedly raise and lower your arms outstretched to each side.

(3) Reverse your flag or ensign so that it flies upside down.

(4) At night, blink out an SOS signal (three dots, three dashes, three dots) with a white range light, a spotlight or a high-powered flashlight.

(5) Send up an orange smoke marker flare for aerial observation.

(6) Light a fire in a pail or other metal container, using oil or kerosene—but never gasoline!

(7) Fire a gun at one-minute intervals (fire up in the air only so there is absolutely no danger of hitting anything).

(8) Sound your horn, bell or whistle rapidly and repeatedly.

(9) Send up emergency rocket flares (special kits are available for small boats), or fire flare pistols at short intervals.

(10) Wave hand flares, showing red light at night and orange smoke in the daytime.

In choosing which devices to use, keep the visibility factor strongly in mind. If you run out of gas in spite of all precautions, drop anchor out of the channel, signal for help and hope someone will stop. *Stay with your boat.*

Marine Emergency and Distress Information Sheet U.S. Coast Guard

Speak Slowly and Clearly

Call: (1) If you are in *distress* (i.e., when threatened by grave and imminent danger), transmit the International Distress Call on either 2182 KHz or 156.8 MHz—"*Mayday Mayday Mayday This Is* (your vessel's call and name repeated *three* times)."*

(2) If you need *information or assistance from the Coast Guard* (other than in a distress), call *Coast Guard* on either 2182 KHz or 156.8 MHz (the Distress and Calling Frequencies). In this situation you will normally be shifted to a common working frequency allowing the *distress* frequencies to remain open.

*The Radiotelephone Alarm Signal (if available) should be transmitted prior to the Distress Call for approximately one minute. The Radiotelephone Alarm Signal consists of two audio tones, of different pitch, transmitted alternately. Its purpose is to attract the attention of persons on watch and shall only be used to announce that a distress call or message is about to follow.

If aboard a vessel in trouble—give:

(1) *Who* you are (your vessel's call and name).

(2) *Where* you are (your vessel's position in latitude/longitude or true bearing and distance in nautical miles from a widely known geographical point; local names known only in the immediate vicinity are confusing).

(3) *What* is wrong (nature of distress, or difficulty if not in distress).

(4) Kind of assistance desired.

(5) Number of persons aboard and the condition of any injured.

(6) Present seaworthiness of your vessel.

(7) Description of your vessel—length, type, cabin, masts, power, color of hull, superstructure and trim.

(8) Your listening frequency and schedule.

Accident Reports

A written report must be submitted to the Coast Guard within five days if a person is incapacitated by an injury for more than twenty-four hours or if there is physical damage in excess of $100. As of July 1973, authorities must be *immediately* notified of boating casualties involving death or disappearance.

The report must contain numbers and names of vessels, location, date and time of accident, names and addresses of operators, nature and extent of injuries, names and addresses of persons injured or killed and a description of the accident. Accident forms are available at all Coast Guard Stations and Marine Inspection Offices.

Loading Your Boat

Some manufacturers display a metal capacity plate on their boats showing the recommended weight capacity, usually indicating the number of people that particular boat can carry safely as well as the total capacity of the boat in pounds. In addition, there is a general rule of thumb used to determine the number of persons a boat of normal shape can carry under normal weather conditions. It is expressed in the formula:

$$\text{Number of persons} = \frac{L \times B}{15}$$

L = Overall length, B = Maximum width (dimensions in feet and tenths)

It is also important to check the total weight-carrying capacity of the boat considering the actual weight of the engine fuel and equipment plus the weight of the passengers. This is expressed in the formula:

7.5 x L x B x De = pounds for persons, engine, fuel and equipment.

De = Minimum Effective Depth of the boat Measure De at the lowest point that water can enter.

It is necessary also to consider the weather and water conditions. If the water is rough the number of persons carried should be reduced.

Man Overboard

It is essential that every houseboat skipper know what to do if someone falls overboard. Your houseboat guests may be complete novices at sea, a child may get overexcited at play—and suddenly it happens. Here is a summary of the Coast Guard recommendations of what to do:

First, swing the stern of your boat away from the man overboard. This will reduce the danger of injury from the propeller.

Next, throw out a lifesaving device, whether the person in question can swim or not. Life rings are best, but as speed is essential, use the first thing at hand—a life vest or jacket, a buoyant cushion, a water-ski vest or any similar safety device.

At no time lose sight of the man overboard. Assign someone to watch him. If the accident occurs at night, train a light on him if possible.

If prevailing conditions permit, approach the man overboard downwind or into the waves. In really bad weather, use your common sense.

If you have a good swimmer aboard, he can don a life preserver with a line attached and get into the water to assist the person in distress.

Be extremely careful when you bring in the accident victim. He will probably be frightened and exhausted. If he is hurt as well, he will find it particularly difficult to climb aboard. If you bring him in over the stern, be sure to stop the propeller first.

Emergency First-Aid

Everyone hopes, of course, that no mishap will ever occur aboard his houseboat. But since accidents can and do happen at any time, it is important to know the essentials of first-aid. Here are some basic procedures:

Artificial respiration: When the brain is deprived of oxygen, it begins to lose its function and all effort to breathe stops. Since it is impossible to survive more than a few minutes without oxygen, it is essential to start the victim breathing again as quickly as possible.

Currently, mouth-to-mouth respiration is recommended as the best method. Here's how to perform it:

(1) Place the unconscious victim on his back. If there is any foreign matter visible in the mouth, wipe it away quickly with your fingers. You can first cover your fingers with a cloth if you like.

(2) Tilt the head back so that the chin is pointing upward, then pull the jaw out as far as possible (see Fig. 1).

(3) Open your mouth and place it tightly over the victim's. At the same time, pinch his nostrils closed, either with your fingers or with pressure from your cheek (see Fig. 2). Or close the victim's mouth and place your mouth over his nose. Air can be blown either into the victim's mouth or his nose. Even if his teeth are clenched, air will penetrate through them into his lungs.

(4) Remove your mouth, turn your head to the side and listen attentively for a returning rush of air, indicating an air exchange (see Fig. 3). Watch as well for the rise and fall of the victim's chest. Repeat the blowing effort at the rate of about twelve breaths per minute for an adult. For a child, take shallow breaths appropriate to his lung capacity—about twenty per minute.

(5) If you are not getting an air exchange, recheck the position of the victim's head and jaw. If there is still no exchange, quickly turn the victim on his side and administer several sharp blows between the shoulder blades to dislodge any foreign matter. Again, sweep your fingers through the victim's mouth, as deep into the throat as necessary to remove possible foreign matter. Often a person who has fallen overboard has swallowed large amounts of water, which may lead to regurgitation. Should this occur, turn the victim's face to one side to allow drainage without choking.

Severe cuts: In cases where blood gushes from an artery or vein, pressure applied on the bleeding part will generally stop the flow. Then fold a piece of cloth into a pad (or use a sterile gauze pad) and bear down hard on the wound

Mouth-to-Mouth Resuscitation:

Fig. 1. Clean mouth and throat of foreign matter before beginning. Close victim's nose with your right hand and hold lower jaw upward so that it juts out.

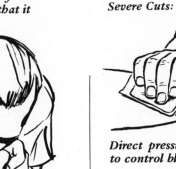

Severe Cuts:

Direct pressure on a wound with a clean cloth to control bleeding.

Fig. 2. Inspiration

Compressing the brachial artery will help control bleeding in an arm or hand.

Fig. 3. Expiration

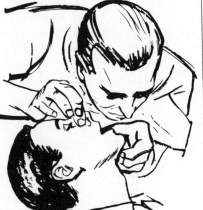

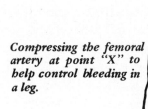

Compressing the femoral artery at point "X" to help control bleeding in a leg.

Fig. 4. To clear air passageway:
Hold child with head down and strike on back.

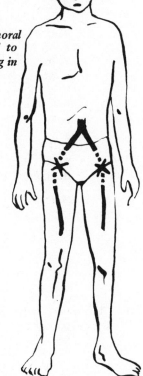

Turn patient on side and administer sharp blows between the shoulder blades to jar foreign material free.

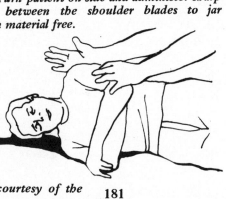

Illustrations pp. 181 and 183 courtesy of the American National Red Cross.

before tying the pad firmly into place with a bandage.

If bleeding is so severe that you are unable to stop it with pressure, apply a tourniquet. Begin by twisting a handkerchief into a bandage two inches wide. Wrap it around the wounded limb about an inch from the wound, between the wound and the heart. Lay a stick on top and tie a knot around it. Turn the stick until bleeding stops. Keep in mind, however, that tourniquets are extremely dangerous because of the possibility of gangrene. Get under way immediately to look for a doctor, loosening the tourniquet every twenty minutes to allow some circulation.

Poisoning: Somebody aboard ship just might accidentally swallow a poisonous substance. Generally it is important to take action at once. For such things as turpentine, insecticides, rat poison, nail-polish remover, most pills, carbolic acid, etc., induce vomiting at once with the aid of four or five glasses of lukewarm water, salt water, soda water or milk and raw eggs.

Here is a specific list of antidotes for some other poisons.

Acids: Give a glass of water to dilute the acid. Then give milk of magnesia or a baking soda solution.

Alkalies (lye, caustic soda, etc.): Give vinegar, lemon juice, or sour milk, follow with white of egg, milk, gelatin, starch or flour pastes and a pint of olive oil or salad oil.

Iodine: Induce vomiting or give starch water, then give a thick starch paste, a thick flour solution or milk.

Matches (phosphorous): Do not give milk, fats or oils. Give hydrogen peroxide—or flour, then Epsom salts.

Mushrooms: Give large amounts of water. Apply heat to stomach. Give strong tea, then castor oil.

If the particular item swallowed lists an antidote on the label, follow these directions as closely as possible, since you should not induce vomiting for every type of poison. If the victim seems to be in shock, raise his feet eighteen inches higher than his head and keep him warm with blankets and a hot-water bottle.

Sunstroke: Sunstroke is caused by overexposure to direct sun. The victim's face becomes red, hot and dry. Frequently he has a headache and a pounding pulse. The body skin becomes hot and dry, perspiration ceases and in severe cases the victim loses consciousness. Should someone aboard be stricken, the first thing to do is start out for a doctor. Next, move the patient to a cool, shady spot and prop up his head and shoulders. Remove his clothes, then try to cool him off by sponging with cold water, or applying compresses made of dripping wet shirts. Ice may be used as well. Continue cold sponge baths until temperature returns to normal.

Heat exhaustion: Too much heat can also produce a form of shock known as heat exhaustion. The symptoms, in contrast to sunstroke, are a pale face; rapid, weak pulse; dizziness; cramps; moist, clammy skin; and a low temperature. To treat, move the victim to a cool place and stretch him out on his back with his feet raised and his head low. Cover him securely with a blanket to maintain body temperature, and give hot tea or cocoa with sugar.

Sunburn: Apply burn ointment, baking soda paste or Vaseline. Keep skin covered from the air.

Sprains: Sprains can occur when jumping on or off your houseboat or when exploring ashore. They can be quite painful and will begin to swell at once. Immediately raise the injured limb and apply cool compresses. Ice bags or very cold water may be used.

Burns: For first degree burns (where the skin simply turns red) use cold water or ice cubes immediately. Keep burn underwater until there is little or no pain. If there are no ice cubes or cold water, apply sterile dressing. For second degree burns (blisters form) cover with dry, sterile gauze bandage. For third degree burns (flesh charred, skin may be burned away) wrap a clean sheet or similar garment around the victim,

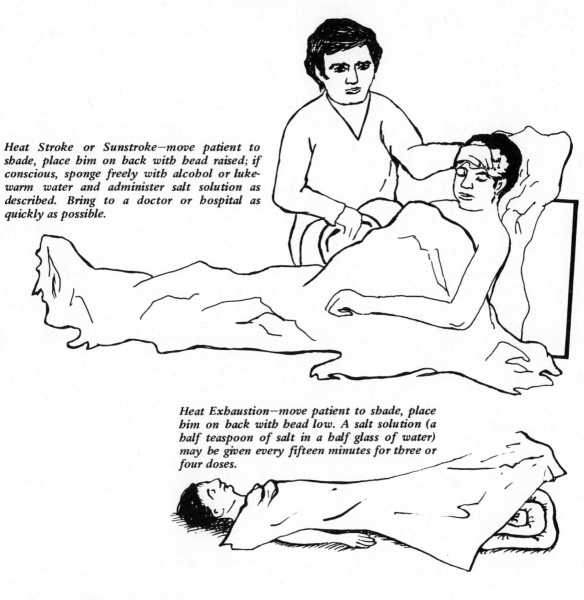

Heat Stroke or Sunstroke—move patient to shade, place him on back with head raised; if conscious, sponge freely with alcohol or lukewarm water and administer salt solution as described. Bring to a doctor or hospital as quickly as possible.

Heat Exhaustion—move patient to shade, place him on back with head low. A salt solution (a half teaspoon of salt in a half glass of water) may be given every fifteen minutes for three or four doses.

Bandage for temporary support of sprained ankle.

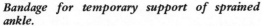

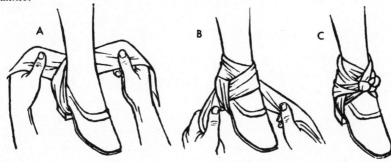

A   B   C

keep warm and rush to a doctor. (Do not try to remove clothing.) Treat for shock by keeping the patient in a prone position and raising his feet.

Nosebleed: Sit down, tilt head back, breathe through mouth and press bleeding nostril four or five minutes to form a clot. Ice held against the other side of the nose may help. If bleeding continues, pack the nostril with a strip of gauze. Do not blow nose for several hours.

Fishhook wound: Push hook full circle up through the flesh instead of backing it out. Cut off barb with wire-cutting pliers, then slip hook back out. If you have no wire-cutting pliers, cut out hook with a sterilized razor blade.

Infected wound: Soak in very hot water every six hours. If swelling does not recede, see a doctor. See a doctor for any sizeable wound.

Poison oak or ivy: If you get off the boat to do some exploring, you may run into one or both of these. Wash exposed area three or four times with a strong lathering soap, then cover with a dressing soaked with a solution of baking soda or Epsom salt. Calamine lotion may also be applied to relieve itching. To keep it from spreading, avoid oily ointments and do not scratch.

Diarrhea: Cut down on fruit and increase intake of dairy products. Drink plenty of water to prevent dehydration.

Insect Bites: Insect bites usually produce acid reactions, so you should apply a neutralizer such as baking soda or household ammonia diluted in water. Remove bee, wasp or hornet stingers from the flesh with tweezers.

Snakebite: If possible call a doctor. If no doctor is available take the following steps:

(1) Apply a tight bandage above the wound.

(2) Paint the wound with iodine or alcohol. Sterilize a knife or razor blade (this can be done with a flame) and make an X-shaped cut through the fang mark.

(3) Apply suction to the cuts to remove the poison. Many first-aid kits contain a suction or bulb syringe. (There are also separate snakebite kits on the market.) If there is no suction device, suck the wound by mouth and spit out the poison (be sure you have no open sores or cuts in your mouth). Apply suction 15 minutes each hour, for several hours.

(4) If the poison spreads, move the bandage higher and make additional cuts where the swelling is bad.

First-Aid Kits

There are several first-aid kits on the market that are specifically designed for boat use. One such model has a cylindrical bulkhead-mounted aluminum case; another boasts a waterproof plastic case that will float. Whatever type of kit you choose, it should be small, lightweight and have a waterproof, nonrusting container.

Your kit should contain the following items: Two 1-inch adhesive compresses; two 2-inch bandage compresses, two 3-inch bandage compresses, four 3 by 3 inch gauze roller bandages; burn ointment. For larger wounds, three units of plain, absorbent gauze (measuring about one-half square yard each); two units of plain, absorbent gauze (about 1 square yard each).

You will also want to have band-aids, gauze pads, two-inch adhesive tape, elastic bandages, salt tablets and a first-aid handbook. And do not forget to tuck in boric acid powder for chafing, eyewash and a snakebite kit—as well as a 40-inch triangular bandage to use as an arm sling. Scissors to cut bandages and tweezers to remove splinters are additional musts.

Additional Safety Information Publications

Various agencies of the government, notably the Government Printing Office and the U.S. Coast Guard, offer a variety of free or nominally priced pamphlets and booklets that can be

184

Bon voyage! Have a safe and happy trip.

studied or carried aboard for an additional edge on boating safety.

From the Boating Safety Branches of the Coast Guard (those District headquarters marked with an asterisk on the list on p. 42), the following, among others, are available:

"Pleasure Craft: Federal Requirements for Boats" (CG-290)

"Marine Communications for the Boating Public" (CG-423)

"Emergency Repairs Afloat" (CG-151)

From the Superintendent of Documents, Government Printing Office, Washington, D.C. 20402:

"The Skipper's Course"

"Official U.S. Coast Guard Recreational Boating Guide"

From the National Ocean Survey, Distribution Division (44), 6501 Lafayette Ave., Riverdale, Md. 20840:

Nautical Chart Catalogs:

No. 1 Atlantic and Gulf Coasts

No. 2 Pacific Coast and Hawaii

No. 3 Alaska

By keeping a weather eye out for trouble and possessing the equipment and knowledge necessary to cope with an emergency should it arise, you will cut shipboard risks to a minimum.
All aboard! Have a safe and pleasant cruise!

Where to Write for State
Travel and Boating Information

ALABAMA

Water Safety Division, Department of Conservation
Administration Building
Montgomery, Ala. 36104

ALASKA

Alaska Travel Division
PO Box 2391
Juneau, Ak. 99801

ARIZONA

Arizona Development Board
1500 W. Jefferson St.
Phoenix, Ariz. 85007

Division of Publications and Travel
State Highway Department
Phoenix, Ariz. 85007

ARKANSAS

Department of Parks and Tourism
149 State Capitol
Little Rock, Ark. 72201

Arkansas Game and Fish Commission
#2 Capitol Mall
Little Rock, Ark. 72201

CALIFORNIA

Department of Navigation and Ocean Development
Sacramento, Calif. 95814

California State Chamber of Commerce
Travel and Recreation Department
350 Bush St.
San Francisco, Calif. 94101

COLORADO

Division of Commerce and Development
Denver, Colo. 80203

CONNECTICUT

Connecticut Development Commission
Hartford, Conn. 06106

Connecticut Boating Safety Commission
Department of Environmental Protection
Hartford, Conn. 06115

DELAWARE

Bureau of Travel Development
45 The Green
Dover, Del. 19901

Legislative Reference Bureau of Delaware
Dover, Del. 19901

DISTRICT OF COLUMBIA

Washington Convention & Visitors Bureau
Washington, D.C. 20001

Greater National Capital Committee
Board of Trade
Washington, D.C. 20001

FLORIDA

(Comprehensive booklet, "Florida Boating," available)
Florida Development Commission
Tallahassee, Fla. 32304

GEORGIA

Tourist Division
Department of Industry and Trade
PO Box 38097
Atlanta, Ga. 30334

Department of Natural Resources
270 Washington St.
Atlanta, Ga. 30334

IDAHO

Idaho Travel
State Capitol
Boise, Id. 83707

ILLINOIS

Illinois Information Service
Springfield, Ill. 62708

Department of Conservation
605 State Office Building
400 S. Spring St.
Springfield, Ill. 62706

INDIANA

Department of Commerce
336 State House
Indianapolis, Ind. 46206

IOWA

Iowa Development Commission
200 Jewett Building
Des Moines, Ia. 50309

KANSAS

Tourist Travel Division
Kansas Industrial Development Commission
State Office Building
Topeka, Kans. 66603

KENTUCKY

Tourist and Travel Division
Department of Public Information
State Office Building
Frankfort, Ky. 40601

Division of Water Enforcement
State Office Building
Frankfort, Ky. 40601

LOUISIANA

Louisiana Tourist Bureau
Baton Rouge, La. 70821

MAINE

Maine Department of Commerce and Industry
State Office Building
Augusta, Maine 04330

MARYLAND

Maryland Division of Tourism
Annapolis, Md. 21401

Department of Natural Resources
State Office Building
Annapolis, Md. 21401

MASSACHUSETTS

The Commonwealth of Massachusetts
Department of Commerce and
    Development Division of Tourism
Boston, Mass. 02105

Division of Motorboats
100 Nashua St.
Boston, Mass. 02114

MICHIGAN

Waterways Commission
Mason Building
Detroit, Mich. 48926

Michigan Tourist Council
300 S. Capitol Ave.
Lansing, Mich. 48926

MINNESOTA

Tourist Information
Department of Economic Development
57 W. Seventh St.
St. Paul, Minn. 55101

Vacation Center
160 State Office Building
St. Paul, Minn. 55101

MISSISSIPPI

Mississippi Boat and Water Safety Commission
Robert E. Lee Building
Jackson, Miss. 39205

MISSOURI

Missouri State Division of Commerce
and Industrial Development
Jefferson City, Mo. 65101

MONTANA

Montana Highway Commission
Advertising Department
Helena, Mont. 59601

Montana Fish and Game Department
State Advertising Department
Helena, Mont. 59601

NEBRASKA

Nebraska Information & Tourism
Lincoln, Neb. 68509

Nebraska Game, Recreation and Parks Commission
9th Floor, Capitol Building
Lincoln, Neb. 68509

NEVADA

Economic Development Department
Carson City, Nev. 89701

Boat Registration Section
Department of Motor Vehicles
Carson City, Nev. 89701

NEW HAMPSHIRE

New Hampshire Division of Economic Development
Concord, N.H. 03301

NEW JERSEY

Department of Labor and Industry
Division of Economic Development
Labor and Industry Building
PO Box 2766
Trenton, N.J. 08625

NEW MEXICO

State Tourist Division
302 Galisteo St.
Santa Fe, N.M. 87501

Director, State Parks Commission
141 DeVargas St.
Santa Fe, N.M. 87501

NEW YORK

The Travel Bureau
New York State Department of Commerce
112 State St.
Albany, N.Y. 12207

New York State Conservation Department
Division of Motorboats
Albany, N.Y. 12207

Waterways Maintenance Subdivision
State Department of Transportation
1220 Washington Ave.
Albany, N.Y. 12226

NORTH CAROLINA

Travel and Promotion Division
Department of Conservation and Development
Raleigh, N.C. 27611

NORTH DAKOTA

North Dakota Highway Department
Capitol Building
Bismarck, N.D. 58501

OHIO

Ohio Division of Watercraft
1350 Holly Ave.
Columbus, Oh. 43212

OKLAHOMA

Oklahoma Tourism and Recreation Department
Will Rogers Memorial Building
Oklahoma City, Okla. 73105

Oklahoma Planning & Resources Board
Boat & Water Safety Division
Will Rogers Memorial Building
Oklahoma City, Okla. 73105

OREGON

Travel Information Division
State Highway Building
Salem, Oreg. 97301

State Marine Board
506 Public Service Building
Salem, Oreg. 97301

PENNSYLVANIA

Department of Environmental Resources
PO Box 1467
Harrisburg, Pa. 17105

RHODE ISLAND

Development Council
Tourist Promotion Division
49 Hayes St.
Providence, R.I. 02908

SOUTH CAROLINA

State Development Board
PO Box 927
Columbia, S.C. 29201

SOUTH DAKOTA

Publicity Director
Department of Highways
Pierre, S.D. 57501

TENNESSEE

Division of State Information
Department of Conservation
Nashville, Tenn. 37202

TEXAS

Texas Highway Department
Travel & Information Division
Austin, Tex. 78710

UTAH

Utah Travel Department
Salt Lake City, Ut. 84114

Boating Division
State Park and Recreation Commission
19 W. South Temple
Salt Lake City, Ut. 84101

187

VERMONT

Vermont Development Department
Publicity Division
Montpelier, Vt. 05602

VIRGINIA

Department of Conservation & Economic Development
Virginia Travel Service
911 E. Broad St.
Richmond, Va. 23219

WASHINGTON

Travel Promotion Division
Department of Commerce & Economic Development
Olympia, Wash. 98501

WEST VIRGINIA

Department of Commerce and Travel
State Capitol Building
Charleston, W. Va. 25305

WISCONSIN

Vacation and Travel Service
Department of Natural Resources
Madison, Wis. 53701

WYOMING

Travel Commission
2320 Capitol Ave.
Cheyenne, Wyo. 82001

Selected Sources for Additional Information on U.S. Houseboating Waters

Alabama Power Company Lakes (map and brochure) Alabama Power Company, 600 N. 18th St., Birmingham, Ala. 35202

Army Corps of Engineers Reservoirs. Includes such reservoirs as Lake Ouachita, Ark.; the Ouachita and Black Rivers Navigation Project; Grenada Lake, Mississippi, Lake Greeson, Ark.; Lake Sharpe Reservoir, South Dakota; Oahe Reservoir, North/South Dakota; the Mississippi River; Lake Texoma; and others.

U.S. Army Corps of Engineers, Washington, D.C. 20001. Or contact the District Office in your area (see telephone directory).

Army Corps of Engineers Addresses for special areas

Intercoastal Waterway, Gulf Section—Apalachee Bay, Fla., to New Orleans

District Engineer
U.S. Army Engineer District, Mobile
PO Box 1169
Mobile, Ala. 36601

Intercoastal Waterway—New Orleans to Port Arthur, Texas, including Atchafalaya and Calcasieu rivers

District Engineer
U.S. Army Engineer District, New Orleans
PO Box 60267
New Orleans, La. 70160

Intercoastal Waterway—Port Arthur to Brownsville, Texas

District Engineer
U.S. Army Engineer District, Galveston
PO Box 1229
Galveston, Tex. 77551

Lake Texoma

U.S. Army Engineer District, Tulsa
Tulsa, Okla. 74101

Middle Mississippi

District Engineer
U.S. Army Engineer District, St. Louis
906 Olive St.
St. Louis, Mo. 63101

Upper Mississippi River and tributaries

Division Engineer
U.S. Army Engineer Division, North Central
536 S. Clark St.
Chicago, Ill. 60605

The Missouri River and tributaries

Division Engineer
U.S. Army Engineer Division, Missouri River
PO Box 103, Downtown Station
Omaha, Neb. 68101

The Ohio River and tributaries

Division Engineer
U.S. Army Engineer Division, Ohio River
PO Box 1159
Cincinnati, Oh. 45201

Southern Mississippi, Mississippi River Commission

Mississippi River Commission
U.S. Army Engineer District
Vicksburg, Miss. 39180

Summersville Reservoir

U.S. Army District, Huntington
Huntington, W. Va. 25701

White River and tributaries above Batesville, Ark.; Arkansas River and tributaries; the Red River and tributaries, Fulton, Ark.

Division Engineer
U.S. Army Engineer Division
1114 Commerce St.
Dallas, Tex. 75202

Other Sources of Information

Bureau of Reclamation Lakes includes Salton Sea, Calif.; Trinity Lake; Lake Shasta, Calif.; Blue Mesa Res., Colorado; Navajo Res., Colorado-New Mexico; Hungry Horse Res., Montana; Elephant Butte Res., New Mexico; Flaming Gorge Res., Utah, Wyoming.

Bureau of Reclamation
Department of the Interior
Washington, D.C. 20001

California Waters Boating Facilities Guide for Northern Area or Southern Area

Division of Small Craft Harbors
1416 Ninth St.
Sacramento, Calif. 95814

Canadian Charts

Dominion Hydrographer
Canadian Hydrographic Service
Surveys and Mapping Branch
249 Queen St.
Ottawa, Ontario, Canada

Chesapeake Bay "Guide for Cruising Maryland Waters"

Board of Natural Resources
State Office Building
Annapolis, Md. 21401

Charts of Inland Waters

National Ocean Survey
Lake Survey Center
630 Federal Building
Detroit, Mich. 48226

National Park Service Waters

National Park Service
Department of the Interior
Washington, D.C. 20240

Includes the following national parks:

Acadia, Maine; Everglades, Florida; Great Smoky Mountains, Tennessee and North Carolina; Isle Royal, Michigan; Virgin Islands, Virgin Islands.

The following national recreation areas:

Amistad, Texas; Arbuckle, Oklahoma; Big Horn Canyon, Wyoming-Montana; Coulee Dam, Washington; Flaming Gorge, Utah-Wyoming; Glen Canyon, Arizona-Utah; Lake Mead, Arizona-Nevada; Sanford, Texas; Shadow Mountain, Colorado; Whiskey Town-Shasta-Trinity, California. (Some of these are administrated by other agencies.)

Tennessee Valley Lakes

Navigation Charts: TVA Map Service, 110 Pound Building, Chattanooga, Tenn. 37401

For additional information on TVA lakes: TVA Information Office, New Sprankle Building, Knoxville, Tenn. 37902

New York

The following chart kits are available from the New York State Conservation Dept., Division of Motorboats, Albany, N.Y. 12226

Cruise 'N Chart Kit #1   The Hudson River, the Champlain Canal, Lake Champlain

Cruise 'N Chart Kit #2   The Erie Canal, the Oswego Canal, the Cayuga-Seneca Canal

Cruise 'N Chart Kit #3   Lake Erie, the Welland Canal, Lake Ontario, the St. Lawrence River

Charts also available from:

National Ocean Survey
Lake Survey Center
630 Federal Building
Detroit, Mich. 48226

Map of the New York State Barge Canal System available from:

Waterways Maintenance Subdivision
New York State Department of Transportation
Albany, N.Y. 12226

U.S. Charts

"Coast Pilot," eight volumes with annual supplements

1. Atlantic Coast Section A, St. Croix River to Cape Cod

2. Atlantic Coast Section B, Cape Cod to Sandy Hook

3. Atlantic Coast Section C, Sandy Hook to Cape Henry

4. Atlantic Coast Section D, Cape Henry to Key West, including Chesapeake Bay Internance and Intercoastal Waterway between Norfolk and Key West

5. Gulf Coast, Puerto Rico and Virgin Islands

6. Pacific Coast California, Oregon, Washington, Hawaii 300

7. Southeast Alaska, Dixon entrance to Yakutat

8. Alaska, Cape Spencer to Arctic Ocean

Published by National Ocean Survey
Distribution Division (44)
6501 Lafayette Ave.
Riverdale, Md. 20840

Houseboat Rental Directory

Rent-A-Cruise of America
PO Box 3558
Springfield, Mo. 65804
Phone 417-883-5544
Locations throughout
the U.S.

Arizona

Canyon Tours Inc.
Wahweap Lodge & Marina
PO Box 1597
Page, Az. 86040
(Lake Powell)

Arkansas

Mountain Harbor Resort
Mount Ida, Ark. 71957
(Lake Ouachita)

California

S & H Houseboat Rentals
Rte 1 PO Box 514
Antioch, Calif. 94509
(Calif. Delta)

Carter's Deluxe Houseboats
Bethel Island, Calif. 94511
(Calif. Delta)

Delta Cruz
PO Box 392
Bethel Island, Calif. 94511
(Calif. Delta)

Lazy Days Vacations
PO Box 736
Brentwood, Calif. 95690
(Calif. Delta)

Lake Shasta Houseboat Co.
PO Box 727
Central Valley, Calif. 96019
(Lake Shasta)

El Cerrito Travel Center
11909 San Pablo Ave.
El Cerrito, Calif. 94530

Land N' Sea Sports
37365 Centralmont Pl.
Fremont, Calif. 94536
(Calif. Delta—S.F. Bay)

Ted Turner Yacht Brokerage
PO Box 69385
Los Angeles, Calif. 90069
(Southern Calif. Coast)

Castaway Houseboat Rental
PO Box 384
Nice, Calif. 95464
(Clear Lake)

Richard's Yacht Center
404 Dutch Slough Rd.
Oakley, Calif. 94561
(Calif. Delta)

Margus Houseboats
PO Box 1258
Project City, Calif. 96079
(Lake Shasta)

Bridge Bay Resort
10300 Bridge Bay Rd.
Redding, Calif. 96001
(Lake Shasta)

Holiday Flotels
PO Box 336
Redding, Calif. 96001
(Lake Shasta)

Jones Valley Resort & Marina
8800 Bear Mountain
Redding, Calif. 96001
(Lake Shasta)

Westaire Flotels
757 Coronado St.
Redding, Calif. 96001
(Lake Shasta)

New Marina Houseboats
345 N. Center St.
Sacramento, Calif. 95202
(Calif. Delta)

Stancha Distributors
7401 Chantilly Lane
Sacramento, Calif. 95828
(Northern Calif.)

Land N' Sea
Tahoe Keys Marina
PO Box 8432
South Lake Tahoe, Calif. 95705
(Lake Tahoe)

Holiday Flotels
PO Box 8771
Stockton, Calif. 95204
(Calif. Delta)

Ladd's Stockton Marina
PO Box 1285
Stockton, Calif. 95204
(Calif. Delta)

Stockton Luxury Houseboats
PO Box 295
Stockton, Calif. 95201
(Calif. Delta)

Tiki Lagoon, Resort Marina
12988 W. McDonald Rd.
Stockton, Calif. 95206
(Calif. Delta)

Windmill Cove Marina
Royal Flotel Houseboats
3630 Holt Rd.
Stockton, Calif. 95206
(Calif. Delta)

Shasta Lake Cruisers
PO Box 666
Summit City, Calif. 96089
(Lake Shasta)

Holiday Flotels Trinity
PO Drawer Ar
Weaverville, Calif. 96093
(Trinity Lake)

R. E. Flotels
PO Box 1026
Weaverville, Calif. 96093
(Trinity Lake)

International Houseboats Inc.
21112 Ventura Blvd.
Woodland Hills, Calif. 91364
(Calif. Delta)

Florida

Rent-A Houseboat
PO Box 1821
Daytona Beach, Fla. 32015

Flamingo Houseboat Corp.
Flamingo, Fla. 33030
(Everglades National Park)

Bahia Mar Yacht Rental, Inc.
Fort Lauderdale, Fla. 33316
(All of Florida coast)

Carefree Houseboat Rentals
1011 San Carlos Blvd.
Fort Lauderdale, Fla. 33931
(Florida's southwest coast)

Florida Houseboat Rentals, Inc.
523 Bahama Dr.
Indian Harbor Beach, Fla. 32937
(Florida Inland Waters)

Florida Keys Houseboat Rentals & Sales
PO Box 1077
Marathon, Fla. 33050
(Florida Keys)

Rent-A-Cruise of America
19400 Collins Ave.
Miami, Fla. 33160

Lazy River Houseboats, Inc.
Stuart, Fla. 33494
(Intracoastal Waterway: Florida east
coast; Okeechobee Waterway, east to
west coast)

Hawaii

Kona Marine Services
PO Box 905
Kailua-Kona, Hi. 96740

Idaho

Priest Lake Marina
Rte 5
Priest River, Id. 83856
(Priest Lake)

Sun Up Bay Resort
Worley, Id. 83876
(Coeur d'Alene Lake, St. Joe
River and Coeur d'Alene River)

Illinois

Pirate's Cove Marina
PO Box 2046
Carbondale, Ill. 62901
(Crab Orchard Lake)

Rent-A-Cruise of Illinois
104 Warren
De Kalb, Ill. 60115
(Illinois River)

Inda's Imports
630 Bucklin St.
LaSalle, Ill. 61301

Northbridge Marine
McHenry, Ill. 60050

Floatel, Inc.
Ottawa, Ill. 61350

Seaway Marina
7012 N. Galena Rd.
Peoria, Ill. 61614
(Illinois River)

Quinsippi Houseboat Rental & Sales
600 Adams St.
Quincy, Ill. 62301

Savanna River Cruises
PO Box 61074
Savanna, Ill. 61074
(Mississippi Waterways)

Starved Rock Marina
PO Box 356
Utica, Ill. 61373
(Illinois Waterway)

Illinois Floatel, Inc.
1835 Mayfair Ave.
Westchester, Ill. 60153

Venture Boating
151 Travers Ave.
Wheaton, Ill. 60187

Indiana

Rent-A-Cruise of Monroe
PO Box 256
Columbus, Ind. 47201
(Monroe Lake)

Rent-A-Cruise of Monroe
PO Box 44
Smithville, Ind. 47458
(Monroe Lake)

Iowa

Dubuque Yacht Basin
PO Box 465
Dubuque, Ia. 52001
(Mississippi River,
Dubuque area)

Boatels Div. McGregor Development
McGregor, Ia. 52157
(Mississippi River—Guttenberg, Ia.
to LaCrosse, Wis.)

Kansas

Houseboat Holidays
331 W. 5th
Junction City, Kans. 66441

Kentucky

Grider Hill Boat Dock
Hwy 734
Albany, Ky. 42602
(Lake Cumberland)

Leisure Cruise
Box 266
Kuttawa, Ky. 42055

Fairview Boat Harbor
4001 Upper River Rd.
Louisville, Ky. 40207
(Ohio River)

Waco Aran Houseboat Rental
Rte 4
Paducah, Ky. 42001
(Kentucky and Barkley lakes)

Maryland

Potomac Leisure Cruises Inc.
Fort Washington Marina
Fort Washington, Md.
(Potomac River, Chesapeake Bay)

Anchor Away, Inc.
West River Marina (Annapolis area)
Galesville, Md. 20765
(Chesapeake Bay and Intracoastal
Waterways)

Massachusetts

"Variance"
229 Newbury St.
Boston, Mass. 02116
(Bar Harbor, Me., to Westport, Conn.)

Houseboat Vacations
Longview Ave.
Hinsdale, Mass. 01235
(Lake Champlain, Hudson
River and Lake Winnipesaukee)

Minnesota

Minnetonka Boat Works
Afton, Minn. 55001

Rent-A-Boat
PO Box 248
Babbitt, Minn. 55706

Snug Harbor Houseboats
Rte 1
Brainerd, Minn. 56401

"Voyaguaire" Houseboats
Crane Lake, Minn. 55725
(Minnesota-Canadian border
area, New Voyageurs
National Park)

Lunder's Haven-in-the-Pines
Resorts & Houseboats
Cross Lake, Minn. 56442

Northernaire Floating Lodges
International Falls, Minn. 56649
(Rainy Lake)

Port of Sunnyside
Stillwater, Minn. 55082

Vermillion Houseboat Rentals
PO Box C
Tower, Minn. 55790
(Vermillion Lake)

Hiawatha Valley Cruises Inc.
Wabasha, Minn. 55981

Fisher's Houseboats
PO Box 488
Walker, Minn. 56484
(Leech Lake)

Missouri

Rent-A-Cruise of the Lake
  of the Ozarks
St. Rd. No. P
Gravois Mills, Mo. 65037
(Lake of the Ozarks)

Holiday Beach Marina
Pomme de Terre Dam
Hermitage, Mo. 65668
(Lake Pomme de Terre)

Kimberling Cove Marina
PO Box 3426
Kimberling City, Mo. 65686
(Table Rock Reservoir)

Water House Rentals
Lake Rd. 13-50-3
Kimberling City, Mo. 65686

Four Seasons Marina
The Lodge of the Four Seasons
Lake Ozark, Mo. 65049
(Lake of the Ozarks)

House of Martin Sales Enterprise
PO Box 9111
St. Louis, Mo. 63117
(Alton Lake and waters of the
Mississippi and Illinois rivers
above Alton, Ill.)

Drake Marina
Star Rte 1, PO Box 272
Sunrise Beach, Mo. 65079
(Lake of the Ozarks)

Nebraska

Stardust River Cruises
PO Box 224
Ponca, Neb. 68770
(Missouri River)

New Jersey

Port O'Call Cruises
25 Beechwood Pl.
Fair Haven, N.J. 07701
(Jersey shore-Barnegat Bay)

Capt. Richie's Marina
E. Lacey Rd.
Forked River, N.J. 08731
(Barnegat and Great bays)

New York

Bonnie Castle Yacht Basin
PO Box 368
Alexandria Bay, N.Y. 13607

Charley's Marina
Sisson St.
Alexandria Bay, N.Y. 13607
(1000 Islands–St. Lawrence Seaway)

Hutchinson's Boat Works
Bethune St.
Alexandria Bay, N.Y. 13607

Van's Motor Marine
Sisson St.
Alexandria Bay, N.Y. 13607

Rent-A-Cruise of Catskill
5 W. Bridge St.
Catskill, N.Y. 12414
(Hudson River-Erie Canal-Champlain
Lake, etc.)

The Iroquois Rental Corp.
PO Box 389
Geneva, N.Y. 14456

Rent-A-Cruise of the Finger Lakes
620 W. Broad St.
Horseheads, N.Y. 14845

Olde Port Harbor
702 W. Buffalo St.
Ithaca, N.Y. 14850
(Finger Lakes)

Carib Explorers
605 Third Ave.
New York City, N.Y. 10016
(U.S. Virgin Islands out
of St. Thomas)

Rent-A-Cruise of New York
645 11th Ave.
New York City, N.Y. 10036
(Florida, Bahamas, Virgin
Islands, N.Y. State)

Black Creek Marina
20 Black Creek Rd.
Rochester, N.Y. 14623
(Erie Barge Canal, Finger
Lakes)

Houseboat Holidays of
  Adirondacks
Sacandega Marina
Rochester, N.Y.
(Great Sacandega Lake)

Houseboat Holidays
109 S. Monroe St.
Watkins Glen, N.Y. 14891

Ohio

Anderson Ferry Marina
4333 River Rd.
Cincinnati, Oh. 45204

Hendricks Creek Resort (Burkesville)
PO Box 2170 RRG
N. Canton, Oh. 44720

Oklahoma

Emery Maritime Associates
Applegate Cove Marina
Star Route 4
Sallisaw, Okla. 74955
(Robert S. Kerr Reservoir
and Arkansas River
Navigation System)

Tennessee

Sequoyah Lodge & Marina
Rte 1
Andersonville, Tenn. 37705
(Norris Lake)

Riverdale Resort & Marina
Buchanan, Tenn. 38222
(Kentucky Lake and Lake
Barkley, Tennessee River)

Hixon Marina, Inc.
PO Box 51
Hixon, Tenn. 37343

Kilgore's Flat Hollow Marina
La Follette, Tenn. 37765
(Norris Lake)

Newport Resort
Rte 1
Spring City, Tenn. 37381
(Watts Bar Lake)

Spring City Resort
Rte 2 New Lake Rd.
Spring City, Tenn. 37381
(Watts Bar Lake, Tennessee River)

Texas

Dome RV & Marine
Holt at Engelmohr
PO Box 20267 Astrodome Sta.
Houston, Tex. 77025
(Gulf Coast)

Utah

Halls Crossing
Blanding, Ut. 84511
(Lake Powell)

Bullfrog Resort & Marina
Hanksville, Ut. 84734
(Lake Powell)

Hite Marina, Inc.
PO Box 1
Hanksville, Ut. 84734

Vermont

Point Bay Marina
Thompsons Point
Charlotte, Vt. 05445

Ipanema Corp.
PO Box 207
Chester, Vt. 05413

Washington

Recreational Facilities Inc.
PO Box 726
Anacortes, Wash. 98221

Beacon Marine
Pasco Port Dock
PO Box 2601
Pasco, Wash. 99301
(Columbia and Snake rivers,
Wallula and Sacamaua lakes)

Ike's Marina
6623 N. Division
Spokane, Wash. 99208
(Lake Coeur d'Alene)

Wisconsin

Alma Marina
Alma, Wis. 54610

Cruising Houseboats, Inc.
8250 N. Oriole
Niles, Ill. 60648 (winter address)
Alma, Wis. 54610 (summer address)

Carri Craft Houseboat Rental
200 Leffert St.
Berlin, Wis. 54923

Holiday Harbor
Rte 3 F
Eagle River, Wis. 54521

Party Doll Fleet, Inc.
RR 2
Fremont, Wis. 54940

Bill's Skipper Buds
127 Marina Dr.
La Crosse, Wis. 54601

Holiday Vacation Cruises
1933 Rose St.
La Crosse, Wis. 54601
(Mississippi River)

Upper Mississippi Cruises
2039 Rose (St. Hwy 53)
La Crosse, Wis. 54601
(Upper Mississippi River)

Family Houseboating
PO Box 380
Prairie DuChien, Wis. 53821
(Upper Mississippi River—Dubuque,
Iowa, to La Crosse, Wis.)

This list is necessarily incomplete since new rental locations are constantly being added.

An up-to-date list can be obtained, for $1 by writing for the:

Recreation Rental Guide
23945 Craftsman Rd.
Calabasas, Calif. 91302

Manufacturers of Disposable Paper Products

Snug Eze
1001 S. Mattis Ave.
Champaign, Ill. 61820

Iroquois Paper Co.
2220 W. 56th St.
Chicago, Ill. 60636

Kendall Company
Fiber Products Division
Walpole, Mass. 02081

Good Knight Enterprises
PO Box 571
Enid, Okla. 73701

Kimlon Disposable Linens
    Contact:
Robert G. Frechette
Cooper/Strock/Scannell
208 E. Wisconsin Ave.
Milwaukee, Wis. 53202

Blanket	$2.98
Sleeping bags	3.98
Sleeping bag liner	1.49
Laundry-free bed sheets, pair	1.79
Infant's pillow cases, six for	1.29
Crib sheets, six for	3.98

A Guide to Boats on the Market (1973)

Cruising and Pontoon Houseboats

	Hull Mat'l	Length	Beam	Draft	Sleeping Capacity	Basic Power	Suggested Retail Price
Aluminum Cruisers, Inc. Standiford Field Louisville, Ky. 40213	Alum.	41'	13'6"	28"	6	2-225	$ 27,250
Alwest 153 Donald Winnipeg, Can.	Alum.	38'	11'	39"	6	I/0 2-225	$ 25,000
	Alum.	38'	11'	39"	6	I/0 2-225	$ 28,000
Americana Living Cruisers Suite 220 Columbian Title Building Topeka, Kans. 66612	Alum.	52'	15'	3'	6	I/0 2-225	$ 65,000 up
Boatel Company, Inc. 811 E. Maple Mora, Minn. 55051	Fiberglass	47'	13'	28"	8	2-250 V-drive	$ 36,695
	Fiberglass	37'	12'	26"	8	I/0 225	$ 17,385
	Steel	42'	12'	16"	9	OB	$ 11,975
Burns-Craft 2940 E. Avalon Ave. Muscle Shoals, Ala. 35660	Fiberglass	32'	12'	16"	6	225 V-8	$ 11,994
	Fiberglass	35'	12'	17"	6	225 V-8	$ 13,670
	Fiberglass	43'	12'	18"	6	T225 V-8	$ 22,400
	Fiberglass	45'	15'	30"	6	T225 V-8	$ 24,400
	Fiberglass	50'	15'	30"	6	T225 V-8	$ 31,670
Chris-Craft PO Box 860 Pompano Beach, Fla. 33061	Fiberglass	34'	12'10"	36½"	6	2-200 Chris-Craft transdrive	$ 19,425
Coleman-Saling Mfg. Co., Inc. Industrial Dr. Morgantown, Ky. 42261	Steel	36'	9'		7	120 Merc	$ 12,204.50
	Steel	42'	10'		7	165 Merc	$ 14,393.50
	Steel	45'	10'		8	225 Merc	$ 16,521.75
	Steel	51'	10'		8	325 Merc	$ 21,822.45
Cruise-A-Home, Inc. 1028 Norton Ave. Everett, Wash. 98201	Fiberglass	40'	12'	34"	6	2-I/0 & V gas/diesel	$ 23,190
	Fiberglass	31'	11'8"	36"	4	S & T I/0	$ 18,450

Company	Hull	Length	Beam	Clearance	Sleeps	Power	Price
Georgian Steel Boats Div. of Abicon Ltd. 516 Regent St. PO Box 815 Niagara on the Lake, Ontario, Can.	Steel	42'7"	12'	30"	6	Single 225 I/O	$ 17,600
	Steel	37'7"	12'	30"	6	2-155 I/O	$ 23,975
	Steel	32'7"	12'	32"	8	2-225 I/O	$ 27,200
Gibson Fiberglass Products, Inc. 308 Church St. Goodlettsville, Tenn. 37072	Fiberglass	30'	12'	19"	6	225 Chry.	$ 10,295
	Fiberglass	36'	12'	19"	6-8	225 Chry.	$ 11,295
	Fiberglass	42'	12'	19"	6-8	225 Chry.	$ 18,295
Hallmark Yachts, Inc. Bldg. 692, Smyrna Airport Smyrna, Tenn. 37167	Fiberglass	37'	12'	34"	6	S/225 I/O	$ 13,995
	Fiberglass	43'	12'	34"	6	T/255 V-drive	$ 21,000
Harbor House Div. Holiday Rambler Corp. Hwy 19 Wakarusa, Ind. 46573	Alum.	46'	13'6"	36"	6-10	2-255 Merc	$ 48,000
	Alum.	46'	13'6"	38"	6-10	210 Cat.	$ 65,000
Holiday Mansion (Division of Mohawk, Inc.) 615 East Pacific Salina, Kans. 67401	Alum.-steel	51'	13'6"	18"	6-8	2-130 I/O	$ 22,995
	Alum.-steel	47'	12'	14"	6-10	OB	$ 13,987
	Alum.-steel	41'	12'	14"	8-10	OB	$ 9,882
	Alum.-steel	38'	10'-12'	14"	6-8	OB	$ 8,245
	Alum.-steel	33'	10'	14"	6	OB	$ 5,995
House Boating Corp. of America PO Box 950 365 Maple St. Gallatin, Tenn. 37066	Steel	38'	12'10"	15"	6	Merc or Waukesha OB/I/0	$ 9,895
	Steel	43'	12'10"	15"	8	Merc or Waukesha OB/I/0	$ 12,230
	Steel	48'	12'10"	15"	8	Merc or Waukesha OB/I/0	$ 15,630
Kayot, Inc., Marine Division 500 Kayot Boulevard PO Box 789 Mankato, Minn. 56001	Steel	30'	10'		4	75	$ 7,250
	Alum.	30'	10'		4	75	$ 8,125
	Steel	40'	12'		9	85	$ 11,990

Cruising and Pontoon Houseboats

	Hull Mat'l	Length	Beam	Draft	Sleeping Capacity	Basic Power	Suggested Retail Price
Kings Craft Corp. PO Box 2306 Florence, Ala. 35630	Alum.	35'	12'	30"	6	**225 Merc or 225 Chry.	$ 16,995 Single $ 20,625 Twin
	Alum.	40'	12'	31"	8	**225 Merc or 225 Chry.	$ 21,450 Twin
	Alum.	44'	15'	32"	8	**225 Merc or 225 Chry.	$ 32,350 Twin
	Alum.	55'	15'	34"	10	**225 Merc or 225 Chry.	$ 48,000 Twin
Lazy Days Manufacturing Co., Inc. Holiday Road Buford, Ga. 30518	Alum.	50'	14'6"	30"	6	Twin 225 Merc	$ 31,667
	Alum.	56'	14'6"	30"	8	Twin 225 Merc	$ 36,542
	Alum.	55'	14'6"	36"	6	Twin 255 Merc	$ 39,022
	Alum.	61'	14'6"	36"	8	Twin 255 Merc	$ 44,997
Leisure Craft Div. Westates Truck Equip. Corp. 3641 Haven Ave. Menlo Park, Calif. 94025	Alum.	35'	12'	18"	6	OB 55 h.p.	$ 11,100
	Alum.	42'	12'	18"	8	OB 55 h.p.	$ 14,500
	Alum.	44'	14'	18"	10	OB 55 h.p.	$ 16,100
Maurell Products Inc. 2711 S.M. 52 Owosso, Mich. 48867	Alum.	30'	8'	9"	4	OB 40 h.p.	$ 4,585
	Alum.	35'	8'	11"	6	OB 60 h.p.	$ 5,275
	Alum.	35'	10'	14"	6	OB 60 h.p.	$ 6,395
	Alum.	35'	10'	14"	6	OB 70 h.p.	$ 6,995
Maxa Industries, Inc. 1603 East Florida Springfield, Mo. 65803	Steel	32'	10'	14"	6	OB or I/0	$ 7,495
Mon Ark Boat Co. PO Box 210 Monticello, Ark. 71655	Alum.	58'	18'	48"	4		

Company	Material	Length	Beam		People	Engine	Price
Nauta-Line, Inc. 1 Nauta-Line Dr. Hendersonville, Tenn. 37075	Fiberglass	34'	12'	21"	8	Single 225 I/O	$ 20,695
	Fiberglass	43'	14'	22"	8	T/225 I/O	
	Fiberglass	48'	14'	26"	8	T/325 V-drive	
Pacemaker Corporation PO Box 337 Egg Harbor City, N.J. 08215	Fiberglass	35'2"	12'	22"	6	gas (2) 220 h.p.	
Rainbow Industries 304 N.W. Norris Fwy. Lake City, Tenn. 37769	Steel	32'	11'	36"	6	I/O 120 up	$ 6,500 w/o p
	Steel	40'	12'	36"	8		$ 7,745 w/o p
	Steel	50'	13'	36"	8		$ 12,900
River Queen Boat Works 6655 E. Dunes Hwy. Gary, Ind. 46403	Steel	40'	13'	19"	6-8	255-450 h.p. gas	$ 18,750 Single
PO Box 379 Douglas, Mich. 49408	Steel or alum.	50'	15'	24"	10	450-600 h.p. gas or diesel	
	Steel or alum.	60'	15'	24"	12	diesel to 600 h.p.	
Sea Line 4302 Jackson Hwy. Sheffield, Ala. 35660	Fiberglass	50'	14'	36"	8	I/O single 225 or 2-225	$ 28,500 Single $ 31,357 Twin
	Fiberglass	39'	14'	36"	6	I/O single 225 or 2-225	$ 25,500 Single $ 28,350 Twin
Sea Rover Marine Div. APECO Corp. 1301 Bay St. S.E. St. Petersburg, Fla. 33701	Fiberglass	36'	12'	19"	6-8	T 165 Waukesha	
	Fiberglass	•36'	12'	19"	4-6	T 165 Waukesha	
	Fiberglass	36'	12'	19"	8-10	T 165 Waukesha	

Cruising and Pontoon Houseboats

	Hull Mat'l	Length	Beam	Draft	Sleeping Capacity	Basic Power	Suggested Retail Price
Sport Craft Houck Rd. Perry, Fla. 32347	Fiberglass	30'	12'		8	2-188	$ 15,224
	Fiberglass	24'6"	8'		5	OB only	$ 4,995
Stardust Cruiser Mfg. Co. PO Box 5262 Chattanooga, Tenn. 37406	Steel	57'	13'	36"	6-10	2-225 h.p. w/o power	$ 26,500
	Steel	52'	13'	36"	6-8	2-225 h.p. w/o power	$ 21,500
	Steel	44'	12'	36"	6-8	1 or 2-225 h.p. w/o power	$ 17,500
	Steel	40'	11'	30"	6-8	OB or 225 h.p. w/o power	$ 9,950
Suburban Industries 944 E. Lincoln Banning, Calif. 92220	Fiberglass	34'8"	11'6"	15"	6	2 OMC 120 h.p.	$ 14,500
Uniflite, Inc. 9th & Harris Ave. Bellingham, Wash. 98225	Fiberglass	36'3"	12'4"	30"TS1/0 32"TSI	6	225 Chry.	$ 28,218 I/0 $ 29,007 I/0 $ 30,776 I/0 W/FB
Watercraft, Inc. PO Box 857 Gallatin, Tenn. 37066	Alum.	45'	14'	11"	8	225 V-drives h.p.	$ 31,500
	Alum.	50'	14'	12"	8	225 V-drives h.p.	$ 33,500
	Alum.	55'	14'	13"	8	225 V-drives h.p.	$ 44,500

Trailerable Houseboats

	Hull Mat'l	Length	Beam	Draft	Sleeping Capacity	Basic Power	Suggested Retail Price

Manufacturer	Material	Length	Width	Draft	Capacity	Power	Price
Arcmarine Corp. 2370 N. Flower Santa Ana, Calif. 92706	Fiberglass	28'	12'	6"-8"	Depends on house	OB to 130	$ 12,995
	Fiberglass	28'	12'	8"	6 up	OB to 130	
	Fiberglass	28'	12'	6"-8"		OB to 130	
Cargile, Inc. PO Box 11499 999 Polk Ave. Nashville, Tenn. 37211	Fiberglass	28'	8'	34"	10	165 h.p. Waukesha	
Conrad Inc. PO Box 88 Houghton, Ia. 52631	Steel	8'	4'6"		6	OB or I/0	
Farenwald Enterprises of Fla.	Fiberglass	24'1½"	8'	15"	4	I/0 165	$ 9,796
Div. of Farenwald Ent. Inc. 330 Millwood Rd. Lancaster, Pa. 17602	Fiberglass	24'1½"	8'	15"	4	OB	$ 6,474
Glendale Plastics	Fiberglass	18'5"	8'	11"	4	OB 85	$ 4,975
Div. of Glendale Mobile Homes Ltd. 145 Queen St. Strathroy, Ontario, Can.	Fiberglass	18'5"	8'	11"	4	OB 85	$ 4,825
Harris Flote-Bote (Div. Harris Mfg. Corp.) 2801 W. State Blvd. Fort Wayne, Ind. 46808	Alum.	16'	8'				
	Alum.	20'	8'				
	Alum.	24'	8'				
	Alum.	28'	8'				
	Alum.	28'	8'				
Kennedy Houseboats, Inc. PO Box 338 Miller, S.D. 57362		37'	10'	6"-10"	7	OB 55 h.p.	$ 9,950
		30'	8'	6"-8"	4	OB 20 h.p.	$ 5,695
		27'	8'	6"-8"	2	OB 20 h.p.	$ 4,995
Land N' Sea Craft, Inc. 1813 S. Tenth St. San Jose, Calif. 95112	Fiberglass	28'	8'	14½"	7-9	200 h.p. I/0	
	Fiberglass	28'	8'	14½"	4	200 h.p. I/0	

	Hull Mat'l	Length	Beam	Draft	Sleeping Capacity	Basic Power	Suggested Retail Price
Rent-A-Cruise of America, Inc. 2274 E. Sunshine Springfield, Mo. 65804	Fiberglass	32'	10'	10"	8	OB 55 h.p.	$ 18,500
Ryan Boat Co. 16324 S. Main Gardena, Calif. 70248	Fiberglass	28'	8'	10"	6		$ 9,685
Ship-A-Shore 1313 E. Jefferson Mishawaka, Ind. 46544	Royalex plastic	23'	7'11¾"	5"-9"	6		$ 11,625
Steury Corporation 310 Steury Ave. Goshen, Ind. 56526	Fiberglass	23'	8'		5	I/O 188 h.p. Merc	$ 5,625
Trail or Float 6438 Bonner Dr. Vancouver, Wash. 98665	Fiberglass	25'	13'	8"	5	OB 40 h.p.	
Trail-It Zoach Mfg. Co. Inc.	Steel	28'	8'	12"	5	Optional OB	$ 8,975
4549 N.E. 22nd St. Des Moines, Ia. 50313	Steel	28'	8'	12"	5	Optional OB	$ 8,975
	Steel	28'	8'	12"	5	Optional OB	$ 9,650
Yachtster PO Box 507 Salina, Kan. 67401	Fiberglass	28'	8'	23"	6	I/O 170 h.p.	$ 12,950
	Fiberglass	28'	8'	23"	6	I/O 170 h.p.	$ 6,995
	Fiberglass	28'	8'	23"	6	I/O 170 h.p.	$ 13,950
Yukon-Delta Inc. 405 Jay Dee St. Elkhart, Ind. 46514	Fiberglass	25'	7'6"		4	OB to 100 h.p.	$ 3,995

Boat Kits

	Hull Mat'l	Length	Beam	Draft	Sleeping Capacity	Basic Power	Suggested Retail Price

Manufacturer	Material	Length	Beam	Draft	Capacity	Power	Price
Arcmarine Corporation, 2370 N. Flower, Santa Ana, Calif. 92706	Fiberglass	28'	12'	6"-8"	4-8	OB to 130	$ 2,875
Champion Boats of Calif., 3076 Saticoy, N. Hollywood, Calif. 91605	Fiberglass	23'	8'	16"	2-6	OB to 55 h.p.	
Glen-Marine Designs, 9152 Rosecrans, Bellflower, Calif. 90706 (Prices for plans only.)	Sheet plywood	12', 16', 20', 21' & 28' models	8'	9"			$ 10
	Sheet plywood	20'1"	7'11"	9"	4	OB or I/0	$ 28
	Sheet plywood	23'4"	7'11"	9"	5	OB or I/0	$ 35
	Sheet plywood	24'11"	8'	9"	4	OB or I/0	$ 37
	Sheet plywood	33'	12'	10"	6	OB or I/0	$ 49
	Sheet plywood	29'	10'2"	11"	6	OB or I/0	$ 45
Luger, 3800 W. Hwy. 13, Burnsville, Minn.	Plywood fiberglass covered	22'	8'	8"-30"	6	OB or I/0	$ 1,450
	Plywood fiberglass covered		8'	8"-30"	4	OB or I/0	$ 1,300
Rotocast Plastic Products Inc., 67 N.W. 36 Ave., Miami, Fla. 33147		24'	8'-12'			OB 40 h.p.	$ 975
		30'	10'-12'			OB 40 h.p.	$ 1,163
		36'	10'-12'			OB 50-60 h.p.	$ 1,380
		42'	12'-15'			OB 100 h.p.	$ 1,586
Sea and Air Products, Inc., Rockland Rd., Norwalk, Conn. 06856	Fiberglass	26'	8'				$ 2,755
	Fiberglass	26'	10'				$ 2,915
	Fiberglass	34'	12'				$ 5,095
	Fiberglass	34'	14'				$ 5,295

FCC Field Offices

Alabama, Mobile 36602
439 U.S. Courthouse & Custom House

Alaska, Anchorage 99501
54 U.S. Post Office & Courthouse Building
PO Box 644

California, Los Angeles 90012
U.S. Courthouse, Room 1754
312 N. Spring St.

California, San Diego 92101
Fox Theatre, 1245 7th Ave.

California, San Francisco 94111
323 A Custom House
555 Battery St.

California, San Pedro 90731
300 S. Ferry St., Room 2525
Terminal Island

Colorado, Denver 80202
504 New Custom House, 19th
between California and Stout Streets

District Of Columbia 20554
Room 216, 1919 M St., N.W.

Florida, Miami 33130
51 S.W. First Ave., Room 919

Florida, Tampa 33602
738 Federal Office Building
500 Zack St.

Georgia, Atlanta 30303
1602 Gas Light Tower
235 Peachtree St. N.E.

Georgia, Savannah 31402
238 Federal Office Building, PO Box 8004

Hawaii, Honolulu 96808
502 Federal Building, PO Box 1021

Illinois, Chicago 60604
219 S. Dearborn St.

Louisiana, New Orleans 70130
829 Federal Office Building
600 South St.

Maryland, Baltimore 21201
819 Federal Building
31 Hopkins Plaza

Massachusetts, Boston 02109
1600 Custom House

Michigan, Detroit 48226
1054 New Federal Building

Minnesota, St. Paul 55101
691 Federal Building & U.S. Courthouse
4th and Robert Streets

Missouri, Kansas City 64106
1703 Federal Building
601 E. 12th St.

New York, Buffalo 14202
905 Federal Building

New York, New York 10014
748 Federal Building
641 Washington St.

Oregon, Portland 97204
314 Multnomah Building
319 S.W. Pine St.

Pennsylvania, Philadelphia 19106
1005 U.S. Custom House

Puerto Rico, San Juan 00903
322-323 Federal Building
PO Box 2987

Texas, Beaumont 77701
323 Federal Building
300 Willow St.

Texas, Dallas 75202
1100 Commerce St.

Texas, Houston 77002
New Federal Office Building
515 Rusk Ave., Room 5636

Virginia, Norfolk 23502
870 N. Military Hwy.

Washington, Seattle 98104
8012 Federal Office Building
1st Ave. and Marion

INDEX

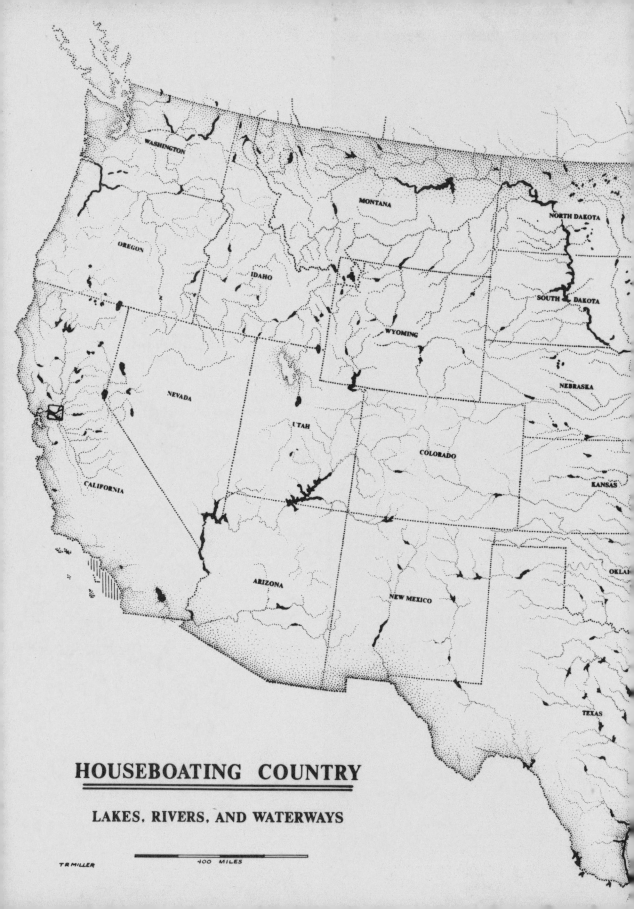

HOUSEBOATING COUNTRY

LAKES, RIVERS, AND WATERWAYS

T.R. MILLER   400 MILES